Social Identities and Political Cultures in Italy

Catholic, Communist and Leghist Communities between Civicness and Localism

Anna Cento Bull

Berghahn Books
New York • Oxford

First published in 2000 by **Berghahn Books**

www.berghahnbooks.com

© 2000 Anna Cento Bull

Library of Congress Cataloging-in-Publication Data

Cento Bull, Anna, 1951–
  Social identities and political cultures in Italy: Catholic, Communist
  and Leghist
communities between civicness and localism / Anna Bull.
  p. cm.
Includes bibliographical references and index
ISBN 1-57181-944-4 (alk. paper)
  1. Political culture – Italy – Erba.   2. Political culture – Italy – Sesto
San Giovanni.   3. Group identity–Italy–Erba.   4. Group culture – Italy
– Sesto San Giovanni.   5. Regionalism – Italy.   6. Italy – Politics and
government – 1994-I.   Title

JA75.7 .C42 2000-07-27
306.2-0945-21 – dc21   99-086562

British Library Cataloguing in Publication Data

A catalogue record for this book is available from the British
Library.

Printed in the United States on acid-free paper

ISBN 1-57181-944-4 (paperback)

For My Father

Contents

List of tables and figures

loyalties, rather than as essential components of nationhood, ultimately becomes counterproductive' (Jenkins and Copsey 1996: 112). By contrast, Italy is generally considered as possessing a weak national identity in the face of strong local and regional sentiments. Yet these differences may mask the resilience, in both countries, of sub-national identities, which may or may not come into conflict with national loyalties.

The research project led to a number of publications, mainly in the form of articles in refereed journals, some of whose findings are reproduced in this volume. In particular, some of the findings presented in Chapter 5 and some of the issues addressed in Part II originally appeared in two articles, one published in *Modern Italy* (Autumn 1996) and one in *West European Politics* (April 1997). Some other findings, reproduced in Chapter 1, originally appeared in *European Urban and Regional Studies* (January 1997). The project did not, however, lead to a joint comparative book on Italy and France, for a variety of reasons. The most important of these was a markedly different degree of success in the number of responses to the questionnaire which formed the main survey tool (see Introduction). The rate of success was much higher in Italy than in France, thus creating problems for systematic comparative analysis. The second reason was a decision to revise and extend the comparative research project to include Spain, with the aim of collecting a new body of information on European political culture, based more on qualitative than quantitative research methods, thus privileging structured interviews rather than a survey by questionnaire. This research project is still under way.

The decision to produce a volume exclusively on Italy was, nevertheless, predicated only minimally upon the uneven success of the questionnaire survey in the two countries. The main aim of the research project referred to above was to produce data which would be meaningful for comparisons within each country, as well as across them. The research questions were formulated in order to probe the relationship between long-term structural and cultural change, and to explore the interconnections between social identities and spatial relations (Rees 1985: 3), both within the national context and within a cross-national perspective. In other words, comparisons between the two localities chosen in Italy (and between the two chosen in France) were fully self-standing, addressing theoretical and socio-political issues of crucial importance for an understanding of change and continuity in each country following the end of the Cold War and recent political instability. This was particularly true in the case of Italy, as a discussion of the research questions underpinning this book will clarify. The volume does, nevertheless, rely in part upon the findings related to the two French sites, since a direct comparison between localities (and regions) across two different countries can greatly add to our understanding of both sub-national and national sociocultural processes. Some of the findings for France will also appear in a separate volume which is being prepared for Berghahn Books by my research collaborator and colleague, Dr Susan Milner.

Acknowledgements

This book would not have been possible without the help of numerous people and institutions. I would like first of all to thank all 888 respondents to the survey by questionnaire which was carried out in Erba (Como) and Sesto San Giovanni (Milan) in February-March 1994. The questionnaire, reproduced in the Appendix, was long and time-consuming, yet the response rate was positive beyond all expectations. I would also like to thank my Research Assistant, Sarah Wild, who carried out most of the fieldwork in both towns, and whose commitment and enthusiasm greatly contributed to the successful completion of the survey.

A special word of thanks should go to Giuseppe Vignati of the *Istituto per la Storia della Resistenza e del Movimento Operaio Sesto San Giovanni-Milano*, the Sesto-based *Partito Democratico della Sinistra*, and two Mayors of Sesto, Sig. Giuseppe Carrà and Sig. Filippo Pennati. My thanks also go to the numerous officials of the trade union movement who gave their help and assistance to ensure that the questionnaires could be distributed at the workplaces, and also volunteered for interviews. The attitude of the main left-wing organisations in the town vis-à-vis the disclosure of information was one of complete openness and accessibility.

In Erba the research was assisted by officials of the local section of the *Lega Nord*, as well as by small business owner-managers, many of whom also filled in copies of the questionnaire. I am grateful to Marco Romanello, then a member of the Northern League and Mayor of the town, for granting me an interview. In Erba the fieldwork was also greatly helped by the assistance of a locally-based Research Officer, Maria Appiani.

In the U.K., I wish to thank Paul Christie of BUCS (University of Bath Computing Services) and Chris Williams, Chief Technician of the Department of European Studies and Modern Languages, for helping a computer semi-illiterate like me through the intricacies of the SPSS program. I also wish to thank Jill O'Brien, whose administrative and clerical support has been simply invaluable. Academically, I am extremely grateful to Roger Eatwell, Mark Gilbert, and above all Hanna Diamond, for their comments on the first draft of the manuscript. My gratitude also goes to Professor Gino Bedani for his useful comments as an external referee for this book. Financially, the research was made possible by a generous grant from the University of Bath Research Strategy Fund.

Finally, I wish to thank Susan Milner, my departmental colleague and collaborator in the research project upon which this book is based, for our regular and fruitful exchange of ideas and opinions, as well as for helping to devise the research and survey questions. A last thank you should go to my husband, David, for becoming increasingly resigned to the fact that research is one of my passions and takes up a good deal of my time, and for discovering golf as his own special interest.

political party (Sani 1992, Pasquino and McCarthy 1993, Mannheimer and Sani 1994). The subtext of many recent works on Italy, therefore, has been the need to emphasise the increasing 'normalisation' of Italian politics and society, and the end of the country's eternally anomalous and exceptional status in a European context and in the developed world.

The second factor, which brought the attention of many scholars from different academic disciplines to explore social and political change in Italy, originates from the so-called *Tangentopoli* (or Kickback City) Scandal, which started in early 1992 in a fairly subdued way and gradually assumed gigantic proportions. The scandal revealed repeated and systematic practices of bribery and corruption, involving all the major political parties, and contributed in no small way to the disappearance of many of them and the success of new ones. On the one hand, the scandal reinforced the interpretations outlined above. On the other hand, it raised new important questions in relation to Italy's presumed 'modernity' and 'normality'. Admittedly, the scandal could be imputed almost exclusively to a corrupt and obsolete political system which was by then on its way out. However, many scholars pointed their fingers at Italian society, putting the blame on a persisting culture of familism and particularism (della Porta 1992, Ginsborg 1994, 1995 and 1998, Sapelli 1995a and 1995b). Italy's 'exceptionalism', which had been thrown out by political analysts, was thus fully reinstated by sociologists, historians and social anthropologists.

The third factor revolves around the rise and success of a new regionalist political party – the *Lega Nord* (Northern League) – which in the early 1990s stood for federalism and later moved on to secessionism. In the early days, following the end of the Cold War and the *Tangentopoli* scandal, this party was seen primarily as a product of voters' protest and reaction against the malfunctioning of the Italian state, and therefore as another sign of the process of modernisation of Italian political institutions (Diamanti 1990, Moioli 1990, Mannheimer 1991, Corbetta 1993, Leonardi and Kovacs 1993). Later, when the party accentuated its radical, populist image and its ethno-regionalist stance, it became evident that these traits sat uneasily with the idea that the unfolding of Italy's political and institutional crisis would witness the emergence of pragmatic parties supported by an electorate exercising a rational choice and free of any emotional form of identification with a political movement. Both the 'modern character' of the Northern League phenomenon and the 'normalisation' of Italian politics were thus put into question (Cento Bull 1992 and 1993, Diamanti 1993, Cartocci 1994, Barraclough 1996).

A single thread connects the various approaches outlined above, despite their obvious differences and even contradictions. This thread is the idea of modernity and modernisation. Traditional modernisation theories argued that the process of industrialisation would be accompanied by the related phenomena of urbanisation, political mobilisation and cultural uniformity. 'The traditional view of social development was that these processes would sever ties with local communities and that "tribal" affiliations would give way to new attachments at national level. Urbanisation would lead to a convergence of economic and social systems towards a global pattern, consisting of a comparatively small number of relatively homogeneous "nation-states"' (Richmond 1988: 151). Politically, this convergence was seen as resulting from the rise of the middle classes accompanying a general rise in living standards, and found expression in a falling-off of ideological conflict.

Reassessing the degree of change (but also continuity) in Italy's social identities and political cultures also means reassessing concepts of modernity and modernisation. The validity of these concepts has recently been questioned from various quarters and they have already been proved at odds with Italy's post-war development. Before outlining the research questions, it is helpful to have a closer look at the main characteristics of post-war Italian society and politics, taking into account the dualistic way in which they have been analysed and interpreted to date.

Contextualising the research: Italy's path to modernity in the 'convergence' approach

After 1945, despite being to all intents and purposes a liberal-democratic country enjoying a new Constitution (from January 1948), new political institutions and free elections based on universal suffrage, Italy was considered a special case. What made the country an anomaly compared to other Western European States was the Cold War and the K (communist) factor, i.e., the presence of a Communist Party enjoying close links with Moscow. The party was viewed by the Italian political Right and its American allies primarily as a tool in the hands of the Soviet Union, implanted from the outside, rather than rooted from within. The most important consequence of this situation was the so-called *conventio ad excludendum*, in other words, the tacit understanding that the Communist Party had to be excluded from government at all costs. This led to a political system in which there was no alternation in power between two parties or coalitions of parties. The Christian Democratic Party occupied the centre ground of the political spectrum and was permanently in government, in coalition with smaller parties situated either to its right or to its left.

The 'anomalous' status of Italian politics in Western Europe was accompanied by socio-economic development in many ways comparable to that experienced by the rest of Europe. Thanks to the 'economic miracle' of the late 1950s and early 1960s – when Italian industry expanded at an annual rate of 8 percent and exports almost doubled – the growth of consumerism, the development of the media and particularly of television, a secularised, modernised, standardised, and, according to some commentators, depressingly uniform society and culture began to take shape. It is indeed possible to view Italy's development between the 1950s and the 1980s as a linear process where sub-national identities increasingly faded and the integration of the lower classes into the nation-state was finally achieved, thanks to economic growth, clientelism and consumerism. The 1970s, in particular, were years of increasing liberalisation and secularisation of Italian society, with new social and pressure groups demanding greater civil liberties and new rights for women. Divorce, abortion and new legislation relating to the family were introduced. Admittedly, the student protests of 1967–1968, originating from the failures of the education system but soon turning into a full-scale attack on the political system, the industrial workers' struggles for higher wages and widespread rights in the Autumn of 1969, not to mention 'red terrorism' in the 1970s, were all inspired by revolutionary and anti-capitalist ideologies and do not point to social and cultural integration. Nevertheless, they can also be seen as the last remnant of a revolutionary syndicalist, anti-parliamentary and anti-liberal tradition, or, alternatively, as representing confused aspirations for greater democracy. At any rate, by the 1980s, the high tide of protests and agitation had already ebbed, and the power of the unions had decreased. 'Proletarian' culture had lost much of its appeal, and new values based on individualism and personal success had emerged.

In accordance with the linear interpretation outlined above, the decades 1960–1990 would appear to have been characterised by a serious dislocation between the political system, which was blocked because of the Cold War, and the Italian economy and society, which were experiencing great change. After the rigid socio-political confrontations and authoritarian style of government of the 1950s, the political system did, in fact, attempt to change, with the 'opening to the Left' in 1963, i.e., the transition from centre–right to centre–left coalition governments. One of the objectives of this transition was precisely to widen the social basis of consensus for the democratic system through a package of social reforms. In the 1970s the political system again appeared on the verge of substantial changes, when the Communist Party enjoyed a surge in popularity and distanced itself from Moscow, going as far as to accept Italy's membership of NATO. These were the years when Berlinguer, the leader of the Communist Party, launched the idea of a 'historic compromise', or political collaboration with the Christian Democrats. The 'opening to the Left' of 1963, the 'historic compromise' of 1976–79, and the return to centre-left coalition governments in the 1980s, show how ideological conflict had given way to a particular modus vivendi between the parties, defined by Lijphart (1977 and 1984) as 'consensual democracy'. By this term Lijphart refers to a political system where rigid ideological and cultural divisions lead the political forces towards a mutual understanding and a compromising attitude, which, in turn, lead to political immobilism.

After the collapse of Italy's First Republic in the early 1990s, following the end of the Cold War, both Christian Democracy and the Communist Party disappeared from the political scene. The former collapsed at the 1994 general elections and was replaced by a number of smaller lay parties which have maintained their Christian roots, the largest of these being renamed *Partito Popolare Italiano* (PPI) after the Catholic party which existed in Italy in the inter-war period (1919-1926). The latter changed its name in 1991, becoming the Democratic Party of the Left (PDS). In 1994, the success of an entirely new party, Berlusconi's *Forza Italia*, heavily drawing on the mass media and appealing to socially and culturally undifferentiated Italians, seemed to reinforce the interpretation that Italy was on course towards the development of a majoritarian political system, where voters expressed their preferences on the basis of party programmes and candidates, rather than ideological allegiances (Mannheimer and Sani 1994). The PDS, in alliance with the PPI and other minor parties, went on to form a centre-left coalition, the *Ulivo*, while *Forza Italia* became the largest party within a centre-right coalition, the *Polo*, which included the ex-neo-fascist party (*Alleanza Nazionale*). As in the famous book by Fukuyama (1992), Italy seemed to have reached the 'End of History'. Modernisation theories appeared vindicated. Gone were the traditional and conflicting ideologies of political Catholicism and communism (not to mention neo-fascism), whose declared enemy was liberalism. The latter now dominated unchallenged, so much so that both the Democratic Party of the Left and *Alleanza Nazionale* (the heir to the neo-fascist party) proclaimed their democratic and liberal credentials. At last, Italy would be able to look forward to a renewal of its political system along the lines of its European neighbours.

Contextualising the research: Italy's path to modernity in the 'divergence' approach

It is possible, however, to take the view that Italy's cultural standardisation since the 1950s masked the re-creation of regional socio-economic structures and boundaries. As Bagnasco pointed out in 1977, there was not one but three Italies: the North-West, characterised by urban development, large industrial plants and a well developed services sector; the North-East and Centre, characterised by small-scale industrialisation, the persistence of primary and social networks and an informal economy; and the South, superficially modernised but economically underdeveloped despite massive state intervention. The North-West presented a more pluralist and individualist political culture; the North-East and Centre the resilience of traditional subcultures, performing a similar role beyond their ideological differences; the South was still embedded in a culture of clientelism and patronage. Italy had industrialised but, as in its rural days, it continued to present clear-cut territorial divisions. In this case, as we shall see, the smooth transition of its political system to some form of majoritarian rule is not a foregone conclusion.

Much of the industrialisation of Italy, in fact, did not follow the route modernisation theories predicted – it was accompanied by limited urbanisation, and although political mobilisation and cultural uniformity were high, they were also at odds with the formation of a centralised 'nation-state' (Bull and Corner 1993). Continuity with the old rural economy and society, on the other hand, brought minimal social conflict and disruption (Fuà and Zacchia 1983). A historical process of diffuse, small-scale industrialisation

6

resulted in the formation of small-business communities where social and economic ties overlapped. Firms were run by local families and the community formed both a socio-cultural referent and a specific economic organisation. This type of development was not uniform across the peninsula. The 'divergence' interpretation thus hinges upon this uneven socio-economic development, which was accompanied by remarkably resilient forms of political localism.

Economically and socially, Italy's north-eastern regions form part, together with the central regions, of what Bagnasco identified, back in 1977, as 'The Third Italy', with reference to the prevailing model of small-scale industrialisation, low social polarisation, and the persistence of strong kinship and social networks. Politically, the north-eastern regions were traditionally Catholic ('white') areas which voted regularly for the Christian Democratic Party from 1946 until the late 1980s. In this they differed from the central regions which were traditionally socialist and communist ('red') areas, where the Communist Party remained the dominant party throughout the post-war period. These two political traditions are generally known to Italian scholars as territorial political subcultures, due to their shared ideology and moral values, high degree of identification with a political party, strong community values, and the identification of a common 'enemy', which took the form of both liberalism and socialism in the 'white' areas, and liberalism and Catholicism in the 'red' ones. Trigilia defined a territorial political subculture as referring to 'some areas dominated by a specific political tradition, where a complex network of institutions – parties, interest groups, cultural and welfare associations – are well rooted in the local society and of the same politico-ideological origins' (Trigilia 1986: 13, Galli et al.1968). A territorial subculture indicates only limited integration into the national body politic and, indeed, both the Catholic and socialist subcultures in the North-East and Centre of Italy put up a defence of the local and regional society against the processes of modernisation, urbanisation and proletarianisation seen as endorsed by the central state.

It can therefore be said that both the North-East and Centre presented specific socio-economic and politico-ideological characteristics, which could have formed the basis, in the post-war period, for the emergence of strong regional identities and even regionalist political movements. Yet this did not happen, due primarily to two main factors. The first factor was ideological, in that both

contend that this continuing insistence on linear development and binary opposites represents the wrong approach to studies on socio-political change.

Scholars have moved a long way from the idea that economic and social modernisation is a uniform process, bringing with it cultural homogenisation and indifferentiation. Whereas today's mass media and global communication technologies reinforce both individualism and the development of a national (but also increasingly global) culture, they may also 'strengthen ties at the local level' (Griswold 1994: 153). As Griswold explained: 'because cultural objects are interpreted not in isolation, but by interacting human beings, it seems likely that distinct interpretations, or reinterpretations, will continue to emerge from groups having distinct experiences' (Ibid.: 91). In other words, global communication technologies will not necessarily lead to the break-up of local and regional communities, although they may add another layer of identity to human beings located in spatial communities. In this respect, the construction of a national culture and identity may be superseded by the development of both a global and a local and regional cultural dimension. Sub-national boundaries, of a socio-economic as well as of a cultural nature, have not necessarily been eliminated. Perhaps, therefore, the time has now come to acknowledge that Italy is not an anomaly in this respect and that a homogeneous national culture is as elusive in Italy as it is in most other western states, which have to contend with social fragmentation, ethnic divisions, spatial subcultures and differing economic structures.

In view of the above, the research project upon which this book is based explicitly adopted the notion of political culture, a concept which, as Wildavski (1998: 10) pointed out, 'is currently undergoing something of a renaissance'. As Welch (1993: 164) forcefully argued, the concept of political culture can help scholars overcome the division between structure and culture, because it emphasises the social construction of cultural meanings. Culture, he wrote, 'is not a set of givens; it is a process, and "political culture" refers to that process in its political aspects'. More specifically, he suggested that the notion of political culture had the merit of doing away 'with an account of politics that ignores meanings and culture, and an account of culture that ignores issues of politics and power' (Ibid.: 165). In its current use, the concept of political culture also fully acknowledges the need to explore issues of identity, not only at the national but also at the sub-national level. In the past, one of the main limitations of this concept was its unquestioned association with the national level, so much so that comparative research tended to be cross-national, 'despite strong evidence suggesting that variations in political attitudes and values within countries are often greater than those between countries' (Wildavski 1998: 4). This is one of the reasons why the research project on Italy and France mentioned in the Preface focused on cross-regional, as well as cross-national, comparisons. The aim was to explore the relationship between local and regional socio-political subcultures and the national environment, with a view to establishing whether there existed congruence and convergence between the two, or whether significant differences, and possibly competing allegiances, could be detected.

The present volume, therefore, sets out to evaluate in more detail the complex relationships between individual, community, local, regional, national, class and religious identities. It also aims to ascertain the extent to which such identities sustain and feed political orientations and voting behaviour. Although there has been a proliferation of studies concerning socio-political change in Italy, there is clearly a need to test the various interpretations emerging from these studies more systematically than before. This volume addresses, explores and tests the following controversial issues, which are steeped in the 'convergence' versus 'divergence' debate:

1. Individualism versus familism. As discussed in the previous sections, Italians are deemed either to have developed increasingly individualist values or to have remained attached to particularist, family-based values. Both propositions can easily be tested. In the first case, it should be possible to detect a clear generational gap in values, since value-changes tend to be more marked among the young. This should be accompanied by negligible gender and/or locality variations. In the second case, no generational gap should emerge, while there could be significant differences by gender and/or locality, testifying to the continuing importance of the local and spatial milieux and of the family as a 'filter' through which external 'modernising' cultural and social influences are mitigated and even neutralised.

2. Horizontal versus vertical associationism. Individualist values are generally associated with non-ascriptive interpersonal relations, which are based both on free choice and on equal (horizontal) terms. Such relations are considered typical of

modern societies. Conversely, particularist values are associated with ascriptive and fixed interpersonal relations, based on birth rather than choice and on unequal (vertical) terms. Such relations are seen as pertaining to pre-modern societies. For these assumptions to be considered valid, it should be possible to establish a significant correlation between, on the one hand, individualist values, weak kinship and friendship ties, and a high degree of horizontal associationism, and, on the other hand, familist values, strong kinship and friendship ties, and a low degree of horizontal associationism.

3. Religious versus secularist values. Modern societies tend to be secularist societies. Italy is a country which has undergone an intense process of secularisation, which is said to have contributed both to the emergence of individualist values and to the demise of the Christian Democratic Party. Religious values are associated with familist, conservative, non-liberal attitudes and ascriptive interpersonal relations. Is this a true picture of Italian Catholics?

4. Sub-national versus national orientations. To what extent are Italians' social identities predicated on territory (the town or region they live in), rather than on other factors, such as social status, religious beliefs, age, education and gender? In a modern, undifferentiated society, people's values, it is alleged, do not significantly differ on the basis of territory. The nation-building process leads to a culturally as well as administratively unitary state, which, in Europe at least, developed class-based cleavages in the course of the industrialisation process, but also shed locally- and regionally-based subcultures. Yet in Italy, as we saw, regional subcultures persisted well into the post-war period, although they are now judged to have seriously weakened. The role of sub-national factors of identity will be fully investigated in the following chapters.

5. Rational versus traditional voting behaviour. It is postulated that a clear-cut separation exists between the behaviour of the electorate in modern and in traditional societies. Voting behaviour in the former is presumed to be individualist and free, cast independently of one's own family and friends, and with little consideration for loyalty, tradition or class. The opposite seemingly applies to pre-modern societies. The appearance of a generational gap in voting behaviour would be in line with the emergence of a modern and rational electorate, while negligible differences in terms of gender and locality should be detected.

Religious or secularist beliefs could also influence the way people vote, and account for their lesser or greater propensity to adopt a more rational approach to voting.

6. Persistence or demise of territorial and/or class political sub-cultures. As in the case of social identities, political beliefs (as well as voting behaviour) in modern societies should not show significant sub-national, territorial variations. There may, of course, be variations in terms of age, education or social status. Nowadays, however, even class has become associated with traditional societies, since modernity has brought, according to various analysts, an increasing uncoupling between political and voting attitudes and class (known as 'partisan dealignment'). The issue of whether the electorate is still influenced by considerations of territory or class is fully explored in the course of this book.

The issues requiring further testing determined to a large extent the characteristics of the fieldwork and the case-studies and led to three key elements being prioritised in the choice of samples. The first element was a clear working-class profile of the people who took part in the survey, to test the resilience or demise of class as a factor of social identities, political values and voting behaviour. The second element was a tradition of political localism in the two areas chosen for the survey, to test its resilience or demise as a major factor in shaping social identities and political culture. As a third element, each area needed to be representative of one of the two main political and ideological traditions in Italy other than liberalism, i.e., communism and Catholicism. This also ensured that it would be possible to judge whether both political traditions or subcultures had weakened to the same extent or unevenly, as well as to examine the influence of religion in modern day Italy. Secondary considerations included the need to achieve a balanced distribution of the samples in terms of the age and gender of respondents as far as possible.

The data collected was used to assess the relative importance of various factors of social identities and political culture in determining the position of each locality in the continuity/change map. It was then possible to elaborate from the data more generally applicable explanations to account for old and new lines of division resting on practices of sociability, cultural and political experiences, thus contributing to an understanding of contemporary society and above all of 'modernity'.

The empirical work was conducted in two northern towns, whose characteristics are described below. I am fully aware that the choice of the localities leaves open the question of the South. Clearly, much work needs to be done in other parts of the country for a truly comparative picture to emerge of the different socio-political cultures which operate at the sub-national level. It is also important to acknowledge that neither the 'North' nor the 'South' constitute homogeneous and undifferentiated entities, a point which will be made throughout this book and which has been argued quite forcefully by various Southern scholars and intellectuals with reference to their region. The more we move away from a uniform or a simple dualistic approach to Italian society and culture, the better we are in a position to understand the complex configuration and specific needs and resources of different social, institutional and political environments.

The two case-studies

The two areas chosen were Sesto San Giovanni, an industrial suburb of Milan renowned until recently for its large-scale industry and solidarist values, with a high degree of trade-union militancy and a high percentage of votes for the parties of the left, and Erba (Como), a small town characterised by small-scale industry and located in a predominantly Catholic area previously represented by the Christian Democratic Party. Both areas have seen the demise of their traditional dominant parties, but in different contexts. Sesto was a rural/textile village at the beginning of the century, when large metal and mechanical industries, largely dependent on state orders, were set up in the area: Breda in 1903 (Breda had 4,500 workers before the First World War), Ercole Marelli in 1905, Falck and OSVA in 1906. In 1951 93 percent of the working population were employed in manufacturing industry, decreasing slightly to 87 percent in 1961. Between 1901 and 1931 the population of the town rose from 7,032 to 32,820. Of this increment, 61 percent was due to immigration from other northern provinces. After the Second World War Sesto experienced considerable immigration from the South, and enjoyed three decades of growth, between 1951 and 1981, when the population more than doubled, from 45,000 to 95,000.

In recent times Sesto has undergone substantial socio-economic changes. Since the 1970s there has been a dramatic loss of employment in the large plants, only partially offset by an expansion of small- and medium-sized industry. Of the large plants set up in the area since the beginning of the century, only one, Falck, remains a major employer. An exodus of industrial workers dismissed from the large factories has been accompanied by an emerging image of the town as a 'residential suburb' of Milan. In 1971, 79 percent of the local working population was still employed in manufacturing industry, by 1991 the percentage had gone down to 43 percent. The town experienced a decline in population: from 97,716 in 1975 to 95,127 in 1982, and 89,128 in 1990. The annual loss due to migration in the period 1982–90 was 1 percent. Unemployment in the mid-1990s stood at about 10 percent. Recently there has been some immigration from outside the European Union (EU), but in 1993 registered extra-EU immigrants numbered only 952, or 1.1 percent of residents. Immigration has recently changed: now it consists mainly of tertiary sector employees from the city of Milan, thanks to the increasing attractiveness of Sesto's new housing estates to middle-class families, both for their affordable prices and for the town's closeness to Milan, to which it is linked via the underground. Many of these new immigrants are single people, who now make up roughly one-third of all residents. Urban development has been marked by the different types of immigration. In the 1960s there was typical 'industrial style' housing – the so-called dormitories – followed in the 1970s by more residential-type housing, in line with the emerging image of Sesto as a 'residential suburb' of Milan.

Sesto's long-standing political culture has already been mentioned. Sesto was known until recently as the 'Stalingrad of Italy'. The town won the Gold Medal for Military Valour for its role in the Italian Resistance. It was badly hit by German and fascist occupation during the war, when many local people were deported to German concentration camps. The Resistance further cemented local identity around communist organisations and ideals. This is now changing, however. Votes for the Communist Party decreased from 40.79 percent in 1983 to 34.90 percent in 1987 and 21.87 percent in 1994 (29.55 percent if one adds the votes of Communist Refoundation, the other offspring of the Communist Party). First the Northern League, then Berlusconi's *Forza Italia*, attracted considerable support among the local electorate. The Northern League gained 16 percent of the votes in 1992, but this went down to 13 percent in 1994, when *Forza Italia* unexpectedly became the first party in the town, with 27 percent of the votes. More importantly, at the March 1994 political elections the parties of the left for the first time since 1946 did not obtain a majority of votes and the candidate of the right was elected. However, at the administrative elections that followed in June 1994 the candidate of the left (a PDS-led alliance, without the Socialist Party, which had collapsed due to the *Tangentopoli* scandal) was elected mayor. At the 1996 political elections the left-wing coalition, the *Ulivo*, regained a majority in the town. The socio-economic changes outlined above, in particular the decline in the size of the Sesto working class, can explain the failure of the left coalition at the 1994 general elections to a certain extent. Left-wing organisations in the town, however, have also started to change, after a period of sterile defence of the status quo in the 1970s and early 1980s. In particular, the Democratic Party of the Left (PDS, now DS, or Left Democrats), the main heir to the Italian Communist Party, has begun to woo the increasingly middle-class electorate.

Erba is a rather different proposition and contrasts neatly with Sesto both in terms of socio-economic development and in terms of political behaviour. Erba was also a rural/textile village at the beginning of the century. In 1901 it had a population of 1,934, which increased to 4,572 in 1911, 16,286 in 1981, and levelled off to 15,764 in 1991. The increase in population was steady but not dramatic, unlike Sesto, reflecting the fact that the transition from a rural to an industrial society was a gradual process in the whole province where Erba is located, and benefited the countryside as much as the towns. Most of the new entrepreneurs came from sharecropping households: artisan workshops 'grew like mushrooms' after 1945, consolidating into small- and medium-sized firms in the 1960s and 1970s. The town is representative of the northern Italian model of 'diffused industrialisation', characterised by the prevalence of small- and medium-sized industrial plants diffused over the territory. Strictly speaking, however, it is not an 'industrial district', i.e., an area characterised by a geographical concentration of small- and medium-sized firms operating in the same industrial sector. In terms of the research project a deliberate decision was taken to exclude the possibility of additional factors (such as an 'industrial district' configuration) from distorting the findings. The town has a variety of industries with a predominance of firms employing 100–200 workers. This model, unlike the one prevalent in Sesto, has not, on the surface at least, undergone substantial change over the years, yet the political configuration of the town has greatly changed, as in Sesto.

Erba was characterised politically by an inter-classist and Catholic subculture, but like Sesto it has seen the demise of its traditional dominant party, although in different contexts. Catholic predominance dates back to the 1880s, when landowners relied on the Church and its influence among sharecroppers. It then re-emerged after the fascist period. Christian Democracy (DC) commanded a comfortable majority after the Second World War and even in 1976 – at a time of increasing support for the left in Italy – it polled 48 percent in the town. In 1992 this decreased to 26 percent, on a par with the Northern League. In 1994 the *Partito Popolare Italiano* (PPI, the main heir to the DC) polled 11 percent, the League 26 percent, and *Forza Italia* 26 percent. In 1996 the Northern League obtained 32 percent of votes, the *Polo* 36.9 percent, the *Ulivo* 31.1 percent. Thus the town has recently seen an upsurge in support for the Northern League, a party which has been defined variously as populist, subcultural, racist and even fascist. The Northern League, it has been maintained, has made inroads into all social groups, therefore recreating the inter-classism which characterised the Christian Democratic Party, whose electorate is deemed to have shifted in great numbers to the Northern League. Christian Democracy's domination thus seems to have been replaced by electoral fluidity. Do we have to conclude that the local subculture has broken down?

The following chapters will assess the extent of the process of partisan dealignment and individualism in voting behaviour or, conversely, the degree to which voters, both male and female, still subscribe to a territorial or class subculture and values. The possible emergence of gender-based discrepancies in voting behaviour and values will also be explored, and their significance in terms of electoral outcomes and political influence examined. First, however, the survey and the characteristics of the samples upon which it was based need to be briefly described.

Fieldwork

The research which forms the backbone of this book was carried out in various phases, reflecting its wide scope in comparative terms, since it involved comparing not only two different sites within Italy, but also, as mentioned in the Preface, matching these two sites with two others in France. The first phase of the research was a pilot project carried out over a six-month period

(January–July 1994), which was financed by the University of Bath. A research assistant distributed questionnaires devised in both Italian and French. In order to do this, she first had to build a network of contacts, relying to a large extent on the goodwill of left-wing associations in the two industrial suburbs, and of owner-managers of small and medium-sized firms in the two industrial towns (as well as Catholic associations in Erba). On the other hand, the assistant was left free to distribute the questionnaires inside the industrial plants to all workers, including non-unionised workers. Whilst this approach may have had the effect of skewing the samples, it was adopted deliberately, since the aim, in the two industrial suburbs, was to target respondents with a traditional left-wing subculture as much as possible, in order to assess changes in their beliefs and attitudes. As many representatives of left-wing organisations told us repeatedly, particularly in Sesto, they now accepted that they no longer knew how workers voted or felt on many sensitive issues, such as immigration. Indeed, the Mayor of Sesto, Sig. Pennati, told me in an interview that he suspected that many workers in the town belonged to some left-wing organisations, such as trade unions, but had voted for a radical-right party, such as the Northern League.

These contacts proved much easier to achieve in Italy than in France, and the rate of return was much higher for Italy than for France. There appeared to be two main reasons for this different rate of success in the fieldwork. First, Italian respondents proved remarkably willing to answer questions on party preferences, whereas French respondents were much more reluctant. This was in some ways surprising, since Italy has notoriously been considered a 'difficult' country for surveys on political attitudes and voting behaviour. The survey suggested that the greater openness of Italian respondents in both localities was due to the liberating effects of the end of the Cold War and the collapse of the old ideological divisions. Suddenly, it was no longer considered shameful or dangerous to declare one's own preference for an ex-communist party or an ex-neo-fascist one: the fact that they were post-ideological parties removed both the stigma and the risk. As for Northern League voters, they were, if anything, proud of their party and its programme. The second aspect that seemed to put French respondents on their guard concerned questions relating to immigration. The growing success of the *Front National* in France at that time and the moral stigma attached to this party, as well as the greater proportions and impact of recent extra-EU immigration in that country, help explain the reticence of French respondents compared to the openness of the Italians.

In total, 443 questionnaires were filled in by workers at a few large factories in Sesto, including Falck, Breda, ABB and Giem, as well as by unemployed people (via the local *Ufficio di Colloca-mento*). A total of 445 questionnaires were filled in by blue- and white-collar workers at various medium-sized manufacturing firms in Erba, as well as by artisans and small entrepreneurs. The data provided by the questionnaires was fed into a computer, thus much of the evidence offered in this volume is based on a computer analysis of 888 questionnaires, using the SPSS program. This analysis was backed up by a detailed manual analysis of 277 responses, which allowed me to gain some extremely valuable insights into the personality and attitudes of the respondents. Many, in fact, had gone to great lengths to convey their values and beliefs, complementing the more standard replies with consider-ations and opinions of their own, by annotating comments on the margins.

The questionnaire, which is reproduced in the Appendix, focused on multiple social identities as well as political behaviour at local level. The more general questions dealt with socio-economic and family background, geographical origins, kinship relations, embeddedness in the local community, degree of religiosity, degree of political participation, local/regional/national identities, and approval/disapproval of main political institutions. Whenever poss-ible respondents were asked to state how their values/criteria/per-ceptions had changed compared to five–ten years before. Specific questions dealt with voting behaviour of the respondents and their parents in the 1987 and 1992 political elections as well as the 1993 administrative elections, voting intentions for the 1994 political elections, and criteria for party preferences. The role of the two most important integrating forces in society, the family and religion, was explored in some depth. A third factor of social identity, class, was also prioritised in the questions. The main object was to exam-ine the interplay of these social identities, in the knowledge that the process of working-class bonding was inserted into pre-existing structures of social relationships such as kinship and family net-works, national and local loyalties, and religious affiliation. Gen-dered attitudes were systematically explored. In addition to the questionnaires, interviews with local politicians, administrators, trade unionists, and members of various associations were carried out. In particular, one-to-one interviews were conducted with representatives of the CGIL trade union, exponents of the Democratic Party of the Left (the ex-Communist Party) and the Northern League, an ex-Mayor and the then Mayor of Sesto and the then Mayor of Erba. Past and present electoral results for both localities and socio-economic statistics also formed the basis of this study.

As for the characteristics of the samples, in Sesto respondents, as already mentioned, were predominantly blue- or white-collar factory workers or unemployed. In Erba they were mainly blue- and white-collar factory workers, but there was also a significant sub-sample of artisans and small entrepreneurs. This was deliberate, since the main aim of the research was to analyse the extent to which territorial (as well as class) subcultures in Italy were breaking down, therefore it was important to target those people who were most likely to have been (and possibly still were) staunch supporters of a specific subculture. In Sesto the most likely supporters of the communist subculture, with its emphasis on class and trade-unionist solidarity, were undoubtedly industrial workers, and this is why they were prioritised to the extent that most questionnaires were actually distributed inside the various factories, with the approval of trade-union shop stewards. In Erba, given that the Catholic subculture was closely correlated to the socio-economic configuration of this area, the aim was to target a sample of respondents representative not just of the working class, but also of those social groups more directly linked to the local economic model: industrial workers employed in small- and medium-sized plants, private-sector employees, and artisans and small entrepreneurs. Thus the socio-economic status of respondents was the main criteria adopted when distributing the questionnaire, although attention was also paid to achieving a balance in terms of both gender and age.

As it turned out, in Sesto roughly two-thirds of respondents were men, and one third were women. In Erba, 60 percent of respondents were men, 40 percent women. In terms of age, the Sesto sample contained a smaller percentage of young people, less than a quarter as opposed to a third in Erba. Although this could be due to a sample quirk, it more probably reflects the fact that large firms in Italy have stopped recruiting in any significant numbers and indeed have been shedding labour. Small- and medium-sized firms in Erba appear to have been better able to sustain employment, in line with Italy's successful model of small-scale industry. In terms of geographical origins, 27 percent of respondents in Sesto and 42.4 percent in Erba had been born in the locality, with another 29.9 percent in Sesto and 32.2 percent in Erba being born in another commune within the same province, reflecting above all the type of population growth experienced by the two towns since the early part of the century. Lastly, in terms of degree of religiosity, 51 percent in Sesto and 74.1 percent in Erba were practising Catholics, as was expected given that the latter is located in a traditional 'white' subcultural area.

The structure of the book

The book is divided in two parts. Part I deals with social identities, Part II with political cultures. Each Part is made up of three chapters, plus an introduction and a conclusion. In the Introduction to Part I, issues related to the continuing importance of kinship, friendship and social networks in Italy are addressed and discussed, with a view to assessing recent controversial debates, revolving particularly around the political and public consequences of their alleged resilience. The book then proceeds to shed new light upon these issues on the basis of the evidence gathered in the fieldwork described in the previous section. Chapter 1 addresses the question of whether kinship and social networks are indeed still as important in Italian society as it is commonly alleged, and concludes that this is certainly the case. To this end the chapter offers new evidence which shows that, in this respect at least, there is little to distinguish between the two towns chosen as casestudies, despite their very different background in terms of socioeconomic development and political culture. A comparison between Sesto and Vénissieux, one of the French sites looked at as part of the wider research project discussed above, further substantiates this finding, by presenting a picture of stark dissimilarities between these two localities in terms of their social identities, despite their economic and political comparability. Chapter 2 then deals with the issue of associationism, aiming to establish whether dense kinship and social networks (as well as Catholic beliefs) have a detrimental impact upon the quantity and quality of horizontal associationism and civic engagement, as argued by some sociologists and political analysts. After a careful analysis of the relevant survey data, the chapter concludes that by and large there is no proven direct correlation between strong kinship ties and a low level of public engagement, or indeed between Catholic values and beliefs and 'asocial' behaviour. The findings presented in the chapter also reveal that people in Erba and Sesto tend to behave differently on the basis of the town they live in and the local subculture they partake of, rather than on the basis of the intensity of their kinship ties or degree of religiosity. To explore this in some depth, Chapter 3 examines the continuing importance of localism in Italy and concludes that a territorial subculture continues to shape people's identities to a larger extent than either social status, religion, gender or age. Of all these, it is gender which, surprisingly, emerges as the next most important factor in accounting for differing social identities. The Conclusion to Part I reinstates the importance of local subcultures – and not just kinship and social networks – in determining people's attitudes and beliefs in Italy. It also establishes that women are decidedly less committed to a territorial subculture than men and somewhat less family-orientated. Finally, it postulates that these findings have important implications for political and voting behaviour, which are then analysed in Part II.

The Introduction to Part II addresses recent controversial debates revolving around the issues of people's attitudes to sociopolitical change and of the resilience or demise of political subcultures and 'loyal' voting behaviour. These debates have found a new urgency, as we saw, following Italian political events since the fall of the Berlin Wall in 1989, particularly the collapse of antiliberal ideologies such as communism and neo-fascism, and the disappearance of the dominant post-war party, the Christian Democratic Party. Chapter 4 examines in some detail political attitudes and beliefs, focusing in particular on the positioning of respondents in relation to change, by probing their views on policies concerning taxation, privatisation, administrative and institutional reforms, and immigration. It concludes that people positioned themselves vis-à-vis change in ways which were not necessarily consistent – from the perspective of theories of modernisation and modernity – with their positioning in relation to kin, class or political localism. Thus many people who held localist and particularist values were keen to promote change, at least in terms of favouring the implementation of free-market economic policies, while others who held individualist and universalist values were found to be resistant to change. Chapter 5 probes voting behaviour. It brings to light the persistence of 'partisan alignment' in Italy and confirms the identification of substantial groups of working-class voters with a specific political party and tradition. In this respect, the same gender divide, which had been detected in

Part I when analysing people's attachment to subcultural values and identities, reappears when examining voting behaviour. In other words, women were found to be the least loyal to a political tradition when casting their votes, while men were the most loyal. Considerations of loyalty were also weaker among the younger generation, but the gap was not very significant. The chapter also establishes that the family plays a substantial role in determining the way people vote. Finally, Chapter 6 deals with political localism and examines in some depth the reasons for the success of the Northern League among Erba respondents at the 1987, 1992 and 1994 political elections. In particular, the chapter addresses the issue of whether this party represented a form of protest against the old political system, or whether it had established roots among and commanded the loyalty of the local electorate. After analysing the evidence, it concludes that the latter was predominantly the case, and argues that there are common 'threads' linking Christian Democratic and Northern League voters, reinforcing the hypothesis that the Northern League is the political heir of the Catholic subculture in areas of small-scale industry. The Conclusion to Part II stresses the relevance of these findings for an understanding of the evolution of political culture in Italy today. It argues that community and class identities do continue to influence the way people regard political issues and cast their votes, alongside more individual orientations. Localism is an integral component of Italian political culture, and it cannot be discarded in any analysis or vision of political change in Italy.

A final chapter rounds off the arguments developed in the book and reassesses theories of modernity and modernisation in the light of the evidence brought forward in Part I and Part II. It rejects the idea that modernity represents a uniform and universal 'outcome' of a linear development and that strong kinship and friendship ties and particularist and localist values are an indication of a pre-modern society. Both the 'Italian family' and socio-political localism have fully modernised and experienced very considerable mutations. The chapter re-examines the issue of the renewal of the political system and therefore of institutional reform, currently debated in Italy on the basis that the country's institutions need modernising to be able to function properly in a united Europe. It argues that the real issue is whether they need to modernise by importing a foreign model from one of the countries deemed to be already fully modern, or by setting up a political system which is both fit for the twenty-first century and able to build upon the social and cultural traits which are the unique and specific product of Italian history. The chapter concludes by stressing that all the evidence unearthed in the course of the book points to the need to embark upon the latter course.

Part I: Social Identities

Introduction

In recent times, and from different sources, the resilience and vitality of the Italian family have been confirmed (Hollinger and Haller 1990, Barbagli 1991b, De Rose 1992, Bull and Corner 1993, Cavalli and de Lillo 1993, Ginsborg 1994 and 1995, Sapelli 1995b, Quattrociocchi 1996). For some commentators, such as Ginsborg and Sapelli, the continuing importance of primary groups in Italian society has deeply negative consequences upon both the economic and the political sphere (Ginsborg 1995, Sapelli 1995a and 1995b). Ginsborg acknowledges, however, 'the social value of strong kinship relationships' (1995: 5), and this leads him to view the phenomenon in dualistic terms (positive at the social level, negative at the political one). In particular, Ginsborg postulates a close connection between the primacy of family and social networks and 'familism', which he defines as 'a specific relation between family, civil society and the state, in which the values and interests of the family are counterposed to those of the other principal moments of human association' (Ibid.: 5–6). He adds: 'Familism, in my definition, is an inward-looking phenomenon which stunts the growth of modern civil society and deforms the relationship between citizen and state' (Ibid.: 6). Both Ginsborg and Sapelli view familism as the fundamental constituent of Italian socio-political culture and link it to the prevalence of vertical over horizontal associationism and to the inability of the Italian state to develop a modern civic culture. Sapelli (1995b: 91, 1997) refers explicitly to a 'bastardised modernisation (clientelism, kinship ties, amoral familism, extremely rapid growth and the impossibility of laying down institutional rules)'. Both scholars draw a clear distinction between the political culture of Mediterranean societies and that which characterises Northern Europe. Northern Europe – a term which is mainly used to indicate the Protestant North, as it is doubtful whether the authors would include Ireland or Belgium in their paradigm – stands for civic values, public ethics, horizontal associationism (Ginsborg 1995) and for 'individualistic values (respect for oneself and for others within an adherence to cultures of legality and universalism)' (Sapelli 1995b: 86). The ultimate aim is that of a rational, enlightened, civic culture. When judged against this paradigm, Italy is deemed to have failed the test. As Griffin (1997: 153) wrote: 'The question which remains tantalisingly open is whether there are any serious prospects for Italy to develop a mature national, though regionally diversified, civic culture which would enable it to play a full role in the new Europe. [...] For the foreseeable future the country seems doomed to remain polarised indefinitely between a cynical or impotent political class and a sceptical, disaffected electorate'.

The views summarised above are extremely interesting in so far as they raise critical questions in relation to contemporary approaches to the study of social and political cultures. They underline the need for clarification on a theoretical level as well as the need to anchor any 'grand' analysis to empirical research. With regards to the former, the underlying, indeed explicit, assumption behind the approach adopted by the above scholars is a continuing belief in classical political rationalism and the idea of progress. As Gray (1995: 64) put it, 'The idea of progress which the Enlightenment project embodies may be seen as a diachronic statement of the classical conception of natural law. This is the modern conception of human social development as occurring in successive discrete stages, not everywhere the same, but having in common the property of converging on a single form of life, a universal civilisation, rational and cosmopolitan'. He added that the Enlightenment project was closely linked with theories of modernisation, and that both had failed, in his view, particularly 'Enlightenment expectations of the evanescence of particularistic allegiances, national and religious, and of the progressing levelling down, or marginalisation, of cultural difference in human affairs' (Ibid.: 65). One of the most important conclusion Gray draws from his rejection of modernisation theories is that 'allegiance to a liberal state is [..] never primarily to principles which it may be thought to embody, and which are supposed to be compelling for all human beings; it is always to specific institutions, having a specific history, and to the common culture which animates them, which is itself a creature of historical contingency' (Ibid.: 78). It is interesting, from my point of view, that all three scholars mentioned above, Ginsborg, Griffin and Sapelli, recognise the importance of Italy's cultural traditions and 'old values' in determining the resilience and continuity of specific political attitudes and institutions in that country. However, given their belief in political rationalism and modernisation, they are left registering and/or lamenting Italy's inability to complete the transition from x (where x stands for old particularist and clientelist values) to y (where y stands for modern, civic, universalist values).

It is even more interesting to compare their laments with those of Gray himself, when confronted with the consequences of the Anglo-Saxon liberal 'paradigm': 'Communities are scattered to the winds by the gale of creative destruction. Endless "downsizing" and "flattening" of enterprises fosters ubiquitous insecurity and makes loyalty to the company a cruel joke. The celebration of consumer choice, as the only undisputed value in market societies, devalues commitment and stability in personal relationships and encourages the view of marriage and the family as vehicles of self-realisation. The dynamism of market processes dissolves social hierarchies and overturns established expectations. Status is ephemeral, trust frail and contract sovereign' (Gray 1995: 98–9). He adds: 'the US model of individualist market institutions has been distinguished by levels of family breakdown and fractured community, of criminality and of incarceration, that are unknown in other Western countries [...] The US model [...] is not exportable to any society with a less individualist moral and political culture' (Ibid.: 97). Similarly, in a very polemical work, Hutton deplored the destruction of common values in the U.K. as a result of the spread of unrestrained individualism, arguing that: 'Britain's national affairs are reaching explosive levels of stress. The individualist, *laissez-faire* values which imbue the economic and political élite have been found wanting – but with the decline of socialism, there seems to be no coherent alternative in the wings' (Hutton 1996: 23-4).

When one considers that Gray used to extol the virtues of market freedom and Thatcherism, and has now completely shifted his attitude as a result of what he considers the destructive effects of the free market upon social cohesion (Gray 1998), one has a better idea of the limited value of any uncritical and simplistic adherence to untested (and ultimately mythical) paradigms. So much for Sapelli's reference to Italy's 'bastardised modernisation'. It seems clear that we have to accept that there is wide disagreement as to what constitutes a 'virtuous modernisation', or indeed whether such a thing exists at all. As Kellner (1997: 15) recently pointed out, in the aftermath of the collapse of the South Korean economy, which had been heralded in the U.K. as a model for export and 'salvation at home', 'there has seldom been any magic elixir in the success of other countries. Their growth has had a variety of causes, many of them complex, some of them unique to that country's history and culture, and all of them interacting with each other'. He concluded by stressing that among the lessons to be learnt in the U.K. from the South Korean experience was the need 'to develop a more mature political culture in which we can explore British solutions to British problems. It is a cop out to suppose that foreign, off-the-peg economic fashions will wear well in Britain; we should design bespoke clothes of our own. This does not mean we can ignore what happens in other countries. But we should heed their disasters as well as their triumphs. We shall be making progress when we really do manage to keep both in perspective'.

It could be argued that what I have presented so far is by and large an extreme view of modernisation theory. Times have moved on since Almond and Verba's (1963) ethnocentric definition of the 'civic culture' as underpinning stable liberal democracies. Yet I would point out that ethnocentrism has proved extremely enduring and this has hampered the replacement of the ideologically charged concept of the 'civic culture' with the more neutral one of 'political culture'. Political culture 'does not, unlike the civic culture, offer a normative criterion for evaluating the democratic status of an individual state. Political culture in this sense attempts to identify those factors in a political system which have a formative political influence on the individual, the group and the society; it further seeks to evaluate the importance of certain values and norms over the long and short term' (Girvin 1990: 33). It is with the latter meaning that the concept of political culture is used in this volume as an analytical tool. This is not to say that 'political culture' is an unambiguous and uncontested notion. It does, nevertheless, have the merit of ensuring what Welch (1993: 72–4) defined as 'sensitivity to context', i.e., to cultural differences and variations, which occur as much intra-nationally as they do across nations. Emphasising cultural variation may be problematic for comparative research. However, as Welch also noted (1993: 161), comparisons remain valid, provided that they become 'much more specific than they have typically been'.

In this section, I start from the premise that Italy's path to modernisation is neither bastard nor distorted: it is, quite simply, specific and congruent with its history. I also start from the premise that there is no proven connection between the importance of the family in Italy and 'familism' as defined by Ginsborg. There is surprisingly little empirical research underpinning recent debates on Italy's political and civic cultures and the predominance of familism (Eve 1996: 45). In particular, I have not been able to find concrete evidence that strong kinship and social ties are correlated with weak horizontal associationism and vice versa. As Putnam argued, Italian regions differ widely in terms of levels of 'civicness' and degrees of associationism (Putnam 1993). Yet the institution of the family, according to all commentators, remains strong in all areas of the country. In this section I will argue that strong family ties correlate perfectly well with a high degree of participation in horizontal associations. Kinship and friendship ties, in other words, seem to be perfectly compatible with horizontal associationism and indeed may underpin participation in the public sphere as well as civic awareness.

What has been said above does not imply that the continuing importance of kinship and friendship ties in Italy has no bearing upon its social and political culture, compared to, for example, Anglo-Saxon societies. The main difference, however, may lie not so much in weak versus strong horizontal associationism, as in the type of horizontal associations people participate in and above all in the unit of associationism. Anglo-Saxon societies are characterised – it goes without saying – by a long-standing tradition of liberal individualism, where the unit of society is considered to be the single individual, who will join a leisure club, a trade union, a political party, etc., on the basis of an autonomous and rational choice. Reality can only approximate the ideal model, of course, nevertheless in recent times the decreasing importance of the family and unsettling of social communities in Anglo-Saxon societies has accentuated – indeed, for scholars like Gray, exasperated – individualist values at the expense of both the family and the community. In Italy, by contrast, the unit of society continues to be the family rather than the individual, and it is often the family which is the springboard for wider social participation, as well as political values and attitudes. In this context, the emergence in Italy of individualist values, as auspicated by Sapelli, who appears to equate such values with 'virtuous modernisation', is highly problematic. Allegiance to and participation in horizontal associations will not be purely a matter for individual choice, but will also depend on the value orientation and even be predicated upon the social behaviour of family members and friends. Socio-political participation, even voting behaviour (as we shall see later in the book), may turn out to be the result of a group's, as opposed to an individual's, choice.

Of greater interest than the above debates is perhaps the issue of the conflicting and complex ways and contexts in which the interests of the family and other primary groups have continued to prevail over individualism in Italy. An important aspect concerns the transmission of family values across different generations. It would appear that there have been periods of great generational divide in Italy in terms of social and political values, moments of crisis as well as continuity. One such period has been analysed by Gribaudi with reference to working-class families in the urban suburbs of Turin (Gribaudi 1987). The primacy of the family, in other words, has been reasserted in Italy despite both internal and external tensions and crises, rather than being the outcome of a linear and uncontroversial process. The question today, therefore, is whether the resilience of the family in Italy is the result of an uneasy (and possibly fragile) equilibrium between the increasingly individualist strategies of its members or, conversely, reflects the predominance of group strategy and cohesion over individual aspirations. Linked to the above, is the issue of whether the apparent continuity provided by the unbroken importance of the family in Italy today, masks in fact real change in the nature of internal relations within this primary group. Quattrociocchi (1996), for example, has stressed the need to look beyond statistical data (which simply confirms the prevalence of family units comprising two parents and their children) and to capture the very substantial changes which have taken place, particularly the increase in single-child family units and the phenomenon of the 'long family', where children stay at home until their late twenties. The latter trend has, if anything, accentuated in the course of the last decade. Whereas 39 percent of Italians between the ages of 25 and 29 were still living at home in 1990, the figure had risen to 54 percent in 1996; similarly, 21.6 percent of people aged between 30 and 34 stayed at home in 1996, compared with 13.7 percent five years earlier (Puccioni 1998: 22). Bagnasco (1996a: 56) has also argued that much has changed in the Italian family, which has become more 'democratic' and contractual in nature. Thus relations between spouses or partners as well as between parents and children are now increasingly based upon an equal standing and children have much more say in family matters. This represents a far cry from the traditional patriarchal and authoritarian family where socio-political values and patterns of behaviour are simply transmitted from parents to children in a one-way, top-to-bottom, flow.

Finally, there is a need for paying attention to subcultural variations (Topf 1990). Despite the emergence of a post-modern approach to political studies, including political culture (Gibbins 1990, Rengger 1997), it continues to be largely assumed – though generally not by Italian scholars – that social identities and political culture are homogeneous within a given nation-state, that it is therefore possible to generalise about the 'Italian family' or a presumed 'Italian national character'. By doing this, one takes the existence of a 'national culture' as a given and remains within the logic of equating modernity and modernisation with an unproblematic erosion of local and regional identities. The resurgence of ethno-nationalism in both eastern and western Europe and the de-structuring effects of the process of economic globalisation upon nation-states should make one wary of adopting this linear perspective. In the case of Italy, the fragility of the process of constructing a uniform 'language of nationhood' is well documented (Dickie 1993 and 1994, Rusconi 1993, Lepre 1994, Gribaudi 1997).

The two case-studies from which this book has been able to draw new, empirical evidence, with a view to throwing new light upon the issues discussed so far, are both highly relevant in the Italian context. One of the Italian case-studies, Sesto, was known in the past as the Stalingrad of Italy for its working-class culture and communist identity. Today, as was mentioned in the Introduction, Sesto has seen a marked decline in its traditional manufacturing sector and factory organisation, a breakdown of its left-wing collective solidarity, and disaffection with existing political parties. The magnitude of the transition Sesto has experienced in the last twenty years shows some resemblance to that of the Turin suburbs described by Gribaudi (1987) before and during the fascist period. In many respects Sesto is, therefore, an ideal place for studying continuity and change in cultural values, particularly in relation to familism, collective solidarity and individualism. The relevance of Sesto is also apparent when one considers Sapelli's claim that the source of Italy's 'bastardised modernisation' is to be found in the all-too-brief period of industrialisation the country went through. As Sapelli (1995b: 91, 1997) wrote: 'When industrial society arrived in Italy, it seemed to demand forms of mobilisation which were defined by horizontal rather than vertical links, and associated with the kind of virtuous modernisation that people thought would be brought about by large companies and the market. However, in reality, industrial society lasted for too short a time to impose such changes in Italy (only twenty years as opposed to the hundreds of years of the first industrial nations)'.

Interestingly, Sesto industrialised at the beginning of the twentieth century on the basis of large companies, each employing thousands of workers. Its de-industrialisation dates back to the late 1970s, therefore the town experienced one of the longest spells of large-scale industrialisation in the whole of the country. Horizontal associations thrived in the town, which also played a large role in the Italian Resistance (associated by Ginsborg 1995 with civic and republican virtues). If Sapelli's interpretation is correct, then one would expect the family to have lost importance among Sesto citizens and the weakening of the old proletarian collective solidarity to have given way to individualist and universalist values. In other words, one would expect to be able to see the effects of the 'virtuous mobilisation' Sapelli associates with long-term industrial societies. Indeed some scholars have detected the emergence of new individualist and 'market' values among the young in Sesto, together with single issue, new social movements (Berti and Donegà, 1992). In my own research I focused on a social group which has been most directly affected by large-scale industrialisation and investigated the cultural values of industrial workers, both in employment and unemployed, of all ages and both sexes. In order to put my own fieldwork in comparative perspective, I will also make use, in this chapter, of some of the findings of the research project on social identities and political culture in Italy and France I mentioned in the Introduction. This will allow me to compare directly Sesto with Vénissieux (Lyon). Since both areas have a very similar history of large-scale industrialisation followed by de-industrialisation, such a comparison will show whether a similar socio-economic process has been accompanied by similar trajectories in terms of social and political cultures, and/or whether kinship networks retain any role as an integrating force.

The other case-study, Erba, is also highly relevant in view of current debates on familism, individualism and civic values. The town is situated in the middle of a traditionally 'white' – i.e., Catholic and, until recently, Christian Democratic – area. This raises new and important questions. According to Ginsborg, the influence of the Church has played a large part in fostering allegiance to particularist groups such as the family, at the expense of horizontal associationism: 'The church has always stressed the preeminence of the family over society, a preeminence both temporal and ethical. The family is the first natural society and its duties are of a higher order than those of civil society. They are essentially internal rather than external, centred on piety, procreation, the Christian education of children, the indissolubility of marriage' (Ginsborg 1995: 7). Putnam also appeared to suggest that Catholic values are inversely correlated with civic values (Putnam 1993: 176). Erba is clearly a town where we would expect family values and religious affiliation to continue to shape social identities. It remains to be seen whether the town also shows a low degree of associationism, particularly when compared to Sesto, where the influence of religion is much weaker, as we shall see.

It is now time to reassess the interplay between family, religious, individualist and civic values in the light of the evidence I was able to unearth in the course of my research.

1

The Persistence of Family and Friendship Ties

Introduction

In this chapter the continuing importance of kinship and friendship ties in Italy is tested with reference to both Sesto and Erba. The questionnaire which was distributed among respondents in these two localities in the Spring of 1994 contained numerous questions which specifically addressed the issue of family and social values. Question 17 asked respondents to subscribe to the statement which best encapsulated what they considered to be most important in life. The choice was between personal fulfilment and success (individualist values), the family (particularist values), or solidarity (universalist/collective values). In Question 23 respondents were asked whether primary and private associations such as the family and circles of friends, and public environments such as work, politics and leisure, had grown or decreased in importance compared to five to ten years previously. Questions 10 and 11 tested the nature and frequency of contacts between non-cohabiting family members and friends. Other Questions (12 and 14) probed the extent to which respondents were involved in their local community, with particular reference to their relations with neighbours and colleagues. Question 13 addressed the issue of job satisfaction, while Question 15 and Question 16 tested the respondents' desire for job mobility and, in the case of an affirmative reply, specifically asked them what kind of job they aspired to.

Family values

Sesto

The Sesto sample comprised 294 men and 137 women. Roughly a fifth of men and a third of women were aged eighteen to thirty: the majority in this age group were single people living at home. Half of the men and 40 percent of the women were aged between forty and fifty: the majority were married with children. Only 3 percent of all respondents were divorced. A large number of young people were found among the unemployed, in line with official statistics.

The age composition of respondents influenced their marital status, with only 24 percent claiming single status in Sesto. Being single and between eighteen and thirty years of age did not, however, mean living away from one's own family of origin. This is in line with recent findings on the Italian family, which show that children continue to stay at home until they get married (Ginsborg 1994). The mean family size of the samples in Sesto was 3.2 (the median score was 3), above both the local averages as recorded in the 1991 population census and the national average.

The data related to gender, age and family composition indicated a relative stability in terms of personal circumstances. The divorce rate was very low, young people enjoyed the security of their families even in their twenties, and partly thanks to them nearly two members per family were in full-time employment, a finding which suggested relative prosperity as well as stability. In Sesto the stable conditions of the respondents contrasted with the general instability of recent demographic and socio-economic changes. Thus a study by Berti and Donegà (1992) showed that a third of all families in Sesto were made up of just one member (up from a fifth in 1981), the average number of members per family had systematically gone down since 1971 and there had been a very considerable exodus of families made up of middle-aged parents with children.

There is little doubt that the family still plays a fundamentally supportive and socialising role in Sesto. Not only did young people live with their families well into their twenties, they also continued to enjoy very close relations with their relatives after they left home (Table 1.1).

As Table 1.1 shows, a majority of respondents in Sesto (53.5 percent) indicated that family relations with non-cohabiting relatives were both 'frequent and friendly', while less than one-third (29.3

Table 1.1 Relations with non-cohabiting relatives in Sesto

		Frequency	Percent	Valid Percent	Cumulative Percent
Valid	solidarist	53	12.0	13.3	13.3
	frequent and friendly	214	48.3	53.5	66.8
	not very frequent but friendly	117	26.4	29.3	96.0
	infrequent and not very friendly	12	2.7	3.0	99.0
	no contacts	4	0.9	1.0	100.0
	Total	400	90.3	100.0	
Missing		43	9.7		
Total		443	100.0		

percent) declared that they were 'friendly although not frequent'. Slightly more than one in ten (13.3 percent) stated that such relations were 'solidarist', with only 3 percent of respondents reporting that they were 'neither frequent nor friendly'. There were some minor gender differences, with more women than men reporting frequent and friendly relations.

The central role of the family was particularly apparent when the issue of individualism was explored (Table 1.2).

Table 1.2 Respondents' life values in Sesto

		Frequency	Percent	Valid Percent	Cumulative Percent
Valid	personal realisation is most important	67	15.1	16.1	16.1
	family interests come before individual aspirations	182	41.1	43.6	59.7
	the family is a handicap in terms of personal success	7	1.6	1.7	61.4
	solidarity is the most important human value	161	36.3	38.6	100.0
	Total	417	94.1	100.0	
Missing		26	5.9		
Total		443	100.0		

Both the older and younger generations in Sesto declared that family values were more important than individualist ones. Among all respondents, 43.6 percent stated that 'family interests come before individual aspirations'. Only 16.1 percent agreed with the statement 'personal realisation is most important', while 38.6 percent subscribed to solidarist values. Male respondents, in particular, considered the family more important than personal success or even solidarity, perhaps the single most important value in the 'proletarian' subculture. Responses were remarkably similar across all age groups, including young men aged between eighteen and thirty. Women were more divided: a substantial minority subscribed to individual success, but most believed in solidarist values, while many still strongly supported family values. Among women, unlike men, specific age patterns emerged: the family was judged most important in the 41–50 group, solidarity was the value supported by most women in the 31–40 and 18–30 groups. However, a third of young women aged eighteen and thirty put personal fulfilment first, as opposed to a fourth of young male workers.

In view of the relationship hypothesised by Ginsborg (1995) between Catholic beliefs and family values, I decided to analyse the sample data on the basis of the degree of religiosity of respondents. Table 1.3 shows the relative importance of family, individualist, and solidarist values among respondents according to their religious beliefs.

Ginsborg's (1995) hypothesis was confirmed by the data, since attachment to the family was highest among respondents who were practising Catholics. A majority of respondents who attended functions such as Mass on either a regular (50.7 percent) or occasional basis (51.1 percent) subscribed to family values. This applied to both men and women. Conversely, respondents in Sesto who were non-believers put their faith primarily in solidarist values. Yet the data also threw up some unexpected results in relation to gender. In particular, Catholic men in Sesto, whether practising or not, judged the family more important than Catholic women, who tended to subscribe in greater numbers to solidarist values. This trend was also noticeable in Erba, as we shall see, and raises the question of whether Ginsborg underestimated the role played by Catholicism in fostering universalist values, leading to a greater potential for associationism than he anticipated. This issue will be further explored in the next chapter.

It is clear that in Sesto the family provided practical support and a stable environment for the young, and that this included the

Table 1.3 Life values compared to religious values in Sesto

		personal realisation is most important	family interests come before individual aspirations	the family is a handicap in terms of career success	solidarity is the most important human value	Total
Religious values	**Religious believer and regular church attendant**					
	Count	8	37	2	26	73
	% within religious values	11.0%	50.7%	2.7%	35.6%	100.0%
	% of Total	2.0%	9.3%	0.5%	6.5%	18.3%
	believer, irregular church attendant					
	Count	12	67	2	50	131
	% within religious values	9.2%	51.1%	1.5%	38.2%	100%
	% of Total	3.0%	16.8%	.5%	12.5%	32.8%
	believer, non-church attendant					
	Count	33	55	3	37	128
	% within religious values	25.8%	43.0%	2.3%	28.9%	100.0%
	% of Total	8.3%	13.8%	.8%	9.3%	32.0%
	non-believer, irregular church attendant					
	Count	2	7		12	21
	% within religious values	9.5%	33.3%		57.1%	100.0%
	% of Total	.5%	1.8%		3.0%	5.3%
	non-believer, non-church attandant					
	Count	6	10		31	47
	% within religious values	12.8%	21.3%		66.0%	100.0%
	% of Total	1.5%	2.5%		7.8%	11.8%
Total	Count	61	176	7	156	400
	% within religious values	15.3%	44.0%	1.8%	39.0%	100.0%
	% of Total	15.3%	44.0%	1.8%	39.0%	100.0%

unemployed. The majority of households in the Sesto sample, as we saw, featured two or three people in employment. Of the forty-five unemployed young people surveyed, only seven lived alone or lived in a family where all members were unemployed. All the others lived in families where at least one member, but most typically two, were in full-time employment. I did not detect any sign of an isolated and marginalised underclass among this category. As the local Mayor of Sesto confirmed during an interview, in the town the family continues to act as an important buffer against unemployment and provides a valuable bulwark against social disintegration and 'anomie'. This situation may explain why the Sesto local council worries more about the effects of early retirement than about youth unemployment, and recently promoted a scheme for re-employing pensioners in social activities (Membrino 1989).

Respondents in Sesto also declared that the family had recently grown in importance (Figure 1.1).

Figure 1.1 shows that factory workers in Sesto were now attributing greater importance to the family. A clear majority (56.4 percent) stated that the family had become more important in recent years, as opposed to only 2.5 percent who considered it less important. By contrast, respondents indicated that the importance of horizontal associations such as a trade union or a political party had decreased in the last decade. Indeed, about half of the respondents did not even bother to reply to the questions relating to the importance of trade unions or the political environment, whereas

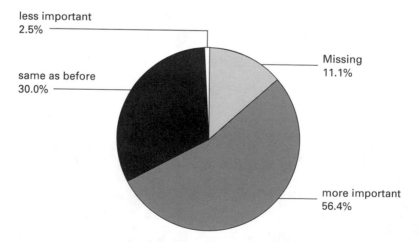

Figure 1.1 Importance of the family in the last ten years in Sesto

most of them chose to answer the questions concerning the importance of the family.

Workers in Sesto were thus showing signs of contemplating 'exit' from public activity altogether, retreating to a private network of family and friends, driven by disappointment and disillusionment, according to the classic Hirschman's theory (Hirschman 1970). Women workers also privileged the family, but to a lesser extent than men. In particular, compared to men, women seemed to have retained time for their friends as well as for politics, leisure activities, and to some extent religion.

The influence of religion was again looked at in relation to the perceived increasing or decreasing importance of the family. Most Catholics in Sesto declared that the family had become more important in the last five to ten years. So did a majority of lay respondents. Interestingly, even among convinced non-believers and non-Church attendants, almost half stated that the family had become more important in recent years. There were, once again, important gender differences. A majority of Catholic men (69.5 percent) stated that the family had become more important in recent years, but so did a clear majority of lay men (61.2 percent). By contrast, among women the distinction Catholic/non-Catholic appeared to be a clear determinant, with roughly two-thirds of Catholic women declaring that the family had become more important, as opposed to barely half of lay female respondents.

These findings indicate that the family has not ceased to function as the basic unit of society in Sesto, despite seventy-odd years of large-scale industrialisation and class-based associationism. Men, in particular, seem to be replacing solidarist values with family (as opposed to individualist) values. The town's social cultures are not those one would expect to find in an industrial suburb grown rapidly as the result of successive waves of immigration and dominated until recently by large firms which were externally owned and controlled. How can this be explained? The answer, of course, lies in the fact that the universalising, anti-particularist effects of large-scale industrialisation postulated by scholars like Sapelli cannot be taken for granted. I will come back to this issue in my conclusions. First, I want to look at family values in Erba.

Erba

In Erba there was a higher percentage of young people among respondents than in Sesto. As we saw, the age composition of respondents influences their marital status, with only a quarter claiming single status in Sesto but two-fifths in Erba. As in Sesto, young people aged between eighteen and thirty years of age continued to live with their family of origin. Indeed, the nearly 40 percent of single people in Erba translates into only 7 percent of people living on their own or outside the family circle. The average family size of the sample in Erba was, as in Sesto, 3.2, above both the local averages as recorded in the 1991 population census and the national average.

Relations between non-cohabiting family members were very close, slightly more so than in Sesto (Table 1.4).

A majority of respondents (55.0 percent) declared that relations with family members were both 'frequent and friendly', and a quarter (24.0 percent) stated that they were 'friendly but not frequent'. A sixth (15.5 percent) stated that such relations were 'solidarist', with only 1.7 percent indicating that they were 'neither friendly nor frequent'. As in Sesto, slightly more women than men enjoyed close family relationships.

Compared to Sesto, in Erba individualist values were more in evidence (Table 1.5). Among all respondents, 18.2 percent agreed with the statement 'personal realisation is most important'. This is not surprising, given the high level of entrepreneurship in the locality and the fact that artisans and small firms owner-managers were also among the respondents. It is perhaps more surprising that individual success was not rated higher, since 38.8 percent put the family ahead of individual aspirations and another 38.8 percent subscribed to solidarist values.

Table 1.4 Relations with non-cohabiting relatives in Erba

		Frequency	Percent	Valid Percent	Cumulative Percent
Valid	solidarist	69	15.5	16.5	16.5
	frequent and friendly	230	51.7	55.0	71.5
	not very frequent but friendly	107	24.0	25.6	97.1
	infrequent and not very friendly	7	1.6	1.7	98.8
	no contacts	5	1.1	1.2	100.0
	Total	418	93.9	100.0	
Missing		27	6.1		
Total		445	100.0		

Table 1.5 Respondents' life values in Erba

		Frequency	Percent	Valid Percent	Cumulative Percent
Valid	personal realisation is most important	81	18.2	18.9	18.9
	family interests come before individual aspirations	166	37.3	38.8	57.7
	the family is a handicap in terms of personal success	15	3.4	3.5	61.2
	solidarity is the most important human value	166	37.3	38.8	100.0
	Total	428	96.2	100.0	
Missing		17	3.8		
	Total	445	100.0		

Men clearly put family values first, indicating that they cherished the family above both individualist and solidarist values, whereas women put solidarity first. Women's understanding of solidarity appeared to be linked to universalist Catholic values, rather than to a class or a group. For this reason, the data contained in Table 1.5 was disaggregated on the basis of religious beliefs, as was done previously for Sesto. The findings for Erba were extremely revealing, particularly when compared to the Sesto ones (Table 1.6).

First, Catholic respondents in Erba proved less likely than Catholic respondents in Sesto to subscribe to family values, and more likely to adhere to either solidarist or individualist values. In particular, Erba respondents who attended Church functions on a regular basis subscribed almost equally to family values (43.2 percent) and to solidarist ones (40.0 percent). In other words, Catholic beliefs did not provide a clear indicator for family values. In addition, responses by sex in the Erba sample did not differ to any considerable extent, in marked contrast to responses by sex in Sesto. In Erba a majority of both Catholic male and female respondents (including practising Catholics) subscribed to solidarist values in preference to family ones. There was also considerable support for individualist values among respondents of both sexes who were believers but were not regular Church attendants.

However, when asked whether the family had changed in

Table 1.6 Life values compared to religious values in Erba

		Life values				
		personal realisation is most important	family interests come before individual aspirations	the family is a handicap in terms of career success	solidarity is the most important human value	Total
Religious values	Religious believer and regular church attendant					
	Count	27	82	5	76	190
	% within religious values	14.2%	43.2%	2.6%	40.0%	100.0%
	% of Total	6.4%	19.5%	1.2%	18.1%	45.1%
	believer, irregular church attendant					
	Count	27	49	3	42	121
	% within religious values	22.3%	40.5%	2.5%	34.7%	100%
	% of Total	6.4%	11.6%	0.7%	10.0%	28.7%
	believer, non-church attendant					
	Count	21	25	4	42	80
	% within religious values	26.3%	31.3%	5.0%	37.5%	100.0%
	% of Total	5.0%	5.9%	1.0%	7.1%	19.0%
	non-believer, irregular church attendant					
	Count	3	5	1	3	12
	% within religious values	25.0%	41.7%	8.3%	25.0%	100.0%
	% of Total	0.7%	1.2%	0.2%	0.7%	2.9%
	non-believer and non-church attandant					
	Count	2	2	2	12	18
	% within religious values	11.1%	11.1%	11.1%	66.7%	100.0%
	% of Total	0.5%	0.5%	0.5%	2.9%	4.3%
Total	Count	80	163	15	163	421
	% within religious values	19.0%	38.7%	3.6%	38.7%	100.0%
	% of Total	19.0%	38.7%	3.6%	38.7%	100.0%

importance in recent years, a majority of Erba respondents (58.2 percent) declared that it had become more important (Figure 1.2). In this respect, responses in Sesto and Erba were comparable, as were responses to the question relating to the importance of trade unions, which in both localities was judged to have greatly decreased. In terms of the importance of the political environment, however, there were some interesting differences between the two towns, with more respondents in Erba than in Sesto indicating that politics was at least as important as in the past.

As far as gender is concerned, in Erba there were hardly any differences in the way men and women regarded the importance of the family in the last ten years. A clear majority in both groups judged that it had become more important. On the other hand, as was detected in Sesto, men indicated primarily that family, friends and work had grown in importance, whereas women showed a higher propensity to privilege other interests outside their circle of family and friends. As in Sesto, the influence of religion was considered in relation to the perceived increasing or decreasing importance of the family. Most Catholics in Erba declared that the family had become more important in the last ten years, as did a majority of lay respondents. However, in Erba the difference between Catholic and lay respondents was more pronounced than in Sesto, whereas gender differences were negligible.

Two preliminary conclusions can be drawn at this stage from the data. First, there seem to be very few differences between Sesto

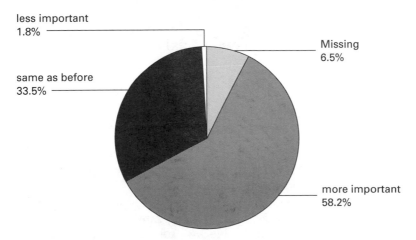

Figure 1.2 Importance of the family in the last ten years in Erba

and Erba in terms of the relative importance of the family, despite the two towns' contrasting socio-economic and cultural history and current environment. Whether the nature of industrialisation was large-scale or small-scale, whether the socio-political culture was communist or Catholic, whether it is an industrial suburb of a large city or a small town situated next to other small towns and villages, the family continues to dominate unchallenged. Feelings of attachment to one's own family were somewhat stronger among Catholic than lay respondents and, in Sesto at least, among men than among women, but the gap did not appear to be significant.

Second, it was established that religious beliefs do not automatically go hand in hand with family values to the exclusion of more public-minded attitudes. There is no denying that there is a correlation between the two sets of values, nonetheless being a Catholic also means being strongly solidarist. In this respect, people in Erba subscribed to solidarist values to the same extent as people in Sesto. The difference, of course, is that solidarism in Erba is universalist, whereas in Sesto it is class-based. While the latter is weakening and being replaced by family values, the former continues to exercise a strong influence upon Erba residents, without supplanting the importance of the family.

It is not just the immediate family, though, which must be taken into account when researching social and political cultures. Networks of friends, neighbours and colleagues can also play important roles in determining patterns of socialisation. It is these networks that will be considered in the next section.

Friendship and social networks

Sesto

In Sesto people enjoyed good relations with their neighbours, and were confident of their friends' support if in need (Tables 1.7 and 1.8).

As Table 1.7 indicates, nearly half of respondents (45.5 percent) stated that they could 'rely on their friends', a third (32.8 percent) indicated that relations with friends were 'cordial', while only one in ten (9.7 percent) declared that they had 'little time for their friends'. Interestingly, more women than men appeared able to rely on their friends. As for neighbours (Table 1.8), roughly half of respondents stated that relations were 'very friendly' (28 percent) or indeed such

Table 1.7 Relations with friends in Sesto

		Frequency	Percent	Valid Percent	Cumulative Percent
Valid	I can rely on them	197	44.5	45.5	45.5
	cordial but each looks after himself/herself	142	32.1	32.8	78.3
	less frequent than previously	52	11.7	12.0	90.3
	I don't have time for my friends	42	9.5	9.7	100.0
	Total	433	97.7	100.0	
Missing		10	2.3		
Total		443	100.0		

Table 1.8 Relations with neighbours in Sesto

		Frequency	Percent	Valid Percent	Cumulative Percent
Valid	very friendly	122	27.5	28.0	28.0
	we help each other	94	21.2	21.6	49.5
	we say hello but that's all	201	45.4	46.1	95.6
	less friendly than previously	2	.5	.5	96.1
	no contacts	10	2.3	2.3	98.4
	rather hostile	7	1.6	1.6	100.0
	Total	436	98.4		
Missing		7	1.6		
Total		443	100.0		

that they 'helped each other' (21.6 percent). The other half declared that they would just 'say hello' to their neighbours, while only 2.3 percent stated that there were no contacts between them and their neighbours. This time it was men, more than women, who declared that they enjoyed very close contacts with their neighbours. Relations at work were also generally good (Table 1.9).

Table 1.9 shows that more than half of respondents (51.4 percent) stated that relations with fellow workers were based on 'mutual trust' and esteem. Another 45.8 percent declared that relations were 'friendly, though not close'. Only 2.8 percent indicated that such relations were based on 'mutual indifference'. None of the respondents indicated that there existed some measure of

Table 1.9 Relations with colleagues at work in Sesto

		Frequency	Percent	Valid Percent	Cumulative Percent
Valid	we trust and respect each other	202	45.6	51.4	51.4
	friendly but not close	180	40.6	45.8	97.2
	there is mainly indifference	11	2.5	2.8	100.0
	Total	393	88.7	100.0	
Missing		50	11.3		
Total		443	100.0		

rivalry with fellow workers. This would suggest that collective solidarity continues to play a part at the workplace, alongside more particularist networks of friends. It would also suggest that individualist values of career advancement (often leading to interpersonal rivalries) had not taken root. There was little difference between the sexes in the responses. As for job satisfaction, here the picture was somewhat less rosy, reflecting the process of de-industrialisation in the town (Table 1.10).

As Table 1.10 shows, respondents were split roughly in half between those who declared themselves to be 'very' or 'moderately' satisfied with their work, and those who were 'not very satisfied' or were 'dissatisfied'. Women were generally less satisfied than men. Not surprisingly, more than half the respondents declared that they wanted to change jobs. Interestingly, given the social and political configuration of Sesto as a working-class town, a majority of people in this category stated that they wanted to become self-employed.

Table 1.10 How satisfied are you with your job? (Sesto)

		Frequency	Percent	Valid Percent	Cumulative Percent
Valid	very satisfied	37	8.4	9.2	9.2
	fairly satisfied	178	40.2	44.4	53.6
	not very satisfied	129	29.1	32.2	85.8
	dissatisfied	57	12.9	14.2	100.0
	Total	401	90.5	100.0	
Missing		42	9.5		
Total		443	100.0		

Erba

Relations with friends in Erba were remarkably similar to – indeed to some extent even closer than – what they were in Sesto (Table 1.11).

As can be seen from Table 1.11, more than half of all respondents in Erba (53.3 percent) stated that they were able to 'rely on their friends'. Fewer than one in ten (8.3 percent) declared that they had 'little time for their friends'. There were some remarkable gender differences. In particular, two women out of three, as opposed to one man out of two, stated that they could rely on their friends. This confirms what had emerged earlier regarding men's greater propensity to focus on family and work in Erba. As for neighbours, the findings are almost the same as for Sesto, except that more women than men in Erba appeared to enjoy close relations with their neighbours (Table 1.12).

Relations with fellow workers were extremely good among Erba respondents, and this applied to both sexes (Table 1.13).

As Table 1.13 shows, a very high percentage of respondents (57.8 percent) declared that relations with colleagues at work were based on 'mutual trust and esteem'. Another 37.5 percent stated that relations were 'friendly but not close', while 4 percent indicated that relations were mutually indifferent. In Erba two respondents (out of 405 who had answered this question) stated that relations at work were based upon rivalry. For what it is worth, both were females. As in the Sesto sample, I am tempted to take these statistics as a sign that solidarity at the workplace has not

Table 1.11 Relations with friends in Erba

		Frequency	Percent	Valid Percent	Cumulative Percent
Valid	I can rely on them	232	52.1	53.3	53.3
	cordial but each looks after himself/herself	112	25.2	25.7	79.1
	less frequent than previously	54	12.1	12.4	91.5
	I don't have time for my friends	36	8.1	8.3	99.8
	Total	435	97.8	100.0	
Missing		10	2.2		
Total		445	100.0		

Table 1.12 Relations with neighbours in Erba

		Frequency	Percent	Valid Percent	Cumulative Percent
Valid	very friendly	123	27.6	28.0	28.0
	we help each other	92	20.7	21.0	49.0
	we say hello but that's all	202	45.4	46.0	95.0
	less friendly than previously	5	1.1	1.1	96.1
	no contacts	12	2.7	2.7	98.9
	rather hostile	5	1.1	1.1	100.0
	Total	439	98.7	100.0	
Missing		6	1.3		
Total		445	100.0		

Table 1.13 Relations with colleagues at work in Erba

		Frequency	Percent	Valid Percent	Cumulative Percent
Valid	we trust and respect each other	234	52.6	57.8	57.8
	friendly but not close	152	34.2	37.5	95.3
	there is mainly indifference	17	3.8	4.2	99.5
	there is mainly rivalry	2	.4	.5	100.0
	Total	405	91.0	100.0	
Missing		40	9.0		
Total		445	100.0		

been replaced by individualist values of career advancement. They appear to suggest that promotion and career advancement take place against a background of mutual support and trust, rather than intense interpersonal competition. As for work satisfaction, this was significantly higher in Erba than in Sesto, with the vast majority of respondents declaring themselves 'very' or 'moderately' satisfied with their work (Table 1.14).

Not surprisingly, the vast majority (77.3 percent) also stated that they had no intention of changing job. The difference with the Sesto findings is striking in this respect and it would appear to confirm what numerous studies on the economy of the 'Third Italy' have highlighted, namely that job satisfaction is higher in small

Table 1.14 How satisfied are you with your job? (Erba)

		Frequency	Percent	Valid Percent	Cumulative Percent
Valid	very satisfied	121	27.2	28.5	28.5
	fairly satisfied	246	55.3	57.9	86.4
	not very satisfied	48	10.8	11.3	97.6
	dissatisfied	10	2.2	2.4	100.0
	Total	425	95.5	100.0	
Missing		20	4.5		
Total		445	100.0		

and medium-sized firms than it is in large ones. This can be attributed to less impersonal work relations, the type of work undertaken (more craft-based in the smaller plants), greater involvement of workers in the running of the firm, or perhaps simply to the fact that small- and medium-sized firms in Erba provide a more stable and secure work environment than large firms in Sesto. The latter have been shedding labour, while the former have continued to take on new staff. Whatever the reasons, job satisfaction appears to be the only area where the personal and social life of respondents in the two localities differed substantially. The findings are less surprising for Erba than they are for Sesto, given the former locality's Catholic tradition, with its emphasis on the family, and its socio-economic characteristics, which have guaranteed the preservation of small businesses sustained by primary ties. The significance of the similarities between Sesto and Erba in terms of the continuing importance of kinship and social networks will become more apparent in the next section, in which I compare Sesto with Vénissieux, an industrial suburb of Lyon. Unlike Sesto and Erba, Sesto and Vénissieux are almost perfectly matched, as we shall see, in terms both of their socio-economic structures and political tradition, yet in terms of social identities the two localities are remarkably different.

A comparison between Sesto San Giovanni (Milan) and Vénissieux (Lyon)

This section draws on the research project on social identities and political culture in Italy and France mentioned in the Preface (Bull and Milner 1997). One of the objects of the project was to compare two areas, Sesto near Milan and Vénissieux near Lyon, which until recently were characterised by a working-class culture and a communist identity, which in turn stemmed from a concentration of large-scale heavy-industry and the presence of powerful trade unions. Both areas have gone through a process of severe de-industrialisation and deep social change, accompanied by significant political developments. One of the questions the research project addressed concerned the role of the family and of social networks in cushioning residents from the impact of socio-economic change and providing a degree of cultural continuity. We postulated that this role would be more in evidence in Italy than in France since, as I remarked in the Introduction to Part I, the resilience and vitality of the Italian family have been confirmed by various sources.

As well as on the basis of their characteristics as declining industrial suburbs of large cities, the two sites were matched in terms of size and composition of the population and the mix of economic activities. Vénissieux is a suburb in the south-east of Lyon, the third largest town in the department. Like Sesto, its population has decreased in recent decades (from 74,347 in 1975 to 64,804 in 1982 and 60,444 in 1990, with an annual loss of 2.8 percent in the period 1982–1990 due to migration). Unemployment is officially around 14.2 percent (10 percent in Sesto), up 7.41 percent since 1993-94; it is, however, concentrated in pockets: 60 percent of the unemployed live in the housing estate of Les Minguettes.

Like Sesto, Vénissieux was a small rural village at the beginning of the century, with a population of just 4,000 in 1911. Shell factories and Berliet set up production during the war, then a variety of industries were established after the war (railway, steel, artificial textiles, electronics, foundries and glass). Berliet, which later became the publicly-owned Renault Véhicules Industriels, has remained a major employer and presence in the commune and is today the largest single employer in the whole region. In many ways the fate of the commune has followed that of the heavy industry which settled there. As for the composition of the population, in 1931, 80 percent of the working population were blue-collar workers. In 1982 only 31.6 percent were blue-collar workers, whereas 22.2 percent were white-collar workers, 13.4 percent technical/supervisory, 22.9 percent inactive. It is also worth noting that both Sesto and Vénissieux (and, by extension, Milan and Lyon) are located in a region containing many small towns which are home to a variety of small- and medium-sized businesses. They are, therefore, long-standing agglomerations of large-scale industry surrounded by a contrasting model of economic development.

Vénissieux, again like Sesto, has always been home to a significant immigrant population. However, whereas in Sesto immigration was initially from neighbouring provinces and regions, and later from the South, in Vénissieux it was predominantly from abroad. In 1931 only 7 percent of workers had been born in the commune, 49 percent were foreign immigrants: there was a strong Italian presence, as well as many Algerians. Vénissieux experienced major changes in the 1960s and 1970s due to urban planning within the context of "Greater Lyon" (Corbel 1983). The result was a large-scale shift of population (especially working-class and immigrant) to Vénissieux, which saw its population boom. This shift created a sense of resentment that Vénissieux was being used as a 'dumping ground'. Severe housing problems developed which have left their legacy today. The housing estate of Les Minguettes was the first 'industrial-style' high-rise development built in France – one set of these tower blocks was demolished in 1994 after lying empty for years. In Sesto, too, in the 1960s there was typical 'industrial-style' housing – the so-called dormitories – but this was followed in the 1970s by more residential type of housing.

As for political behaviour, in Vénissieux, between 1945 and 1981, the average score of the Communist Party at elections, both local and national, equalled 39.38 percent of the electorate (not voters) (Brula 1993). The year 1981 is considered a turning point in terms of support for the Parti Communiste Français (PCF). Since 1981, it has still commanded a relatively stable core vote, but it is shrinking, averaging 15.08 percent of the electorate. Abstentions are on the rise and now exceed the PCF score (40.79 percent average). More importantly perhaps, the *Front National* (FN) has consistently gained in popularity. At the general elections held between 1984 and 1989, the FN in Vénissieux obtained around 14–15.5 percent of the vote. In the presidential election of 1988, Le Pen won 19 percent of the vote. At the regional elections of 1992, the FN score went over 20 percent for the first time (24.5 percent), coming first among all parties present (the PCF obtained 22.86 percent). In the municipal elections of 1995, the FN came second after the left alliance, with 29.56 percent of the vote. Since the late 1980s the FN has become a force to be reckoned with in Vénissieux (Centre d'histoire et d'études 1992). In Sesto, the demise of the PCI-PDS came later, but it has similarly led to an increased vote for the right parties, including the ex-fascist party and the Northern League (see Part II).

Despite the above similarities, the survey conducted among industrial workers in both towns threw up fundamental discrepancies. First, a marked generational break in values was detected in Vénissieux, while it was not much in evidence in Sesto, in line with the rest of Italy. In particular, there was much greater social and civic disaffection among the young and single in Vénissieux than in Sesto (Gérin 1991). Family was held to be an important value for the Vénissians surveyed, but work appeared a more significant socialising factor, particularly in the promotion of political opinions. In terms of the social status of respondents, many women in the Vénissieux sample were the sole breadwinner and there was also a significant number of households with no one in paid employment. Such occurrences were rare in the Sesto sample.

Second, it was also found that social networks of friends, neighbours and colleagues played different roles in the two localities. In Sesto, compared to Vénissieux, many more people were satisfied with their jobs, enjoyed good relations with their neighbours, and were confident of their friends' support if in need. This is not to say that social contacts in Vénissieux were scarce or even non-existent. Relations with family members outside the immediate household were generally considered to be very good among respondents, in line with earlier findings about frequency of family contacts in France (Gotman 1989). In contrast with the denser social networks of Sesto, however, the picture which emerged was one of scattered family units in regular contact.

Third, and most significantly, it was found that there was a congruence between underlying social identities in the two localities and the kind of future they seem to have in store. In Vénissieux, there were severe social problems marked by 'exclusion' of all kinds, expressed in the riots of the 1980s, which prompted President Mitterrand to set up an inquiry into social problems in the big cities and led to the creation of a ministry for urban affairs. The generational and ethnic segmentation of the town, coupled with a growing individualism, prevent the family from contributing to re-cementing the local community. A general feeling of defensiveness is not in itself enough to unite people, and it also has the negative effect of lowering self-esteem unless it leads to specific projects. This task is left to the council, which in turn looks to national government for large-scale schemes of urban regeneration.

In Sesto, too, there is social segmentation, but between a middle class and a working class, rather than a working class and an underclass. Here there have been no episodes of social conflict or public demonstrations by the unemployed, and the working-class family still provides practical as well as affective support for its members, as we saw. The family is at the centre of various relational networks made up of friends, colleagues and neighbours. From a social point of view, the difference between Sesto and the surrounding region of diffused industrialisation is not that great. The persistence of strong kinship and social networks in Sesto may explain the presence of a growing and viable small-business sector originating in large part from local entrepreneurs. Many small firms in Sesto are family-owned and run, and were set up by people who were often previously employed in the large factories (Regalia 1986, Provincia di Milano 1988). It is well known that there is a type of entrepreneurship which stems from industrial decline and which is unlikely to be a motor for new economic activity (Amin et al. 1986, Shutt and Whittington 1987). This is essentially a 'negative' model of entrepreneurial activity that is low-technology and big-firm dependent. Although a similar interpretation has been put forward regarding Sesto's expanding small-business sector (Berti and Donegà 1992), this picture is not consistent with other findings. In particular, according to a study of small- and medium-sized firms operating in Sesto, which was commissioned by the province of Milan, the prospects for this sector were judged promising. It was ascertained that Sesto's small firms did not depend on the local large firms for sales or supplies (Provincia di Milano 1988). They tended to have their own markets outside the town, and had developed their own production system (based on a complex chain of subcontractors, artisans and domestic workers) remarkably similar to that present in traditional and well-established areas of small-scale industry.

In both cases, the left-wing councils have been active in attempting to reverse economic decline and recreating a sense of community. In Vénissieux, the council has focused on three main areas: renovation of housing estates, restoration of the old centre, and integration of the commune into the city. In all three areas the council has gained some notable victories (Bull and Milner 1997) and maintained a high profile. The crucial difference in Sesto is that the local council has acted as one of a number of prominent players, representing both territorial and social interests: thus local, provincial, regional and national actors have all played a role in policy-making. Despite the fact that the main actors did not see eye-to-eye (Bergo and Ferrazza 1987), a consensus finally emerged around the need to promote small-scale development in the manufacturing and services sectors. In 1994, the new centre-left council approved a town-planning scheme which earmarked some areas for small-scale industry, both in traditional and in highly innovative sectors (Comune di Sesto San Giovanni 1993).

What is interesting about Sesto's possible future identity is the fact that this area may be on the verge of being 'subsumed' under the prevailing regional model of development, whereas Vénissieux seems to rely on large-scale national solutions to the problems of de-industrialisation and unemployment it shares with other French urban areas. Nor does Vénissieux represent an isolated case. The French economic and political system, it has been noted, privileges a vertical relationship between the local and the national dimension rather than horizontal links between actors operating in different spheres (Ganne 1991).

There is an invisible but none the less real barrier separating Vénissieux from the small towns of small-scale industry which make up the surrounding region. Vénissieux is unable to shed its image as an industrial suburb of a large city. In this it is not alone. Throughout Europe, as well as in the U.S.A., large industrial conurbations have been facing steep decline, which 'is unlikely to be reversed by policy and planning' (Clark 1989). As Keating (1998: 154) wrote,

> norms of collectivism forged in an era of class struggle may not provide the basis for social cooperation in the modern era, as witnessed by the difficulties of adaptation of old heavy industrial areas formerly dominated by large firms and unionised workforces. Coal miners or steel workers, with their own tradition of class solidarity, are not going to convert themselves overnight into small-business people engaged in networks of solidarity.

Sesto, by contrast, is keen to re-invent its identity as that of a small independent town, dismantling the image of a suburban area in decline. Whether it will succeed is a moot point, nevertheless under the surface, family and social networks appear to have provided a 'soft landing' for local residents after a period of economic decline and de-industrialisation, and they may even form the greatest resource the local council has at its disposal in its attempt to promote regeneration through small-scale industrialisation.

The findings also indicate that nation-specific (or, more appropriately in this case, region-specific) patterns of social cultures and identities prevail over cross-national (cross-regional) similarities. Despite the general socio-economic and political comparability between Sesto and Vénissieux, the two towns are diverging. A common phase as urban conurbations dominated by a small number of large corporations and as centres of trade-union militancy and communist culture has given way to contrasting scenarios.

Conclusions

This chapter has established that kinship, friendship and other social networks remain very strong in (northern) Italy today. Responses in Sesto and Erba confirm recent research findings on kinship and social networks in Italy compared to other advanced countries. As a recent study showed, marriage dissolution in Italy has consistently been much lower than in other Western European countries (De Rose 1992). The same study concluded (p. 90) that in Italy

> family stability today responds to a widespread need for security, in a period in which economic vicissitudes have a strong influence on personal decisions, concerned both with work, and with interpersonal relations. Limited opportunities and a chronic shortage of housing are making it ever more difficult, especially for young people, to leave the parental home, and as a result the asset of a family seems to be becoming increasingly precious, ensuring material and psychological protection and support.

As for friendship and other social networks, it was recently found that, in contrast to other nationalities, for Italians the importance of friends was not inversely proportional to the importance of the family: 'Italians expect social support from both relations and friends' (Hollinger and Haller 1990: 120). Another study found that Italians, both men and women, have a closer relationship with friends than other nationalities, and are much more likely to turn to their friends in case of need (Bruckner and Knaup 1993: 263–64). It was also found that Italians were socially more involved in their local community than at their workplace, and that they recruited two-thirds of their friends from contexts other than work or neighbourhood (Ibid.: 258). This suggests that Italians tend to have a wide range of kinship and social networks upon which they can draw at times of personal distress or economic hardship.

This scenario is precisely the one I had envisaged when choosing Erba as one of the case-studies. The town is, after all, characteristic of Italy's small-business model of development, a model all scholars have linked to strong kinship and social ties. A strong integration between economy, society and politics is typical of the small-business dominated subalpine areas of Italy, with kinship and social networks continuing to play a central role in all three spheres (Bull and Corner 1993). Empirical research has also shown that an important region of small-scale industry, Emilia Romagna, is associated with strong kinship ties (Barbagli 1991b). In her study on the continuing importance of the family in Italy, De Rose (1992: 90) herself concluded by stressing 'the economic value of a stable family in a country like Italy, in which the productivity of family businesses is so high as to constitute the main source of income in small-sized *comuni* in northern and central Italy. Under these circumstances, any attack upon family unity can be extremely damaging and is therefore avoided if at all possible [...]'.

I had not, however, anticipated similar findings in Sesto, given its entirely different socio-economic configuration. To a certain extent I had implicitly taken for granted what Sapelli articulated explicitly, namely, as we saw, that prolonged large-scale industrialisation would lead to a weakening of primary and particularist ties and a parallel strengthening of both universalist and individualist values. These assumptions need to be revised. There are four main considerations stemming from such a revision.

First, the findings indicate that the resilience of primary and particularist ties is not necessarily a function of economic development. By itself, the process of modernisation is compatible with both individualist values (in Anglo-Saxon societies) and particularist ones (in Asian societies as well as Italy). Conversely, particularist values are compatible with both small-scale and large-scale industrialisation.

Second, the findings indicate that the process of cultural modernisation, i.e., the transition from x (where x, as we saw, stands for old particularist values) to y (where y stands for modern, civic, universalist values), is neither linear nor irreversible. The concept of a linear model of development made up of different and distinct phases is particularly problematic. If we replace it with the concept that 'individuals participate in a variety of social dimensions and functions' (Grancelli 1987: 266–7), then it is possible to envisage that each successive layer of 'culture' does not supersede previous layers – in either an individual or a community – unless it is rooted out by some major displacement (e.g. an industrial and/or social revolution). Even when an industrial revolution takes place (and

Sesto, along with some areas of Italy, did experience one), older values and cultures will persist if they continue to find any conceptual and existential space. I remember watching a BBC series on Italy, in the 1980s, entitled *Italians*. One of the programmes in the series was called 'The man from Alfa'. Its caption in the *Radio Times*, 5 December 1984 read, quite presciently, as follows:

> Mauro Fiamenghi inhabits two worlds. From Monday to Friday he's involved in angry meetings at the Alfa Romeo car factory near Milan. He's a quality controller on the production line. Mauro is a Communist and in the thick of his union's fight to resist lay-offs. Feelings run high. There are lightning strikes and demonstrations. He is a moderate, and has been threatened because of his views.
>
> Mauro's other world is a two hour train journey away, high up in the Alps. He goes there every weekend to escape with his wife and young children to their mountain home and to tend his vines. But there's always Monday morning ...

The programme visualised these two worlds with impressive clarity. On the one hand, the smoky, militant, 'modern' atmosphere of the factory, where Mauro and his comrades worked, discussed union matters and politics, and organised collective action. The family had no space there. On the other hand, the quiet, rural, village environment where Mauro knew every other resident and where he was able to 'take on' the role and culture of a small farmer and house-owner. It should be clear from the above that as long as Mauro had the possibility of escaping to a completely different world for some time of his existence at least, he – and his family – were able to conceptualise two contrasting sets of values and two visions of the world alongside each other. There is no reason to believe that the more 'modern' set of values had to supersede the other; on the contrary, we may well picture to ourselves Mauro today, having retired to the Alps and to a rural existence.

Similarly, workers in Sesto participated in at least two social dimensions. Like Mauro Fiamenghi, they worked in large factories, belonged to a union, took part in mass strikes, and subscribed to communist values. Many of them, however, came from neighbouring provinces, such as Brescia, Bergamo, Como, Sondrio, etc. They came, in short, from 'the valleys', to where they returned in their spare time. Indeed, according to an ex-Mayor of Sesto, Sig. Carrà, many people who worked in Sesto commuted daily from the surrounding countryside, by bike, car, train, or coach. He added that

role in the communist subculture appears to have made them more receptive towards new forms of associationism and to have freed them from traditional cultural constraints. Gender differences have thus opened up new perspectives for studying social identities and political cultures in Italy today. Rather than the nature or extent of the industrialisation process, as Sapelli maintained, the main factor behind the persistence of family values may lie in gender relations. The greatest tension between different sets of values may therefore be found within the family itself, whose internal equilibrium in terms of the strategies pursued by its members may have become relatively fragile. In order to allow any conclusion of this kind to be reached, gender differences will continue to be systematically explored at all levels in the following sections.

In the next chapter, I will be looking at the degree and nature of associationism in Sesto and Erba, with a view to establish whether the resilience of family values has hindered participation in, and the development of, horizontal associations. The question of the influence of Catholic beliefs upon social and political participation will also be addressed.

2

Associationism

Introduction

In this chapter the degree of associationism in the two localities will be assessed, on the basis of responses to the survey by questionnaire, which was carried out in both Sesto and Erba in 1994. As Putnam remarked, 'any society [...] is characterised by networks of interpersonal communication and exchange, both formal and informal' (Putnam 1993: 173). Putnam, along with other scholars, distinguished between 'horizontal' networks, 'bringing together agents of equivalent status and power', and 'vertical' networks, 'linking unequal agents in asymmetric relations of hierarchy and dependence'. 'Horizontal' associations contribute to 'effective social collaboration' and to 'effective democratic governance' (Ibid.: 90). In his book Putnam listed a number of 'horizontal' associations, including choral societies, cooperatives, sports clubs, mass-based parties, cultural associations and voluntary unions. Among the 'vertical' associations Putnam focused on two: the Mafia and the institutional Catholic Church. Putnam measured associational life throughout Italy and concluded that it was much more vibrant and widespread in the North than in the South. He also found that good and effective regional government correlated positively with a high degree of civic engagement, and concluded that the northern Italian regions were both the more civic and, consequently, the best administered. Despite acknowledging the existence of two different socio-political traditions in northern Italy – corresponding in modern times to the 'red' (socialist and communist) subculture of the central regions and the 'white' (Catholic) subculture of the north-eastern regions, including part of Lombardy – Putnam argued that, as these were both highly civic areas, they should be treated as one.

As many as possible of the associations classified as 'horizontal' by Putnam were included in the questions put to respondents. Two questions, in particular, probed the level of associationism. The first question (Question 18) was a multiple one. Respondents were asked to what extent (regularly, occasionally or never) they participated in leisure, religious, voluntary, environmental, cultural, charity and professional associations. The second question (Question 22) was also a multiple one, probing the extent of participation by respondents in a political party, a trade union, a cooperative, a local council and a neighbourhood council. Following Tocqueville, Putnam (1993: 92) also argued that newspaper readership correlates positively with associationism: 'Newspapers readers are better informed than non-readers and thus better equipped to participate in civic deliberations. Similarly, newspaper readership is a mark of citizen interest in community affairs'. It is noticeable that Putnam made specific reference, in his book, to local newspapers and the local media, although he did not distinguish in his analysis between readers of local newspapers and readers of the national press. I thought this area of enquiry merited special attention. Accordingly, Question 20 asked respondents how often they read a newspaper, with a view to ascertaining whether they read a local and/or a national, a daily and/or a weekly, newspaper. Finally, Question 21 asked respondents whether they were members of a political, union, industrial/professional or cooperative association.

This chapter aims at establishing the degree of associationism and 'civic-mindedness' in each locality, looking in depth at the relationship between Catholicism and associationism on the one hand, and family values and social participation on the other. As regards the former, both Ginsborg and Putnam argued that Catholic values correlate negatively with associationism. Putnam, in particular, argued openly that 'in Italy [...] the most devout Catholics are the least civic-minded'. He added: 'At the regional level, all manifestations of religiosity and clericalism – attendance at Mass, religious (as opposed to civic) marriages, rejection of divorce, expressions of religious identity in survey – are negatively correlated with civic engagement' (Putnam 1993: 107). A negative correlation between strong kinship and friendship values and associationism was also postulated by both Ginsborg and Sapelli. The principal aim of this chapter is to test the validity of these two interpretations. Although Putnam, in his book, made no distinction between political and apolitical associations, I chose to distinguish between these two types of association in my analysis. The reason for this is that, as Trigilia (1986) remarked many years ago, participation in political associations, as opposed to voluntary, apolitical ones, tends to be higher in areas with a strong socialist and communist subculture, whereas the reverse is true in areas with a traditional Catholic subculture. Putnam, as we saw, chose not to separate the 'red' from the 'white' subculture, yet results could be skewed if one did not take account of such an important difference in socio-political behaviour in Italy.

Apolitical associationism and Catholicism in Sesto and Erba

In order to extract meaningful information from the questionnaire data, an index of associationism was constructed on the basis of responses to Question 18 (a multiple question) (Garvía Soto 1996). For every one of the seven types of association listed in Question 18, each respondent was assigned a 'value'. This corresponded to 0 (Zero) if the respondent did not participate at all in the activities of that type of association, to 1 if the respondent participated on an occasional basis, and 2 if participation took place on a regular basis. The final index for each respondent thus varied potentially from a minimum of 0 (someone who never participated in any of the seven types of association listed) to a maximum of 14 (someone who participated on a regular basis to the activities of all seven types of association).

In addition, a simplified scale of associationism was constructed, with a value out of only 4 assigned to each respondent. The value corresponded to 0 (defined as 'non associationism') for those who never participated in any association. It corresponded to 1 (defined as 'minor associationism') for those who indicated that they participated on an occasional basis to the activities of at least one of the seven types of association listed. The value equalled 2 (defined as 'medium associationism') for those who participated occasionally in two types of association or regularly in one, and 3 (defined as 'major associationism') for those who participated regularly in at least two types of association or occasionally in at least three.

When applied to Sesto and Erba, the scale of associationism resulted as follows:

Table 2.1 Scale of apolitical associationism in Sesto and Erba

AREA		Frequency	Percent	Valid Percent	Cumulative Percent
Sesto					
Missing	System	3	100.0		
Valid	non associationism	78	17.6	22.6	22.6
	minor associationism	105	23.7	30.4	53.0
	medium associationism	114	25.7	33.0	86.1
	major associationism	48	10.8	13.9	100.0
Total		345	77.9	100.0	
Missing		98	22.1		
	Total	443	100.0		
Erba					
Valid	non associationism	103	23.1	25.9	25.9
	minor associationism	90	20.2	22.6	48.5
	medium associationism	110	24.7	27.6	76.1
	major associationism	95	21.3	23.9	100.0
Total		398	89.4	100.0	
Missing		47	10.6		
Total		445	100.0		

As for the index of associationism, it resulted as follows:

Table 2.2 Index of apolitical associationism in Sesto and Erba (T-Test)

AREA		N	Mean	Std. Deviation	Std. Error Mean
			Group Statistics		
Q18	Sesto	347	1.5476	1.4425	7.744E-02
	Erba	400	1.7675	1.6155	8.078E-02

		Levene's Test for Equality of Variances		t-test for Equality of Means				
		F	Sig	t	df	Sig. (2-tailed)	Mean Diff.	Std. Error Diff.
Q18	Equal variances assumed	9.456	.002	−1.950	745	.052	−.2199	.1128
	Equal variances not assumed			−1.966	744.373	.050	−.2199	.1119

As can be seen from Tables 2.1 and 2.2, the level of associationism was decisively higher for Erba than for Sesto. In Erba, 295 respondents out of 445 participated in at least one association, while 47 did not give any indication and 103 did not associate at all. Of the ones who replied to the question, 25.9 percent were 'non associationists', 22.6 percent were 'minor associationists', 27.6 percent were 'medium associationists' and 23.9 were 'major associationists'. In Sesto, 267 respondents out of 443 participated in at least one association, as opposed to 98 who did not reply and 78 who did not participate in any association. Of those who replied, 22.6 percent were 'non associationists', 30.4 percent were 'minor associationists', 33.0 percent were 'medium associationists' and only 13.9 percent were 'major associationists'. This was a somewhat unexpected result, given the strong Catholic orientation of respondents in Erba which, as we saw, has been judged to correlate negatively with the degree of associationism. To test this further, for each locality respondents were disaggregated on the basis of an 'index of religiosity', constructed around Question 19, which asked them whether they were practising Catholics and how often they attended religious functions such as Mass. Respondents were defined as 'Catholics' if they indicated that they were both believers and attended religious functions on either a regular or occasional basis, and 'lay' if they were believers but did not normally attend any religious functions or if they were not believers (whether or not they attended such functions). Not surprisingly,

Table 2.3 Religious values in Sesto and Erba

AREA			Frequency	Percent	Valid Percent	Cumulative Percent
Sesto	Missing	System	3	100.0		
	Valid	Catholic	213	48.1	51.0	51.0
		Lay	205	46.3	49.0	100.0
		Total	418	94.4	100.0	
	Missing		25	5.6		
	Total		443	100.0		
Erba	Valid	Catholic	321	72.1	74.1	74.1
		Lay	112	25.2	25.9	100.0
		Total	433	97.3	100.0	
	Missing		12	2.7		
	Total		445	100.0		

Table 2.4 Scale of apolitical associationism by religious values in Sesto and Erba

AREA			Religious values		Total
			Catholic	Lay	
Sesto	non associationism	Count	29	45	74
		% within religious values	16.8%	28.1%	22.2%
		% of Total	8.7%	13.5%	22.2%
	minor associationism	Count	62	40	102
		% within religious values	35.8%	25.0%	30.6%
		% of Total	18.6%	12.0%	30.6%
	medium associationism	Count	55	56	111
		% within Religious values	31.8%	35.0%	33.3%
		% of Total	16.5%	16.8%	33.3%
	major associationism	Count	27	19	46
		% within Religious values	15.6%	11.9%	13.8%
		% of Total	8.1%	5.7%	13.8%
	Total	Count	173	160	333
		% within Religious values	100.0%	100.0%	100.0%
		% of Total	52.0%	48.0%	100.0%

Erba				
non associationism	Count	72	30	102
	% within religious values	24.9%	29.1%	26.0%
	% of Total	18.4%	7.7%	26.0%
minor associationism	Count	62	28	90
	% within religious values	21.5%	27.2%	23.0%
	% of Total	15.8%	7.1%	23.0%
medium associationism	Count	80	26	106
	% within Religious values	27.7%	25.2%	27.0%
	% of Total	20.4%	6.6%	27.0%
major associationism	Count	75	19	94
	% within Religious values	26.0%	18.4%	24.0%
	% of Total	19.1%	4.8%	24.0%
Total	Count	289	103	392
	% within Religious values	100.0%	100.0%	100.0%
	% of Total	73.7%	26.3%	100.0%

Catholics were found to be more numerous in Erba (74.1 percent of respondents) than in Sesto (51 percent) (Table 2.3).

How did the two groups of respondents (Catholic and lay) fare in the two localities, when judged against the 'scale of associationism' defined above (Table 2.4)?

As Table 2.4 shows, in Sesto there was not a marked difference between lay respondents and their Catholic counterpart in terms of apolitical associationism: 'non associationism' and 'minor associationism' together accounted for 52.6 percent of Catholic respondents and for 53.1 percent of lay respondents. Yet in Erba there was a clear divide between the two categories of respondents: indeed, Catholic respondents associated considerably more than their lay counterpart. Here 'non associationism' and 'minor associationism' accounted for only 46.4 percent of Catholics, as opposed to 56.3 percent of lay people. The difference was especially striking for 'major associationism', with 26.0 percent of Catholics but only 18.4 percent of lay respondents in this category. The index of associationism was also significantly higher for Catholic than for lay respondents in Erba, while it was roughly the same for both groups in Sesto (Table 2.5). Indeed in Erba, following evidence of a linear relationship, a positive bivariate correlation, which measures how variables are related, was found to exist between the degree of religiosity of respondents and participation in apolitical associations. The more religious the respondents, the more likely they were to be active participants, and vice versa.

The difference between the two localities, particularly between the behaviour of Sesto and Erba Catholic respondents, is mostly accounted for by participation in religious associations, which was higher in Erba than in Sesto and was also higher among Erba Catholic respondents compared to Sesto ones. Indeed if one leaves

Table 2.5 Index of apolitical associationism by religious values in Sesto and Erba

Q18 AREA	Religious values	Mean	N	Std. Deviation
Sesto	Catholic	1.5920	174	1.2447
	Lay	1.5217	161	1.6511
	Total	1.5582	335	1.4525
Erba	Catholic	1.8694	291	1.6969
	Lay	1.4757	103	1.3637
	Total	1.7665	394	1.6240

aside participation in religious associations, then the degree of associationism in both Sesto and Erba can be considered roughly on a par.

A few considerations can be made at this point, stemming from the above findings. First, contrary to expectations, devout Catholics can be considerably more civic-minded than non-Catholics, at least as far as apolitical associationism is concerned. Second, devout Catholics appear to be more noticeably civic-minded in the Catholic dominated areas of Italy, where norms of reciprocity, trust and cooperation have traditionally underpinned the religious orientation of residents. Putnam (1993) made no reference to the specific role played by Catholic associations and unions in fostering 'networks of civic engagement' in certain regions of Italy, with the result that he judged the Catholic Church and faith to have played a uniform negative impact across the peninsula. Similar sweeping generalisations apply to Ginsborg (1995), as we saw. Yet numerous studies have highlighted the dynamic role played by Catholic organisations in the north-eastern regions of Italy, so much so that Cartocci recently distinguished between areas characterised by 'conformist Catholicism' (primarily the South), and areas characterised by 'participative Catholicism' (the North-East) (Bagnasco and Trigilia 1984, Cartocci 1994: 159–196). Cartocci himself pointed out that Putnam had ignored this fundamental difference (Cartocci 1994: 194, note 40). Lastly, participation in religious associations appears to add to rather than detract from, the general level of associationism. Thus Catholics in Erba associated more than lay people for the simple reason that they participated in religious associations *as well as* (and not instead of) other forms of associationism. In this respect participation in associations of a religious nature cannot be considered detrimental to public engagement; such associations appear to instil in their members the same virtuous habits of 'co-operation, solidarity, and public-spiritedness' Putnam attributed to non-religious organisations (1993: 89–90).

Apolitical associationism and family values in Sesto and Erba

In order to assess whether family values correlate negatively with associationism, respondents were first subdivided into three categories: the 'individualists', i.e., those who had agreed with the statement that individual fulfilment and advancement was most important in life; the 'familists', i.e., those respondents who had ranked the family above both individual fulfilment and solidarity, and finally the 'solidarists', or all those who had declared that solidarity was the most important value.

Participation in apolitical associations was then considered in the light of the values respondents most cherished in their life. Table 2.6 shows the results.

As it turned out, the 'solidarists' showed the highest degree of associationism (25.1 percent were 'major associationists'), followed by the 'individualists' (18.7 percent) and finally by the 'familists' (among whom only 14.8 percent were 'major associationists'). The hypothesis put forward by Ginsborg thus appears sustained by these findings, even though it should be emphasised that Ginsborg underestimated the continuing importance of solidarism in Italian political culture. Thus the 'familists', despite constituting the largest category in the overall sample and far surpassing the 'individualists', were not a dominant group. Indeed the 'solidarists' were almost as numerous as the 'familists'.

A breakdown of respondents by locality also shows some considerable variations (see Table 2.7).

It turned out that in Sesto the 'familists' associated roughly to the same extent as the 'individualists', and that both groups were clearly surpassed by the 'solidarists'. While only 10.0 percent of the 'individualists' and 9.7 percent of the 'familists' were classified as 'major associationists', the corresponding figure for the 'solidarists' was 21.7 percent. It was in Erba that the 'familists' turned out to be poor participants in apolitical associations compared to the other two groups, even though all categories of respondents in Erba associated considerably more than their Sesto equivalents. In Erba 24.4 percent of the 'individualists', 19.6 percent of the 'familists' and 28.1 percent of the 'solidarists' emerged as 'major associationists'. It was also in Erba that more men than women defined themselves as 'familists'. It was not surprising, therefore, that in Erba women revealed themselves to participate in apolitical associations to a higher degree than men, whereas the opposite was true in Sesto.

In terms of marital status, more unmarried than married respondents participated in this type of association, which suggests a generational cycle, as opposed to a fixed pattern of behaviour. It is only logical that young people without the burden of a family participate more widely in various associations, whereas married people have less time at their disposal, particularly when they also

Table 2.6 Scale of apolitical associationism by life values (All respondents)

		Life values			
		individualist	familist	solidarist	Total
non associationism	Count	41	71	62	174
	% within life values	27.3%	23.8%	22.5%	24.1%
	% of Total	5.7%	9.8%	8.6%	24.1%
minor associationism	Count	37	97	59	193
	% within life values	24.7%	32.6%	21.5%	26.7%
	% of Total	5.1%	13.4%	8.2%	26.7%
medium associationism	Count	44	86	85	215
	% within life values	29.3%	28.9%	30.9%	29.7%
	% of Total	6.1%	11.9%	11.8%	29.7%
major associationism	Count	28	44	69	141
	% within life values	18.7%	14.8%	25.1%	19.5%
	% of Total	3.9%	6.1%	9.5%	19.5%
Total	Count	150	298	275	723
	% within life values	100.0%	100.0%	100.0%	100.0%
	% of Total	20.7%	41.2%	38.0%	100.0%

Table 2.7 Scale of apolitical associationism by life values in Sesto and Erba

AREA			Life values			
			individualist	familist	solidarist	Total
Sesto	non associationism	Count	14	33	26	73
		% within life values	23.3%	22.8%	20.2%	21.9%
		% of Total	4.2%	9.9%	7.8%	21.9%
	minor associationism	Count	21	51	32	104
		% within life values	35.0%	35.2%	24.8%	31.1%
		% of Total	6.3%	15.3%	9.6%	31.1%
	medium associationism	Count	19	47	43	109
		% within life values	31.7%	32.4%	33.3%	32.6%
		% of Total	5.7%	14.1%	12.9%	32.6%
	major associationism	Count	6	14	28	48
		% within life values	10.0%	9.7%	21.7%	14.4%
		% of Total	1.8%	4.2%	8.4%	14.4%
	Total	Count	60	145	129	334
		% within life values	100.0%	100.0%	100.0%	100.0%
		% of Total	18.0%	43.4%	38.6%	100.0%

Erba					
non associationism	Count	27	38	36	101
	% within life values	30.0%	24.8%	24.7%	26.0%
	% of Total	6.9%	9.8%	9.3%	26.0%
minor associationism	Count	16	46	27	89
	% within life values	17.8%	30.1%	18.5%	22.9%
	% of Total	4.1%	11.8%	6.9%	22.9%
medium associationism	Count	25	39	42	106
	% within life values	27.8%	25.5%	28.8%	27.2%
	% of Total	6.4%	10.0%	10.8%	27.2%
major associationism	Count	22	30	41	93
	% within life values	24.4%	19.6%	28.1%	23.9%
	% of Total	5.7%	7.7%	10.5%	23.9%
Total	Count	90	153	146	389
	% within life values	100.0%	100.0%	100.0%	100.0%
	% of Total	23.1%	39.3%	37.5%	100.0%

localities who had stated that relations with family members were 'not very frequent or friendly' subscribed primarily to individualist values.

Political associationism and Catholicism

In the same way as for 'apolitical associationism', my analysis of 'political associationism' started with the construction of an 'index of associationism', followed by a 'scale of associationism' (Garvía Soto 1996). The procedure that was followed was exactly the same as the one described earlier in this chapter. The aim was, once again, to arrive at a simplified 'filter', on the basis of which respondents could be classified as 'non', 'minor', 'medium' or 'major' associationists.

When applied to Sesto and Erba, the scale of political associationism revealed a greater percentage of active respondents in the former locality (Table 2.9). As we saw earlier, the reverse was true in the case of apolitical associationism.

Table 2.9 shows that only 29.3 percent of respondents were 'non associationists' in Sesto, as opposed to 46.5 percent in Erba. The findings confirm what Trigilia had pointed out in 1986, namely that in Italy the 'red subculture' had developed political forms of associationism to a much larger extent than the 'white subculture', which continued to privilege social and voluntary networks of interpersonal communication at the expense of political ones. As I mentioned above, this important distinction was overlooked by Putnam in his recent work. It follows that Catholics should also prove less associative than lay people when it comes to political participation. The findings confirmed this hypothesis (Table 2.10).

As can be seen from Table 2.10, lay people associated substantially more than Catholics in both Sesto and Erba. In the former locality, 64.4 percent of Catholic respondents were either 'non associationists' or 'minor associationists', as opposed to 49.1 percent of lay respondents. By contrast, only 13.3 percent of Catholics were 'major associationists', against 21.7 percent of lay respondents. In Erba, a massive 71.3 percent of Catholic respondents were either 'non associationists' or 'minor associationists'. The corresponding figure for lay respondents was also high: 68.2 percent. Indeed in Sesto political associationism was found to correlate negatively with the index of religiosity: the more religious the

Table 2.9 Scale of political associationism in Sesto and Erba

AREA			Frequency	Percent	Valid Percent	Cumulative Percent
Sesto	Missing	System	3	100.0		
	Valid	non associationism	91	20.5	29.3	29.3
		minor associationism	86	19.4	27.7	56.9
		medium associationism	78	17.6	25.1	82.0
		major associationism	56	12.6	18.0	100.0
		Total	331	70.2	100.0	
	Missing		132	29.8		
	Total		443	100.0		
Erba	Valid	non associationism	159	35.7	46.5	46.5
		minor associationism	80	18.0	23.4	69.9
		medium associationism	62	13.9	18.1	88.0
		major associationism	41	9.2	12.0	100.0
		Total	342	76.9	100.0	
	Missing		103	23.1		
	Total		445	100.0		

respondents, the less likely they were to participate in political associations, and vice versa.

Thus the most associative of all were lay people in Sesto, which is in line with the socialist and communist subculture of the town. In some respects each locality showed specific patterns of behaviour, which cut across the division between Catholics and lay. The most notable case is that of participation in trade-union activities, which was considerably higher among Sesto respondents than among Erba ones, and also higher among Sesto *Catholic* respondents than among Erba *lay* ones. The most logical explanation for this lies in the different socio-cultural characteristics of the two localities. Trade unionism in Italy has traditionally been stronger in areas of large-scale industry than in areas of small-scale industry, as well as in areas with a 'red' subculture as opposed to a 'white' one (Golden 1988). It seems clear that Catholic workers in Sesto

Table 2.10 Scale of political associationism by religious values in Sesto and Erba

AREA			Religious values		
			Catholic	Lay	Total
Sesto	non associationism	Count	42	45	87
		% within religious values	29.4%	28.7%	29.0%
		% of Total	14.0%	15.0%	29.0%
	minor associationism	Count	50	32	82
		% within religious values	35.0%	20.4%	27.3%
		% of Total	16.7%	10.7%	27.3%
	medium associationism	Count	32	46	78
		% within religious values	22.4%	29.3%	26.0%
		% of Total	10.7%	15.3%	26.0%
	major associationism	Count	19	34	53
		% within religious values	13.3%	21.7%	17.7%
		% of Total	6.3%	11.3%	17.7%
	Total	Count	143	157	300
		% within religious values	100.0%	100.0%	100.0%
		% of Total	47.7%	52.3%	100.0%

Erba				
non associationism	Count	116	42	158
	% within religious values	46.2%	49.4%	47.0%
	% of Total	34.5%	12.5%	47.0%
minor associationism	Count	63	16	79
	% within religious values	25.1%	18.8%	23.5%
	% of Total	18.8%	4.8%	23.5%
medium associationism	Count	41	17	58
	% within religious values	16.3%	20.0%	17.3%
	% of Total	12.2%	5.1%	17.3%
major associationism	Count	31	10	41
	% within religious values	12.4%	11.8%	12.2%
	% of Total	9.2%	3.0%	12.2%
Total	Count	251	85	336
	% within religious values	100.0%	100.0%	100.0%
	% of Total	74.7%	25.3%	100.0%

have been influenced by the strong trade-unionist tradition of the town; conversely, lay workers in Erba have largely adopted the predominant local attitude of indifference towards trade union activity.

Similarly, when participation in the activities of a neighbourhood association or a cooperative was explored, it was revealed that respondents in Sesto were more active than respondents in Erba, whatever their religious beliefs. It should be remembered that the cooperative movement in Italy is strongly associated with the 'red' subculture, and Sesto is clearly no exception. On the other hand, the difference between the two localities is less pronounced when participation in a political party is taken into consideration.

The above findings confirm the existence, already detected for apolitical associationism, of a new dimension alongside the Catholic/lay divide postulated by Putnam and Ginsborg. The new dimension corresponds to localism. It is fair to say that Ginsborg (1996) recently acknowledged the importance of localism in northern Italy. As for Putnam, he fully recognised the importance of the local and regional dimension in analysing civic and political culture in Italy, nevertheless he was primarily concerned with the North/South divide and to this end grouped together the northern areas of the 'red' and 'white' subcultures, as Cartocci remarked. In doing so, Putnam failed to identify the specific 'localist' component of north Italian 'civicness', with the result that he equated 'civicness' directly to 'democracy', without addressing the question: 'what type of democracy?' The impersonal, representative democracy of the rule of law or the highly participative but exclusionary democracy which had characterised Italy's city-states, cited by Putnam as an example of 'civic engagement'? I will come back to this crucial issue in the conclusions to this chapter.

Political associationism and family values

When political associationism was taken into consideration, the findings contradicted Ginsborg's assumption that family values and ties would stand in the way of wider civic engagement. In both Sesto and Erba the 'solidarists' were again found to be the most active participants, but this time they were followed by the 'familists', while the 'individualists' turned out to be poor participants. The difference between the 'familists' and the 'individualists' was particularly noticeable in the case of participation in a political party and a trade union. Coupled with the fact that, as we saw, young people were especially numerous among the 'individualists', this suggests that the younger generation tends to participate more in leisure, sport, cultural and voluntary activities, whereas the older generations are more likely to participate in political (and more structured) associations. It was also the case that women participated less than men, particularly in Erba, whereas, as we saw, they were more active in apolitical associations. This finding is in line with various analyses of women's socio-political behaviour, which registered their preference for informal and apolitical associations over formal and political ones (Lovenduski and Hills 1981, Zincone 1985, Lovenduski and Norris 1993). The gender factor appears stronger than the locality factor; in other words, women in both Sesto and Erba behaved in similar ways, rather than 'conforming' to the specific pattern shown by the locality. This was especially true of trade-union behaviour: only 30 percent of men in Sesto were weak participants in trade-union activities, as opposed to a massive 67 percent of women. In this respect, gender appears more resistant to 'localism' than religion.

At this stage it may be interesting to compare political socialisation with associationism. Political socialisation refers to people's acquisition of ideas, attitudes and values related to the political system and institutions. Political socialisation takes place throughout people's lives and in different environments, ranging from the family to the workplace. Question 28 asked respondents where they had formed their political ideas: the choice was between family, friends, church, school, work, union and party. They were allowed to choose more than one of these answers. Tables 2.11 and 2.12 show which environment(s) played a major part in shaping the political opinions of respondents in Sesto and Erba.

True to their specific socio-economic characteristics, the two localities differed sharply in terms of political socialisation. Workers in Sesto (particularly men) had been influenced primarily by the workplace (often in conjunction with the union and/or with the family), whereas respondents in Erba (both male and female) had been influenced predominantly by the family and by friends (sometimes in conjunction with the workplace). The strong socialising influence of large-scale industry in areas like Sesto, as well as its ability to counteract (although in many cases simply to reinforce) the influence of primary groups is thus confirmed. In this respect, Sapelli was correct in judging large-scale industrialisation as capable of transforming people's attitudes and values. By

Table 2.11 Where respondents had formed their political ideas (Sesto): (Percentages)

	Men	Women
Family	35	57
Friends	23	31
Work	64	34
Union	17	6
Party	6	4
School	7	16
Church	3	3
Total numbers	(264)	(118)

Please note that respondents were allowed to tick more than one box, therefore the percentages do not add up to 100. Most men chose 'work' either on its own or in combination with 'union' and 'family'. Most women chose 'family' either on its own or in combination with 'friends' and 'work'.

Table 2.12 Where respondents had formed their political ideas (Erba): (Percentages)

	Men	Women
Family	52	72
Friends	43	42
Work	35	21
Union	4	2
Party	8	2
School	8	11
Church	9	8
Total numbers	(230)	(168)

Most men and women chose 'family' either on its own or in combination with 'friends'.

contrast, small-scale industry in areas like Erba has little influence on people's values, and in no way counterbalances the predominance of the family as an agent of socialisation.

It would be wrong, however, to infer from the above (as Sapelli did), that political socialisation in primary groups stands in the way of horizontal associationism. What is true is that Sesto male respondents who had developed their political ideas largely at the workplace were more likely to participate in both a political party and a trade union than respondents who had socialised primarily in the family. What is also true is that women in Sesto did not conform to this pattern, and that respondents in Erba who had socialised in the family or among friends were among the most active participants in horizontal associations. In short, Sapelli's interpretation regarding the socialising effects of large-scale industry is correct but it applies only to male workers participating in a political party or a trade union. It is only if we privilege participation in these associations at the expense of participation in less politically-orientated associations that we can agree with Sapelli that the family has a negative influence upon horizontal associationism.

More importantly, we have now entered a post-industrial phase, with the result that throughout Europe membership and participation in a political party or a trade union are considered to be on the wane, while elections are characterised by 'post-modern' campaigns, dominated by the media, pollsters, and 'strategic marketing' (Norris 1997). The younger generations, in particular, appear to have lost interest in politics and/or to have shifted in large numbers towards participation in single-issue, voluntary and non-partisan associations. Indeed, according to Inglehart (1990: 56), the modern world and modern democracy are characterised by post-materialist values, which place less emphasis on economic growth and job security and greater emphasis on the environment and the quality of life. If trade unionism and political associations of a traditional, class-based, type are increasingly being superseded by less partisan ones, this means that the family may, at least in Italy, be destined to play an even more crucial role as the main agent of socialisation. Such a role is likely to accelerate the move away from class-based associationism but it should not, on the basis of the evidence presented so far, stifle civic engagement and social commitment.

It cannot be denied that, historically, trade unionism and other class-based forms of associationism played a very important role in shaping ideals of solidarity and of a 'common good' and in fostering collective action and horizontal bonds of fellowship. Nevertheless, numerous studies have shown that class-based associations could also be highly exclusionary, often banning women from membership and, in Italy at least, privileging some categories of workers and neglecting others (Procacci 1970, Frader 1981: 203–5, Snell 1981, Seccombe 1986). Other works have shown that organised collective action, generally undertaken by male workers, often rested upon the support of their female family members (Ramella 1975, Gentili Zappi 1991). Conversely, when women became involved in trade-union activity, or in a public protest, they often did so in support of their husbands, sons and brothers, and in the pursuit of a family strategy, rather than in the name of class solidarity (Cento Bull 1989, Palazzi 1990, Tomassini 1991). It was argued in the Introduction to Part I that, since many industrial workers in Italy experienced different social dimensions and contrasting value-systems, the culture associated with large-scale industrialisation and class-based organisations never fully replaced more traditional peasant values. In the light of these recent studies, it should be added that the role played by family networks and values in the development of class-based organisations and solidarist values also needs to be reassessed, since it has almost certainly been underestimated.

Associationism and newspaper readership

A majority of respondents in both localities read at least one daily newspaper on a regular basis, more so in Sesto than in Erba (229 respondents in Erba, 260 in Sesto). Putnam's hypothesis that newspaper readership correlates positively with the index of associationism was confirmed by the survey findings. For both apolitical and political associationism, the correlation existed when the two localities were considered together, and persisted when the data was disaggregated, even though it proved more significant for Sesto than for Erba. Thus people who read a newspaper on a regular basis were also active participants in horizontal associations.

Did Catholics read newspapers to a lesser extent than lay people? According to Putnam (1993: 107), 'of those Italians who attend Mass more than once a week, 52 percent say they rarely read a newspaper and 51 percent say they never discuss politics; among their avowedly irreligious compatriots, the equivalent figures are 13 percent and 17 percent'. The survey findings contrast sharply with this negative portrayal of Italian Catholics. Putnam's treatment of Catholicism as an independent variable serves to distort his figures. Catholicism in Italy is best treated as a dependent variable, precisely because Catholic values and Catholic activism/passivism in the public arena, vary in accordance to geographical areas.

This is not to say that the Catholic/lay divide becomes insignificant when analysing Italian political culture. It simply means that the divide is not a straightforward one between Catholic = uncivic/lay = civic. Rather, both groups can be highly civic (at least in northern Italy), however the nature of their 'civicness' is not directly assimilable and it depends to a large extent on the locality factor. In the case of newspaper readership, this emerged quite clearly when a distinction was made between readership of the national press and readership of the local press. It was then that some interesting findings began to emerge (Tables 2.13 and 2.14).

First, readers of the national press were numerous in both localities, but considerably more so in Sesto than in Erba (Table 2.13). Thus in Sesto 343 respondents declared that they read a national daily newspaper on either a regular or an occasional basis (of which 226 regularly), whereas the corresponding figure for Erba was 315 (151 regularly). The reverse was true when readership of the local press was taken into consideration (Table 2.14). Thus in Sesto only 170 respondents read a local daily newspaper either occasionally or regularly, whereas the corresponding figure for Erba was 320 (higher than the figure for national readership!). Also, in Sesto three times as many respondents read the national press on a regular basis than they read the local one (226 a national newspaper, 64 a local one), while in Erba the two figures were remarkably similar (151 a national paper, 136 a local one). Indeed in Sesto most respondents did not even bother to answer

Table 2.13 Readers of national daily press in Sesto and Erba

AREA			Frequency	Percent	Valid Percent	Cumulative Percent
Sesto	Missing	System	3	100.0		
	Valid	regularly	226	51.0	63.0	63.0
		occasionally	117	26.4	32.6	95.5
		never	16	3.6	4.5	100.0
		Total	359	81.0	100.0	
	Missing		84	19.0		
	Total		443	100.0		
Erba	Valid	regularly	151	33.9	41.6	41.6
		occasionally	164	36.9	45.2	86.8
		never	48	10.8	13.2	100.0
		Total	363	81.6	100.0	
	Missing		82	18.4		
	Total		445	100.0		

Table 2.14 Readers of local daily press in Sesto and Erba

AREA			Frequency	Percent	Valid Percent	Cumulative Percent
	Missing	System	3	100.0		
Sesto	Valid	regularly	64	14.4	32.7	32.7
		occasionally	106	23.9	54.1	86.7
		never	26	5.9	13.3	100.0
		Total	196	44.2	100.0	
	Missing		247	55.8		
	Total		443	100.0		
Erba	Valid	regularly	136	30.6	38.4	38.4
		occasionally	184	41.3	52.0	90.4
		never	34	7.6	9.6	100.0
		Total	354	79.6	100.0	
		Missing	91	20.4		
	Total		445	100.0		

the question on the local press: 55.8 percent of Sesto respondents did not answer the question, as opposed to only 20.4 percent of Erba respondents. By contrast, when asked whether they read the national press, only 19.0 percent of Sesto respondents, and 18.4 percent of Erba respondents failed to respond. Thus readership of a local newspaper, unlike readership of a national one, correlated positively with locality.

Second, in both localities there was a positive correlation between the index of religiosity and readership of the local press (Tables 2.15 and 2.16). Thus Catholics read the local press to a larger extent than lay people: 41.1 percent of Catholics in Sesto and 43.3 percent in Erba read a local daily newspaper regularly, as opposed to 24.7 percent of lay respondents in Sesto and 22.1 percent in Erba (Table 2.16). The greater tendency of Catholics to read the local press went hand in hand with a negative correlation, which applied only to Erba, between the index of religiosity and readership of the national press. In other words, Catholics in Erba tended to read the local press in place of, and not in addition to, the national press: 61.8 percent of Sesto Catholics and 64.4 percent of Sesto lay respondents read a national daily newspaper on a regular basis, but for Erba the figures were 37.5 percent and 52.7 percent respectively (Table 2.15).

The 'locality factor' did not weaken when gender was taken

			Religious values		
AREA			Catholic	Lay	Total
Sesto	readers of national daily press	regularly			
		Count	107	112	219
		% with religious values	61.8%	64.4%	63.1%
		% of Total	30.8%	32.3%	63.1%
	occasionally	Count	60	53	113
		% with religious values	34.7%	30.5%	32.6%
		% of Total	17.3%	15.3%	32.6%
	never	Count	6	9	15
		% with religious values	3.5%	5.2%	4.3%
		% of Total	1.7%	2.6%	4.3%
	Total	Count	173	174	347
		% with religious values	100.0%	100.0%	100.0%
		% of Total	49.9%	50.1%	100.0%
Erba	readers of national daily press	regularly			
		Count	99	49	148
		% with religious values	37.5%	52.7%	41.5%
		% of Total	27.7%	13.7%	41.5%
	occasionally	Count	130	31	161
		% with religious values	49.2%	33.3%	45.1%
		% of Total	36.4%	8.7%	45.1%
	never	Count	35	13	48
		% with religious values	13.3%	14.0%	13.4%
		% of Total	9.8%	3.6%	13.4%
	Total	Count	264	93	357
		% with religious values	100.0%	100.0%	100.0%
		% of Total	73.9%	26.1	100.0%

Table 2.16 Local press readership by religious values in Sesto and Erba

AREA				Religious values		
				Catholic	Lay	Total
Sesto	readers of local daily press	regularly	Count	39	24	63
			% with religious values	41.1%	24.7%	32.8%
			% of Total	20.3%	12.5%	32.8%
		occasionally	Count	50	53	103
			% with religious values	52.6%	54.6%	53.6%
			of Total	26.0%	27.6%	53.6%
		never	Count	6	20	26
			% with religious values	6.3%	20.6%	13.5%
			% of Total	3.1%	10.4%	13.5%
	Total		Count	95	97	192
			% with religious values	100.0%	100.0%	100.0%
			% of Total	49.5%	50.5%	100.0%
Erba	readers of local daily press	regularly	Count	114	19	133
			% with religious values	43.3%	22.1%	38.1%
			% of Total	32.7%	5.4%	38.1%
		occasionally	Count	127	56	183
			% with religious values	48.3%	65.1%	52.4%
			% of Total	36.4%	16.0%	52.4%
		never	Count	22	11	33
			% with religious values	8.4%	12.8%	9.5%
			% of Total	6.3%	3.2%	9.5%
	Total		Count	263	86	349
			% with religious values	100.0%	100.0%	100.0%
			% of Total	75.4%	24.6%	100.0%

into consideration. In other words, as far as newspaper readership is concerned, both women and men conformed to the patterns described above. Despite the fact that in both localities men tended to read a national daily newspaper to a larger extent than women, *women* in Sesto read the national press to a larger extent than *men* in Erba. In particular, 64.7 percent of Sesto male respondents and 57 percent of Sesto female respondents read a national daily newspaper on a regular basis, whereas the corresponding figures for Erba were 44.6 percent and 36.8 percent. In the case of the local press, a high proportion of both men and women in Sesto failed to respond to the question, whereas the reverse applied to Erba.

This data suggests that, despite a generic comparability between the two towns in terms of newspaper readership and in terms of the existence of a positive correlation between newspaper readership and associationism, there were fundamental qualitative differences which reveal a contrasting nature of 'civicness' and associationism in the two areas. Once again a third dimension has emerged which complicates the simple binary opposition between civicness and non-civicness, participation and non-participation, vertical and horizontal associationism. This third dimension is localism and the next chapter will incorporate it fully into a discussion of Italy's social identities and political cultures.

Conclusions

This chapter has analysed the degree of associationism in both Sesto and Erba in relation to such factors as Catholicism, family values and newspaper readership. The results indicate that, contrary to Putnam's interpretation, Catholics are no less civic than lay people, although the nature of their civicness differed considerably. As Trigilia had anticipated in 1986, Catholics in predominantly 'white' areas (such as Erba), privileged participation in apolitical associations at the expense of political ones. By contrast, non-Catholics in predominantly 'red' areas (such as Sesto) participated more often in political associations, particularly a trade union or a political party. Similarly, Catholics in Erba were more avid readers of the local press, whereas non-Catholics in Sesto preferred reading the national press. Putnam singled out readership of the local press as an important index to measure civicness and as 'a mark of citizen interest in community affairs' (1993: 92). From this point of view we would have to conclude that Catholics are more civic-minded than non-Catholics, a conclusion which makes little sense, because the findings are indicative above all of the importance of 'localism' in Italy, rather than of the degree of civicness.

My findings were less unequivocal in relation to the role played by family (particularist) values. Ginsborg's hypothesis that strong family values hindered the development of horizontal association-ism found at least partial confirmation in responses to the survey. In particular, respondents who subscribed to 'familist' values associated less often in apolitical associations than respondents with either 'solidarist' or 'individualist' values. As far as political associations were concerned, however, people with 'familist' val-ues were found to participate to a greater extent than people classi-fied as individualists. The survey also revealed very clearly that strong kinship and friendship ties do not automatically coincide with 'familist' values. On the contrary, respondents who enjoyed very close relations with members of their family and with friends were at least as likely to hold solidarist values as familist values and participated widely in horizontal associations.

Thus it would appear that strong kinship ties do not correlate with weak associationism, even though 'familist' values do to a certain extent. Perhaps it is time to stop blaming the strong Italian family for uncivicness, clientelism and patronage. Such an approach is not sustained by the evidence. It is almost ironic that, while in the Italian context the family is often blamed for clien-telism and corruption, in the U.K. it is cultural individualism which has been seen as the culprit for the increasing episodes of sleaze. As Freedland (1998: 17) commented: 'That British corruption exists is plain; more intriguing is the explanation for it. A standard left response is to blame the culture of deregulation, the get-rich-quick ethos [...] More subtle is the view that the end of trade unionism has fostered a new, aggressive individualism [...] We have long assumed corruption to be a faraway malady – endemic in Italy or Latin America, but hardly a worry here. That attitude probably made things worse, creating a sense of holier-than-thou probity which barred many from seeing the corruption all around them'.

Furthermore, there is a need to take into account important recent research and debates. To blame the political ills of the coun-try on the Italian family serves to reaffirm the validity of interpre-tations which became prominent in the 1950s, such as Banfield's (1958) 'amoral familism' (where the family was seen as the cause of social opportunism and lack of trust), or Almond and Verba's

(1963) 'civic culture' (where Italy was found to possess poor civic values). While it is perfectly legitimate to recognise the resilience of traditional socio-cultural trends in contemporary Italy, it is also necessary to acknowledge that the debate both within and outside Italy has moved on. The family and patronage are two areas where there is a growing consensus among sociologists and historians that old assumptions need to be considerably revised. The following summary of these debates demonstrates how they have a direct bearing on the issues under discussion.

Studies on the 'Italian' family have recently highlighted the variety of family forms and structures across the peninsula. These different family forms are generally seen as stemming from specific rural and land-tenure systems. Barbagli (1991a: 108) identified three main family structures in Italy, each prevalent in a specific socio-geographical area and remarked that 'in Italy, perhaps unlike many other European countries, there was no single system or pattern, but instead a variety of different systems of family formation'. According to Gribaudi (1996: 83–4), the patriarchal family often associated with Italy was absent in the South. Bull and Corner (1993) showed how proto-industrialisation in northern Italy was linked to the existence of a specific family form, originating from the sharecropping system, which survived and indeed contributed to the later process of industrialisation. They argued that the absence of this type of family in the South can help explain why the region failed to develop small-scale, family-based industries, and to give rise to wealthy communities characterised by trust and solidarity, as was the case in the central and north-eastern regions. More recently, Macry (1997: 188–214) re-examined the issue in the light of the new findings and concluded that family structures and values in the South of Italy were indeed profoundly different from those found in the North. Specifically, he argued that the family form which was predominant in the North (originating from the sharecropping system) fostered both intra- and inter- familial collaboration, and depended on a full utilisation of women's work. By contrast, the typical peasant family form prevailing in the southern region was characterised by the exclusion of women from the production process and by inter-family rivalry and mistrust. Thus strong kinship ties in the North actively encouraged collaboration and trust – families were outward-looking as much as they were inward-looking. Conversely, strong kinship ties in the South contrasted with conflictual inter-family relations – families were inward-looking only. Other commentators pointed out that the

South should not be seen as an undifferentiated area and suggested that this applies to family forms as well as to socio-economic configurations. Indeed Trigilia (1992) argued that, historically, some southern regions had rural structures comparable to those in the North and were marked by a widespread presence of semi-autonomous farming families, similar in many ways to the sharecropping families prevalent in many central and northern areas. Trigilia (1992: 131–5) also showed that, in the South, a high historical presence of independent farming families and a strong artisanal tradition correlated positively with economic growth and the creation of a dynamic small-business sector. This finding suggests that endogenous development based on small- and medium-sized firms is not a prerogative of central and northern Italy but can also be detected in some southern regions and forms a viable foundation for economic prosperity.

Just as important as these variations in family forms within Italy, is the change that has occurred in the nature of intra-family relations in the contemporary period. As mentioned in the Introduction, Bagnasco (1996a) argued that such relations are now more contractual, more 'bargained' than they were in the 1950s and 1960s. Children, partly by virtue of their long-term residence with their original family nucleus, are now much more likely to have a say in family matters and participate in decision-making. The result is a more democratic primary group, representing a fairly significant break with the past, which is bound to have an effect upon the wider social and political patterns of participation. More democratic and equal relations within the family can easily reverberate through other associations, helping to establish a climate of consultation and cooperation. As Bagnasco (1996a: 56) put it: 'The way in which hierarchies are perceived within the family has changed, with consequences upon processes of socialisation: the values of obedience and hierarchy make way for those of discussion and agreement, both in the family and in society'. These new family values, in other words, may well be underpinning democratic participation and political pluralism. We can therefore safely conclude that, by themselves, strong family ties do not tell us anything at all about the degree of trust and collaboration in a society, or indeed about the level of horizontal associationism.

Recent debates on the issue of patronage have proved as illuminating and revealing as those on the family. Here the key question is in some ways the opposite of the one we have just addressed. In other words, the question is not 'can we generalise (about the family) and attribute the same (negative) characteristics associated with "amoral familism" to the whole of Italy?'. Rather, the question is: 'Can patronage, usually associated with traditional societies and with the South of Italy in particular, be deemed to apply to the North of Italy as well?'. This question could have far-reaching consequences. According to Putnam, as we saw, patronage (i.e., hierarchical, unequal networks of interpersonal relations) is restricted to the South of Italy, while the modernised and industrialised northern regions are characterised by civic virtues, trust and, above all, horizontal and democratic associations between equal citizens. It has become increasingly clear in the course of this chapter, however, that northern areas can be both civic and relatively 'unmodernised', at least as far as the continuing importance of family and friendship ties, Catholic values, and localism – even parochialism – are concerned.

Offering a fresh perspective on patronage, Moss recently argued that patronage relations, built around the control and dissemination of information, are present throughout Italy. In his view, 'the contrast between north, central and south Italy is better drawn in terms of the quality of patronage relations, not their quantity' (Moss 1995: 85). More importantly, he argued that patronage per se does not have any detrimental effect on horizontal associationism:

> To reinforce the empirically grounded doubts about the picture of a clearly uneven distribution of patronage between north, central and south Italy, a more direct attack can be made on one of the core assumptions which supports it: namely, the alleged incompatibility between clientelism and collective mobilisation which entails that powerful vertical relations must undermine horizontal types of social co-operation. To use Hirschman's terminology, voice and loyalty are essentially incompatible options which work against each other [...] However, if we relax this rigid picture of the political imagination and replace it with the idea of a flexible repertoire, we can consider the possibility that under certain circumstances voice and loyalty can be mutually reinforcing (Ibid.: 71).

Moss added that 'patronage may be a vital factor in permitting people to develop trust in one another and accept the risks of collective action' (Ibid.: 86). In his opinion, patronage in the sharecropping regions of northern Italy had precisely the effect of strengthening horizontal ties and collaboration. He also noted that his aim was 'not to resuscitate patronage as a desirable social relationship, only to suggest that the social and economic consequences of some of its forms are more varied than we have acknowledged' (Ibid.: 72).

Why have these considerations opened up new avenues for an understanding of Italy's socio-political cultures? The answer lies in the fact that, just as the relationship between 'the strong Italian family' and 'uncivicness' has been proven inflexible and untrue, in the same way the straightforward identification of 'hierarchical and vertical associationism' with clientelism and patronage and of 'horizontal and democratic associationism' with the absence of these phenomena, no longer holds. This is where Putnam's argument is perhaps weakest. Putnam identified northern Italy with civicness and democratic institutions. He was aware that many theorists tended to associate civic virtues of the type he described for northern Italy with pre-modern societies: 'Contemporary social thought has borrowed from the nineteenth-century German sociologist Ferdinand Tönnies the distinction between Gemeinschaft and Gesellschaft – that is, between a traditional, small-scale, face-to-face community resting on a universal sense of solidarity and a modern, rationalistic, impersonal society resting on self-interest' (Putnam 1993: 114). Putnam dismissed this thorny issue by stressing that the most civic communities in Italy were to be found in 'the most modern, bustling, affluent, technologically advanced societies on the face of the earth' (Ibid.: 114–15). He did not, however, further investigate the nature and characteristics of northern Italy's modern society. Clearly, for Putnam, 'modernity' is both an uncontroversial and universal concept.

The problem with Putnam's rejection of many theorists' association of the civic community with 'small, close-knit, pre-modern societies, quite unlike the modern world', as he himself put it (Ibid.: 114), lies in the fact that modernisation is conceived as a linear and uniform phenomenon, to be compared and contrasted only with pre- or non-modernisation. In reality, as generally acknowledged by historians, there are different paths to modernisation and one of these paths – the one followed by the central and north-eastern regions of Italy – combined economic modernisation with a 'pre-modern' pattern of cultural values (Bull and Corner 1993). It is interesting that Putnam dealt at some length, in his analysis of northern Italy, with the industrial system typical of these areas, a system consisting of geographical concentrations of small manufacturing units operating in tightly-knit communities characterised by an overlapping of business and family ties, low social and political polarisation, and a high degree of entrepreneurship. He did not, however, remark on its specificity, which other scholars have discussed at some length (Piore and Sabel 1984, Sabel and Zeitlin 1985, Becattini 1987, Bagnasco 1988, Bull and Corner 1993).

This combination of the modern with the (allegedly) pre-modern is generally overlooked by modernisation theory, which is based on the idea of stages of modernity. Thus, in his book *The Consequences of Modernity*, the distinguished sociologist Anthony Giddens (1990: 100–11) neatly separated pre-modern from modern societies, equating the former with kinship ties and a local community, and the latter with disembedded social relations and an abstract, non-spatial community. Once again, the historical process is conceptualised as unfolding in clearly identifiable and compartmentalised stages of development, rather than encompassing complex and non-linear social and cultural change. Similarly, we cannot assume that democracy is uniform in all modern societies: the formation of democratic institutions has to a certain extent followed the different patterns of industrialisation and modernisation. In short, democracy in the central and north-eastern regions of Italy has been largely shaped by the specific pattern of cultural modernisation experienced by these areas and above all by the continuing relevance of 'pre-modern' values, including localist allegiances. This chapter has shown how the localist nature of much of northern Italy's horizontal associationism and civic engagement was underestimated by Putnam, and that the negative consequences of localism were largely ignored by him. One of the reasons for this is that Putnam's book, while dealing ostensibly with Italy, is in fact much more preoccupied with North American society. Northern Italy is thus largely treated as an 'ideal-type' place, where democratic participation and civic engagement could be taken as a model for other advanced societies, judged to be at risk of losing those 'virtues' which sustain a truly democratic system.

To sum up, this chapter has established that northern Italy, including traditionally Catholic areas, is neither as familist and particularist as depicted by Ginsborg, nor as uncontroversially modern and patronage-free as argued by Putnam. Reality is more complex than its representation, and localism can provide us with the key to an understanding of this complexity. The next chapter examines this issue.

3

Localism

Introduction

Localism in Italy is often defined as 'municipalism' and it usually refers to the long-standing tendency of Italians to give their loyalty and allegiance primarily to their village or town, rather than to the nation-state. According to many scholars, this tendency can be traced back to the medieval city-states, which developed predominantly in northern Italy: 'Underneath the surface of the territorial states of the modern period, the vitality of the city-state tradition survived powerfully. [...] In retrospect, it can seem surprising that the new Italian state was able to impose a centralised system of government on a complex of diverse societies marked by a high degree of local particularism' (Lyttelton 1996: 37). It is interesting that Putnam, like Lyttelton, also traces the origins of a specific trait of Italian political culture back to the development of the city-states. Nevertheless the similarity between their positions ends here. Putnam, as we saw, focused exclusively on the city-states as examples of civic virtues, associationism, trust and (with only slight reservations) good and effective government. Lyttelton, by contrast, emphasised localism and particularism. The one does not exclude the other, however, crucially, the one *without* the other offers us an incomplete and ultimately a false picture, as we shall see.

The concept of localism has become increasingly popular among Italian sociologists and political analysts in recent times, and it has been broadened to refer both to specific socio-economic milieux and to an identifiable shared system of values which characterises these same milieux (Diamanti 1996: 30–1). It also implies a fairly high degree of internal cohesion and of 'closure' of a territorial community vis-à-vis the outside world, including the nation-state (Cartocci: 1994). This attitude of 'closure' creates an 'invisible' boundary around the community in question and it often manifests itself in the identification of an external enemy, as well as in the predominance of a specific political orientation and political party. Thus localism is not simply a legacy of the experience of the city-states.

After Unification, the Italian nation-state had only limited success in its attempts to construct a national identity. As well as with class, religious and linguistic cleavages, the new state soon had to contend with strong sub-national political cultures. In the central and north-eastern areas of Italy, the socialist and Catholic movements were able to tap into the vast reservoir of local identities produced by the experience of the city-states, and in turn reinforced these identities by establishing strong roots at municipal level, thanks to the success of socialist and Catholic candidates at local elections and their domination in local government institutions (Cartocci 1991: 572–73). In the case of the Catholic subculture, in particular, the local dimension was prioritised, since the Pope had condemned the new state and forbidden all Catholics, with the *non expedit*, to vote at political elections but had made an exception for local elections (Cartocci 1991: 573). As well as the presence of a dominant political movement, what characterised each subculture was also a vast network of associations and organisations which were either socialist– or Catholic-inspired and which the majority of the local population either belonged to or regularly came into contact with. Each associational network had clear territorial boundaries, which were local and regional as opposed to national. As Cartocci (Ibid.: 573) put it, 'the alienation of the socialist and Catholic masses from the process of nation-building during the first decades after Unification implied therefore a localist dimension'.

Thus, in terms of collective and shared identities, in northern Italy there were both distinct 'local communities', characterised by face-to-face familiarity and social interchange, and 'imagined communities' (such as the 'socialist' or the 'Catholic' community), which coincided with both a global and a regional territory, but not with the nation-state. Indeed each imagined community was imagined in opposition to the nation-state, as well as to each other. To an extent this process was not specific to Italy. According to Keating (1998: 21), in western Europe 'Labour organisation typically began at the local level, where it was usually combined with a commitment to global class solidarity, leaving no special place for the nation-state. In time, labour movements were integrated into national systems of wage bargaining and sought dialogue with national governments, but strong traces of localism remained'. In the case of Italy, however, it was not just a question of localist feelings persisting despite the process of nationalisation. Diamanti (1996: 31) pointed out that after the Second World War localism was actually reinforced in Italy's north-eastern and central regions by the emergence of a specific model of economic development characterised by a predominance of localised clusters of small and medium-sized businesses, a network of small and medium-sized urban areas and the absence of vast conurbations, as well as family and social solidarity. There was therefore a convergence, in areas below the level of the nation-state, between the social, economic and cultural spheres. In this context, collective identities continued to be based largely on a local dimension, whether municipal, provincial or regional.

What has been said above has implications for the type of democracy which is prevalent in many Italian northern areas. As Held (1995) recently reminded us, there are various models of democracy, not a single type. The Italian city-state model was characterised by the inclusion of all members of the commune who participated in its government but the exclusion of the people who lived in the countryside which surrounded the city-state and were subject to its rule. It was a highly participative model of democracy which fitted the small territory and the small number of people to which it applied. In short, civic solidarity and trust were community-based, and each community erected barriers to protect and isolate itself. Putnam (1993: 125) recognised that 'the [...] communes were not democratic in our modern sense, for only a minority of the population were full members'. This important acknowledgement did not, however, lead him to consider whether the more 'undemocratic' traits of the city-states have also left a trace upon contemporary Italian political culture, along with the positive traits he so eloquently portrayed in his book. Does localism, in short, continue to play a role in northern Italy? Does mistrust towards 'outsiders' exist alongside trust towards 'insiders'? Are horizontal associationism and civic virtues compatible with parochial and intolerant attitudes? If so, what kind of democracy exists in northern Italian regions? This chapter will provide some insight into the persistence of localism in some areas of Italy and discuss its consequences.

Geographical mobility

Modern, democratic and meritocratic societies are often associated with a high degree of social mobility, while traditional, deferential and patronage-based societies are generally linked to a low degree of social mobility. The issue of geographical mobility is less widely taken into consideration. Yet it is generally accepted that North American society is characterised by high levels of geographical mobility: people move residence regularly in their lives, and are expected to be prepared to follow job opportunities wherever these arise. The same is true to a large extent of the U.K. (Norris 1997). Italy is a country where people have traditionally emigrated in large numbers, both on a seasonal and a permanent basis, to Europe and to the Americas, as well as internally from the South to the North. In this respect, Italy can be considered as no different from other modern and industrial societies, indeed within Europe Italy has experienced the highest levels of mass emigration apart from Ireland. Yet this picture can be misleading.

Central Italy has been affected by emigration to a much lesser extent than the North-East or the South. In the nineteenth century and in the first half of the twentieth, emigration from the northern regions was to a large extent seasonal, whereas emigration from the South was permanent or semi-permanent. In other words, many people from the North emigrated to France, Germany or Switzerland only in the winter months, and returned home in the Spring, whereas people from the South emigrated long-distance and returned only after a number of years, or did not return at all. In addition, once the north-eastern regions started to industrialise, after the Second World War, emigration came to a halt. After 1945, emigration from the southern regions remained high, but was relatively low from the rest of the country.

Low levels of geographical mobility can foster localism, at least in terms of attachment to a particular locality and relatively scarce knowledge of – and interest in – other social and cultural environments. For this reason I will now examine whether Sesto and Erba show high or low degrees of geographical mobility.

As Table 3.1 indicates, only 27 percent of all respondents in Sesto were born in the town, 29.9 percent in another commune of the province of Milan, 14.4 percent in another commune of northern Italy, and 24.1 percent in the South.

The figures contained in Table 3.1 are indicative of the different waves of immigration experienced by Sesto during the period of

Table 3.1 Place of birth of respondents in Sesto and Erba

AREA			Frequency	Percent	Valid Percent	Cumulative Percent
Sesto	Valid	same commune	111	25.1	27.0	27.0
		another commune in the same province	123	27.8	29.9	56.9
		northern Italy	59	13.3	14.4	71.3
		central Italy	13	2.9	3.2	74.5
		southern Italy	99	22.3	24.1	98.5
		abroad	6	1.4	1.5	100.0
		Total	411	92.8	100.0	
	Missing		32	7.2		
	Total		443	100.0		
Erba	Valid	same commune	183	41.1	42.4	42.4
		another commune in the same province	139	31.2	32.2	74.5
		northern Italy	58	13.0	13.4	88.0
		central Italy	8	1.8	1.9	89.8
		southern Italy	37	8.3	8.6	98.4
		abroad	7	1.6	1.6	100.0
		Total	432	97.1	100.0	
	Missing		13	2.9		
	Total		445	100.0		

industrial expansion: in the initial stages immigration was from neighbouring villages and towns, it later expanded drawing on nearby provinces and regions and, in the 1960s and 1970s, the southern regions. By contrast, 42.4 percent of Erba respondents were born in the town; a further 32.2 percent were born in another commune of the province of Como, and 13.4 percent in another province of the North. Only 8.6 percent were born in the South.

The figures are even more striking if we consider the geographical origins of the parents of respondents. In Sesto only 38.9 percent of the respondents' fathers, and 40.3 percent of their mothers, were born in the town. The corresponding figures for Erba were 64.9 percent and 58.1 percent. 35 percent of the parents of Sesto respondents were born in the South, as opposed to 13 percent in Erba.

It should be clear from the above that the population of the two towns differs sharply. In the case of Erba, the town shows a high level of demographic 'closure' and a minimum degree of socio-geographical disruption. The majority of respondents had lived in the town for at least two generations, and most probably for even longer. This is a somewhat predictable but no less surprising finding, particularly if one considers that Erba is a highly industrial town located in one of the wealthiest and most industrial regions in Italy, it enjoys easy communications with Milan and with Europe, both by road and by railway, it has a well developed banking sector, out of town shopping malls and 'hyper-markets', new housing estates: in short, all the outward signs of modernity which make any one place almost indistinguishable from another. Despite all this, the town has preserved its identity and an unmistakable 'village' atmosphere, with men playing cards in bars, women shopping in the local open market, traditional summer fairs, and church bells chiming all the time. Thus the legacy of the past is very visible in the town, as indeed it is throughout the areas of small-scale industrialisation of northern and central Italy identified by Bagnasco as the 'Third Italy'.

Compared to Erba, Sesto presents a more diversified and 'open' demographic environment, with a much greater population mix. The 'old' industrial and proletarian town lives on in the large factories, many of which are now empty and waiting to be converted into housing estates or new industrial parks, but the town has also taken on the more undifferentiated look of a residential suburb. According to an ex-Mayor of Sesto I interviewed in 1994, the town never experienced residential 'segregation' on the basis of territorial origins: 'They all lived next to one another, Lombards, Calabrians, Sicilians, quite unlike other towns in Lombardy, such as Cologno Monzese, where people from different parts of Italy lived in different suburbs'.

Despite these differences between the two localities, they had something in common which suggests that, quite apart from migratory movements, Italian people have a tendency to settle in a place and live there for the rest of their lives. They are not, in other words, mobile in the same way as people in the U.K. or the U.S.A.; they do not change residence in search of employment, or to study, or when they marry. Figures 3.1 and 3.2 show that only a small minority of respondents in both localities had lived there for less than ten years (9.5 percent in Sesto and 12.8 percent in Erba).

By contrast, 30.9 percent of respondents in Sesto and 50.3 percent in Erba had lived in the town uninterruptedly since they were born, while 43.6 percent of respondents in Sesto and 20.9 percent in Erba had lived there for more than twenty years. Migration thus appears to be a one-off experience of a lifetime, sometimes leading

AREA: 1.00 Sesto

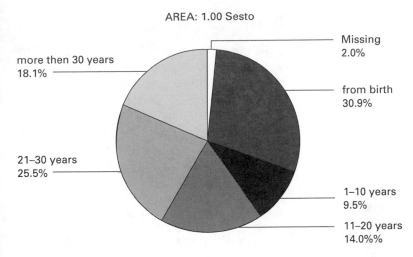

Figure 3.1 Period of residence in the town (Sesto)

AREA 2.00 Erba

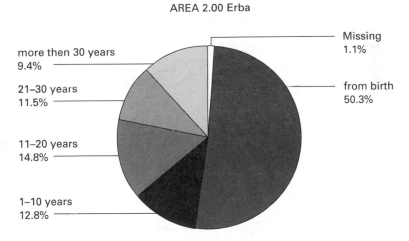

Figure 3.2 Period of residence in the town (Erba)

to the phenomenon known as 'return migration', when people go back to their place of origin after several years' absence. What still seems relatively uncommon is the phenomenon of regular, short- or medium-term mobility within the national territory, with the exception of daily commuting which occurs regularly in both localities.

Territorial allegiances

The questionnaire probed the extent to which people felt attached to a specific territory. Question 32 asked respondents to which collectivity they felt they most belonged: their commune, province, region, the Italian nation-state, Europe or the entire world. Respondents were asked to express their sentiments with a numeric value, ranging from 0 (no sense of belonging) to 9 (maximum feeling of belonging). They were also asked to specify how they valued the different collectivities listed above in comparison to five/ten years previously.

Responses are shown in Table 3.2. For every collectivity, both the mean and median values are given. When the two localities were considered together, the nation-state emerged as the collectivity with the highest mean score (6.7) and a median value of 7, followed by Europe (mean score 6.1, median score 7) and the world (mean score 6.1, median score 7). None of the other collectivities managed a mean score of 6 or a median score of 7.

Table 3.2 Feelings of belonging to various communities at time of survey (0 = no belonging; 9 = maximum belonging)

AREA		Valid (N)	Missing (N)	Mean	Median
	commune	0	3		
	province	0	3		
	region	0	3		
	nation	0	3		
	Europe	0	3		
	world	0	3		
Sesto	commune	233	210	5.7167	6.0000
	province	197	246	5.1777	6.0000
	region	210	233	5.4762	6.0000
	nation	256	187	6.6875	7.5000
	Europe	225	218	6.0222	7.0000
	world	212	231	5.9953	7.0000
Erba	commune	289	156	6.1765	7.0000
	province	253	192	5.4032	6.0000
	region	263	182	5.7110	6.0000
	nation	276	169	6.6522	7.0000
	Europe	257	188	6.1907	7.0000
	world	276	169	6.1196	7.0000

However, when the data was disaggregated by area, a different picture emerged.

As Table 3.2 shows, in Sesto the nation-state came a clear first, with a mean score of 6.6875 and a median score of 7.5, followed by Europe (mean score 6.0222, median score 7) and the 'world' (mean score 5.9953, median score 7). None of the other collectivities in Sesto managed a mean score of 6 or a median score of 7. Also, more people in Sesto expressed a score for the nation-state than they bothered to do for any of the other collectivities. By contrast, in Erba more respondents expressed a score for the local commune than for the other collectivities. The nation-state came first in Erba by virtue of the mean score only (6.6522); nevertheless, the commune, Europe, and the world also received a mean score above 6. In terms of the median score, all four collectivities obtained a score of 7. In short, people in Sesto clearly felt they belonged above all to their nation-state, and to a lesser extent also to Europe. Allegiance to sub-national entities was less strong. In Erba, people felt that they belonged to various collectivities and divided their allegiance almost equally between the sub-national, the national and the supra-national level. In both localities there were no significant generational differences in the way people felt towards the various communities. However, gender differences did make some impact: men in Sesto put the nation-state well above any other collectivity, while Sesto women put both the world and Europe ahead of the nation-state. By contrast, men in Erba put both the commune and Europe on a par with the nation-state, while Erba women felt they belonged above all to the nation-state. In particular, men of all ages in Sesto subscribed to the nation-state above their local community, whereas in Erba men put them on a par. Significantly, in Erba young men aged between eighteen and thirty declared that they belonged above all to the local community, whereas young women in the same age bracket reported feelings of belonging primarily to the nation-state.

The long-term trend is important, too. To what extent do the sentiments expressed by respondents in both Sesto and Erba represent the emergence of something new, rather than a confirmation of long-standing attitudes? The data show that allegiances had shifted considerably in the course of the last five to ten years (Table 3.3).

Taking the two localities together, allegiance to the nation-state proved stable, however other collectivities were more highly esteemed by respondents in 1994 (the time of the survey) than they had been in the past, particularly the commune, Europe and

Table 3.3 Feelings of belonging to various communities 5–10 years previously (0 = no belonging; 9 = maximum belonging)

		N			
AREA		*Valid*	*Missing*	*Mean*	*Median*
	commune	0	3		
	province	0	3		
	region	0	3		
	nation	0	3		
	Europe	0	3		
	world	0	3		
Sesto	commune	198	245	5.5657	6.0000
	province	172	271	5.1860	6.0000
	region	181	262	5.3978	6.0000
	nation	234	209	6.6880	7.0000
	Europe	180	263	5.2667	6.0000
	world	180	263	5.5722	6.0000
Erba	commune	252	193	5.5079	6.0000
	province	231	214	4.9524	6.0000
	region	237	208	5.1772	6.0000
	nation	258	187	6.5078	7.0000
	Europe	228	217	5.4298	6.0000
	world	241	204	5.4315	6.0000

the entire world. This trend applies to both Sesto and Erba, though with some interesting differences. In Sesto it was Europe and the world which commanded greater affection among respondents compared to the past: both gained a median score of 7 in 1994 compared to 6 when respondents were asked to judge them retrospectively. In Erba all three sub-national collectivities, as well as Europe and the world, gained in their standing, from a median score of 6 to one of 7. When gender differences were taken into account, the trend was particularly noticeable among Sesto women and Erba women and men.

Compared to the past, the nation-state appears to have lost some of its appeal and no longer seems destined to command the exclusive loyalty of (northern) Italian citizens. In many ways this can be considered as the logical consequence of the development of the European Project and the increasing awareness and acceptance of the European dimension among ordinary citizens. In the case of Erba, however, the findings also seem to indicate a parallel strengthening of the local, sub-national dimension.

Institutional allegiances

As well as generic feelings of belonging to certain collectivities, the questionnaire also aimed at probing how people judged the performance of different political and economic institutions or organisations at both a national and sub-national level. Question 31 asked respondents to judge the performance of the following institutions and organisations: political parties, trade unions, employers' associations, banks, industry, the Catholic Church, the local and national media, the Judiciary, local, regional and national government, and Parliament. For each of these, respondents had to indicate whether their judgement was positive, satisfactory or negative. Once again, they were also asked to indicate whether and how their opinion had changed compared to five/ten years previously.

The aggregated results indicated that four institutions and/or organisations were given the thumbs down: political parties, trade unions, national government and Parliament. All the others were judged satisfactory, with the exception of the Judiciary whose performance was considered good. Compared to the past, respondents downgraded both political parties and trade unions, while the judgement for the other institutions and organisations remained unchanged.

When the data was disaggregated by locality, there was no change in the way respondents judged the national government or Parliament. However, there was considerable difference in other areas. The performance of trade unions was judged satisfactory or positive in Sesto, but negative in Erba. By contrast, the performance of employers' associations and industry was judged satisfactory or positive by Erba respondents, but poor by Sesto ones. As for local government, Sesto respondents were split almost down the middle, whereas a majority of Erba respondents saw its role in a positive light.

When the data was further disaggregated by gender, the general picture remained unchanged for Erba, where both male and female respondents expressed remarkably similar judgements. In Sesto, however, there was a marked tendency on the part of men to view employers' associations, banks, industry and regional government in a much more negative light than women.

Respondents in Sesto were clearly influenced by considerations of their social class and by the long-standing socialist and communist culture of their town when judging certain associations. In my view, this explains why Sesto male respondents approved of trade unions but disapproved of employers' associations and of industry as a whole. As mentioned in Chapter 1, women in Sesto appear to have been less influenced by the communist, working-class ideology than men. In Erba, by contrast, respondents did not seem to be influenced by the fact that they, too, belonged to the 'working class'. Even if artisans and small entrepreneurs are excluded from the statistics for Erba, the results do not alter. These findings confirm what numerous studies have highlighted in the past, namely that areas of small-scale industrialisation in Italy show low levels of political polarisation, and high levels of inter-class collaboration and social mobility. In other words, there is a continuum linking industrial workers to the self-employed and to small entrepreneurs. This is due to the fact that it is relatively easy to move up from one social category to another and also that there is a high degree of interaction and communication between workers and employers, due both to the small size of the average firm and to the modest social origins of most employers (Franchi and Rieser 1991: 461).

The findings once again appear to confirm Sapelli's view that large-scale industry has been capable of transforming people's attitudes and values. They also substantiate the arguments put forward in Chapter 2, when analysing political socialisation, namely, that large-scale industry promotes a specific type of horizontal associationism, based on class. It does not follow that small-scale industry promotes only particularism, indeed it seems clear that it is capable of breaking down class barriers, thus facilitating the establishment of 'weak ties' across different social groups and networks. In a pioneering study, Granovetter (1985) emphasised the importance of such 'weak ties' in allowing interpersonal contacts and exchange of information to reach beyond internally cohesive groups. While 'strong ties' guarantee that *within* a social network members keep in regular contact and are informed of each other's activities, thus facilitating joint action, it is only 'weak ties' *between* different social networks that prevent each network from becoming self-contained and inward-looking. The paradox of localities like Sesto and Erba is that the former is a perfect example of dense social networking which takes place predominantly within one social group but is also able to cut across local and regional barriers (class is mainly conceived of in a national and international context), while the latter presents dense social networking which cuts across occupational and class barriers but simultaneously remains tied to a specific locality.

Local Issues and Identities

This section will analyse how respondents viewed their town, both in terms of what they considered to be the most pressing issues faced by their local community, and in terms of general feelings of well-being and/or anxiety in relation to life in the town and to current and future trends. Question 36 asked respondents to identify the main issues and problems their community was addressing compared to five/ten years previously. Question 37 asked them to what extent their community had changed as a result of immigration from non-EU countries. Question 39 (a multiple question)) aimed at assessing the extent to which respondents felt that their town possessed a corporate identity and whether such identity was currently 'under threat'.

As far as Question 36 was concerned, respondents differed sharply in the two localities. Sesto respondents cited 'unemployment' as the most pressing issue in their town, whereas Erba respondents indicated a variety of issues, ranging from criminality and drugs to the environment and infrastructures. Respondents in Sesto were also concerned about the 'deterioration of social relations' and 'social and political conflicts', whereas in Erba there was little preoccupation with these issues. Lastly, Sesto respondents indicated that, compared to the past, they were now more worried about unemployment, a finding which clearly reflects the trend towards industrial recession in the town.

Question 37 also threw up considerable differences. Taking the two localities together, nearly half of respondents indicated that immigration from extra-EU countries had been 'minimal', almost a third said 'considerable, but without creating problems of social integration', while 21 percent stated that it had been 'considerable, creating substantial problems for social integration' (Table 3.4).

When the data was disaggregated by area, respondents in Sesto showed a much higher degree of worry and anxiety over this issue than respondents in Erba (Table 3.5).

More than half of Erba respondents declared that immigration from outside the EU had been minimal, but only 38 percent of Sesto respondents felt this way. Conversely, 30 percent of Sesto respondents stated that immigration had been considerable as well as becoming a source of social problems, while only 12.8 percent of Erba respondents agreed with such sentiments. In terms of gender, women were generally more worried than men about the effects of immigration, particularly in Sesto, where 45 percent of

Table 3.4 Respondents' views on extra-EU immigration in their localities (all respondents)

		Frequency	Percent	Valid Percent	Cumulative Percent
Valid	minimal	386	43.3	48.4	48.4
	considerable but without creating social problems	245	27.5	30.7	79.1
	considerable, leading to social problems	167	18.7	20.9	100.0
	Total	798	89.6	100.0	
Missing		90	10.1		
Total		888	100.0		

men stated that immigration to their town had been marginal, compared to only 22 percent of women. By contrast, 24 percent of men considered that immigration had created social problems, whereas 43 percent of women held this opinion.

The most simple interpretation of these findings would be to relate them to current levels of immigration from outside the EU into the two localities. However, official statistics indicate that such levels have been low for both localities: in particular, registered extra-EU immigrants to Sesto numbered only 952 in 1993, or 1.1 percent of residents. Unofficial figures are probably higher, nevertheless my informants in Sesto, including the ex-Mayor, Sig. Carrà, confirmed that extra-EU immigration to the town had been marginal. This suggests that anxiety over extra-EU immigration among Sesto respondents had causes other than the scale of the phenomenon itself. Worries over unemployment, which, as we saw, were widespread among Sesto respondents, probably made them more sensitive to competition from 'outsiders', in the same way as concerns over social relations and conflicts made them view immigration as a source of problems.

These findings contrast both with Sesto's long-standing communist and solidarist culture and the recent popularity of the Northern League in Erba. The latter has often been defined as a racist movement, responsible for 'creating an invasion syndrome among Italians, and a fear of being under siege' (Brierley and Giacometti 1996: 188). Fear of immigration and more generally anxiety over a possible disintegration of social cohesion at the local

Table 3.5 Respondents' views on extra-EU immigration in their localities (responses by area)

AREA			Frequency	Percent	Valid Percent	Cumulative Percent
Sesto	Missing	System	3	100.0		
	Valid	minimal	146	33.0	38.1	38.1
		considerable but without creating social problems	123	27.8	32.1	70.2
		considerable, leading to social problems	114	25.7	29.8	100.0
	Total		383	86.5	100.0	
	Missing		60	13.5		
	Total		443	100.0		
Erba	Valid	minimal	240	53.9	57.8	57.8
		considerable but without creating social problems	122	27.4	29.4	87.2
		considerable, leading to social problems	53	11.9	12.8	100.0
	Total		415	93.3	100.0	
	Missing		30	6.7		
	Total		445	100.0		

level therefore appear to be linked to the underlying economic situation and recent social dynamics of each locality, rather than to political propaganda. In this respect it is quite clear that Sesto is more of a community 'under siege' than Erba. This raises the question of when and how fear of immigration translates into support for a radical right-wing party, as opposed to remaining at the level of unpoliticised feelings and beliefs. The political implications of these findings will be discussed in Part II of this volume, which explores the relationship between anti-immigrant attitudes and party-political preferences, as well as the popularity of the Northern League in Erba and more generally in the traditional Catholic subcultural areas.

Fear of immigration in Sesto was also reflected in responses to Question 39 (Figures 3.3 and 3.4).

When asked whether 'extra-EU immigrants create competition on the labour market', 44.3 percent of Sesto respondents agreed with

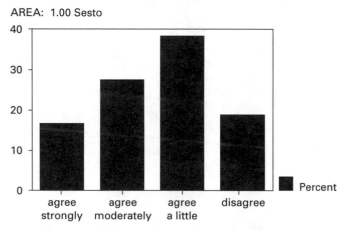

extra-EU immigrants create competition on the labour market

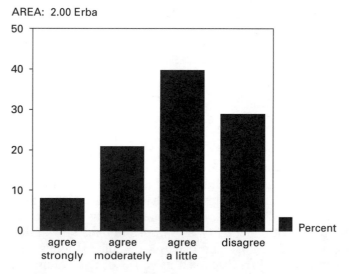

extra-EU immigrants create competition on the labour market

Figure 3.3 Respondents' views on immigrants' competition on the labour market (by area)

the statement either strongly or moderately, but only 29.9 percent of Erba respondents did so (Figure 3.3). Similarly, when asked whether

AREA: 1.00 Sesto

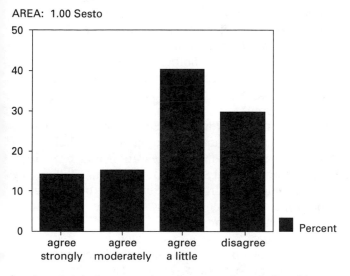

immigrants take houses and services away from Italian citizens

AREA: 2.00 Erba

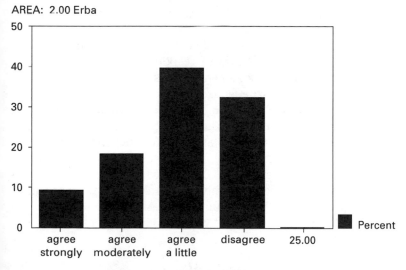

immigrants take houses and services away from Italian citizens

Figure 3.4 Respondents' views on immigrants' competition on the housing market (by area)

'extra-EU immigrants take housing and services away from Italian citizens', 31 percent of respondents in Sesto agreed, as against 26.8 percent in Erba (Figure 3.4). Men in Sesto were particularly worried about competition from immigrants on the labour market.

Finally, on the issue of a 'local identity', Questions 39g to 39l aimed at establishing whether respondents felt that the local community was well integrated from both a socio-economic and cultural point of view. It emerged clearly that in neither locality extra-EU immigration was judged to have had a negative impact on culture and identity. Southern Italian immigrants, however, were viewed differently in the two towns. In Sesto, which, as we saw, experienced substantial immigration from the South of Italy, there was a general feeling that 'ethnic' integration had been fully achieved, thus confirming what Sig. Carrà had told me. In Erba, by contrast, where immigration from the South had been of more modest proportions, respondents showed some reservations regarding social and cultural integration.

When asked whether 'Southerners are well integrated in the town', 39 percent of Sesto respondents strongly agreed and a further 42.1 percent did so moderately. In Erba the figures were 24.6 percent and 48.9 percent respectively. When asked whether 'Southerners threaten the local culture', 67.2 percent of Sesto respondents disagreed completely with the statement, as opposed to 54.1 percent of Erba respondents. Indeed only a *minority* of male respondents in Erba disagreed completely with this statement. The different attitudes of respondents towards southern immigrants can be best explained in terms of the nature of 'culture' in each locality. This issue is taken up in the next section.

As for the impact of the socio-economic environment upon local identity, this was seen as an issue by respondents in Sesto. Asked whether they agreed with the statement 'My town has lost its identity due to economic recession', 58.9 percent of Sesto respondents agreed (25.9 percent strongly, 33 percent moderately). The corresponding figure for Erba was only 18.9 percent (2.9 percent and 16 percent respectively). More women than men shared these sentiments in Sesto (64.1 percent of women, 56 percent of men).

Local cultures

The working-class, socialist subculture which until recently characterised Sesto developed in the early part of the century, alongside large-scale industrialisation. While the myth of the 'Stalingrad of Italy' unfolded, strengthened by successive waves of strikes and industrial action, participation in the Resistance during the Second World War further cemented local identity around communist organisations and ideals. Indeed industrial action and partisan activities almost became one in the Spring of 1943 and 1944, when Sesto was at the forefront of industrial strikes, caused both by economic grievances and anti-fascist as well as anti-German activities. As mentioned in the Introduction, Sesto won the Gold Medal for Military Valour for its role in the Italian Resistance. The Resistance played a dual symbolic role: it was a symbol of national resurgence and of the national struggle for liberation against the Germans but it was also a symbol of the class struggle, representing the anti-fascist working class against the pro-fascist bourgeoisie and capitalist system (Pavone 1991). The myth of the Resistance was thus able to reconcile Sesto's internationalist, class-based communist culture with the Italian nation-state. Successive town administrations (all dominated by the parties of the left), strove to keep alive the memory and symbols of the Resistance, by popularising it in schools, celebrating it at regular intervals, supporting an active local association of veteran partisan fighters, and erecting monuments in honour of the dead.

Alongside this distinctive political identity of the town, sport and other public services were also promoted by its administrators in pursuit of social integration and political consensus. Before the Second World War sport was mainly sponsored and controlled by large local firms, often in competition with the fascist state, which in turn used sport effectively to popularise the regime among industrial workers and particularly the young. In 1954 the Sesto Communist Party set up its own sport society, the *Gruppo Escursionistico Alpinistico Sportivo*, in collaboration with the local council (GEAS 1991). Today Sesto boasts six bowls courts, eleven football pitches, eleven tennis courts, one open-air and two covered swimming pools, two athletic tracks, thirty gyms in school buildings, and one sports centre. In 1992 13,370 people used sport facilities in the town. As a booklet published by the local council in 1992 stated, 'Sesto is not just a working town, it is also recognised as a sports town' (Città di Sesto San Giovanni 1992). In the same year the communist-dominated council confirmed its commitment to all sports activities, 'despite the current economic difficulties'.

With the possible exception of the Resistance myth, the working-class, communist culture of the town was accessible to all 'outsiders' on the basis of their occupation. Being a manual worker in a large factory defined one's own identity and established one's own boundaries in a way which transcended geographical and ethnic origins. As argued in Chapter 1, the 'proletarian' identity did not entirely supersede other forms of belonging, nevertheless it guaranteed that for most of this century social conflicts were exclusively of a class nature.

In Erba the predominant culture was Catholic and inter-classist, with an emphasis on social solidarity and collaboration, conservative values, particularly in relation to civil liberties, and, once economic growth got under way, a strong work ethic and a deep conviction that one can improve one's lot in life through sheer hard work and self-sacrifice. Entrepreneurship became both a vehicle for upward social mobility and a measure of people's worth. Industrialisation in Erba, as in all Italian areas of small-scale industrialisation, guaranteed the persistence of primary ties and localist, community-based allegiances (Bull and Corner 1993). It also brought a heavy predominance of the manufacturing sector, small-size industrial plants, a high degree of social mobility, class collaboration, and a low level of political polarisation. In these areas trust and solidarity – two essential components of a market economy – developed out of living in the same village, speaking the same dialect, sharing family as well as business ties, having comparable social statuses.

Trust and solidarity, therefore, are community-based. A sharp division exists between those who are seen as belonging to the community and those who are considered 'outsiders' (Becattini 1990: 114). The 'outsiders' are not necessarily physically outside the community as long as they are outside the community of small manufacturing producers, i.e., as long as they are not employed in manufacturing or related activities. This explains why in areas like Erba occupations in the public sector and in public administration have always been viewed with contempt and judged to be foreign. 'Outsiders' are also those who do not speak the local dialect. It is interesting to note here that the dialect is still widely used in business transactions involving local entrepreneurs: it is, therefore, yet another factor conducive to trust.

People are generally considered foreigners when they come from a different geographical area, when they are in 'foreign' occupations and/or when they do not share the local productivist and entrepreneurial ethos (CGIL Lombardia-AASTER 1991: 38). In this respect immigrants from southern Italy are considered foreign on all three counts since a) they come from outside the area, b) they are considered to be employed primarily in the public sector and c) they come from a non-industrialised society and do not appear to readily share the productivist ethos of the indigenous population. By contrast, the immigrants from extra-European countries are generally employed in the local factories and are therefore judged to perform a useful role (Ambrosini 1992). The process of exclusion is activated against them when they are considered in excess of the needs of local industry and join the ranks of the unemployed or – even worse in the eyes of the locals – the ranks of beggars and petty criminals.

Unlike Sesto, therefore, Erba possesses a culture and an identity which is only accessible to 'outsiders' if they both share and engage in the productivist and entrepreneurial ethic born out of endogenous development. In reality, it is almost impossible for outsiders to participate in the local enterprising culture given that small firm formation is tied to social factors, such as the family, possession of a small plot of land, mutual trust born out of face-to-face familiarity, use of dialect. As Hellman argued (1997), it is remarkable how Italy, a country where self-employment and small businesses form the backbone of the economy, seemingly denies immigrants access to these forms of economic activity. I believe that the social culture associated with Erba and countless other localities in northern and central Italy goes a long way towards explaining this apparent paradox. Admittedly, it could be argued that becoming a manual worker in a small manufacturing plant can also provide entry to the 'local culture', however, in practice, many people from the South found employment more easily in the public sector than in small businesses, due to 'the high rates of unemployment in the South and the lack of enthusiasm on the part of northerners to take up lower paying public-sector jobs' (Leonardi and Kovacs 1993: 58). Furthermore, as a survey of local employers in industrial towns such as Erba established, they tended to recruit in preference among relatives and friends of existing employees, rather than taking on 'outsiders' (Bull, Pitt and Szarka 1993).

Conclusions

This chapter has provided evidence for the persistence of localism in northern Italy. Attachment and affiliation at local level were especially in evidence in Erba, where loyalty and allegiance to the town (as well as the province and region) rivalled those for the nation-state, and a degree of mistrust towards 'outsiders' (including southern Italians) existed alongside trust among 'insiders'. Clearly, the type of industrialisation experienced by places like Erba contributed substantially to the preservation of traditional community ties and face-to-face familiarity. As noted elsewhere, in many northern areas people industrialised, so to speak, on the spot: they continued to reside in their village or town while witnessing a shifting in the balance between agriculture and industry away from the former (Bull and Corner 1993). Many resorted to cultivating the land in their spare time rather than as their main occupational activity. Many others set up industrial workshops where a cowshed or greenhouses had previously stood. Thus local values changed only gradually and the local culture remained, in some ways quite astonishingly, relatively isolated from and uninfluenced by wider and more cosmopolitan cultural and social movements and trends. In particular, a distinctive working-class culture and ideology failed to emerge: local people shared faith in and support for economic and political institutions which were seen as non-partisan, but also as instrumental in promoting growth and development, such as banks, industry and local government.

By contrast, localism in Sesto was less pronounced. Nevertheless, I would contend that the difference between the two localities is more a question of degrees of localism than a contrast between a particularist and a cosmopolitan culture. Admittedly, Sesto's culture was both class-based and nationally-orientated, as opposed to Erba's which was inter-classist and locally-orientated. However, Sesto also possessed a strong and distinctive local identity, which the local council summed up, as we saw, by referring to Sesto as 'a working town and a sports town'. The Resistance and the 'Stalingrad of Italy' myths also added to the image of Sesto as a unique place within Italy. Recent trends seem to indicate that economic recession, unemployment and a weakening of the traditional working-class ideology in Sesto have led to increasing concerns that the local community is now 'under threat'. The capacity for assimilation of 'outsiders' seems to have weakened, and worries over problems of social integration are coming to the fore. A tendency to distinguish between 'us' and 'them' is becoming apparent in Sesto, too.

In conclusion, civic solidarity and trust continue to a large extent to be community-based and to draw upon localist ties.

Horizontal associationism and civic virtues do not prevent the emergence of intolerant attitudes or at least of feelings of mistrust and concern towards 'outsiders'. Thus civic virtues and localism are mutually compatible, as indeed are civic virtues and deep mistrust for the national government and for Parliament, a sentiment which was pervasive in both localities. In this respect Putnam's argument that the 'civic community' underpins democratic institutions is incomplete, for two main reasons. On the one hand, it overlooks the question of the multiform nature of democracy while, on the other, it fails to address the issue of whether the civic communities of northern Italy underpin democratic institutions at the local and regional level, or at the national level, or both. As Bagnasco pointed out (1994: 102), the Italian case can be best defined in terms of a 'bounded civicness', 'capable at most of weaving short-distance networks of trust, which do not go beyond the boundaries surrounding limited communities'. Failure on Putnam's part to acknowledge the persistence of localism in northern Italy leads him to postulate a simple and direct relationship between public associationism and participation and the correct functioning of a liberal-democratic system. Putnam appears to take for granted that there is a positive correspondence and mutual reinforcement between local and national democratic participation and institutions and never questions the solidity of the Italian nation-state. Yet his book implicitly throws very serious doubts over the future of Italian democracy in the face of deep and unresolved territorial cleavages. The rise of the Northern League Party in the early 1990s was further testimony to the complex and contradictory relationship between 'civic communities' and democracy. Although Putnam (1993: 61) briefly mentioned the Northern League phenomenon in his book, and even referred to its 'veiled racism', he did not probe its relationship with the democratic system. By contrast, in his comment on Putnam's work, Bagnasco (1994: 102) clearly referred to the Northern League as an example of 'limited civicness'. That Putnam underestimated the Northern League only serves to underline the fact that, by failing to acknowledge localism, he also failed to grasp its potentially explosive impact upon the national body politic.

Conclusion to Part I

Italian social cultures have recently been revisited by scholars of
different disciplines in a renewed attempt to identify the main
elements of continuity and change at times of great political turmoil and transition, following the collapse of the 'First Republic' in
the early 1990s. Now that the period dominated by the Cold War
can be encapsulated within a precise time span, and the transition
to a 'Second Republic' is proving less smooth than might have
been expected in the early 1990s, it is as if Italy's intellectual and
political agenda is being directly linked to concerns and debates
which predate that period and go back as far as the process of
Unification. Thus current debates on nationhood, clientelism, corruption and democratic institutions are privileging a long-term
view of historical change.

While Ginsborg and Sapelli, as we saw, put the emphasis on
familism and particularism as an enduring trait in Italian society,
which in their view accounted for the weakness of the state and
central political institutions, others, like Putnam and Cartocci,
emphasised the persistence of sub-national cleavages. Thus Putnam relegated familism and particularism to the southern regions;
in contrast, he stressed the civic virtues, high levels of associationism and trust and effective regional governments of the northern
and central areas. In doing so, however, Putnam underestimated
the localist, subcultural (and in some respects anti-national)
dimension of northern Italy's socio-political identities. As for Cartocci, he accepted that familism and particularism formed two
important characteristics of Italian social culture and that they
were fairly uniformly distributed across the peninsula. He nevertheless argued that 'subcultural solidarities', as present in the central and northern regions of Italy, had effectively contrasted in

those areas the long-standing orientation towards 'familist particularism' (Cartocci 1994: 28).

Chapter 1 threw some new light upon the issue of familism. On the one hand, it showed that the strong family is undoubtedly a homogenising force in Italian society, even in areas which went through a prolonged period of large-scale industrial expansion, substantial population growth due primarily to immigration, and the dominance of left-wing culture and organisations. From this point of view, Italy is more homogeneous than traditional divisions between different models of development led us to believe. In addition, no strong generational difference was detected in the two areas surveyed in terms of attitudes towards the family. Young people, particularly young men, were nearly as much family-orientated as older people. There was more of a gender divide, rather than a generational one. Thus women in both localities appeared to have adopted more pragmatic attitudes than men and to cultivate wider interests outside their circle of family and friends. Also, feelings of solidarity were stronger among women than men.

The chapter also demonstrated, however, that a strong family is not identical to familism and/or cannot be equated to weak civicness. Strong kinship and friendship ties are entirely compatible with, and indeed often sustain, horizontal associationism and civic engagement. This is where sub-national divisions come forcefully back into the picture. The main issue is that the 'Italian family' does not exist, since not one but several family forms can be found in Italy, as we saw in Chapter 2. Therefore, as Macry rightly remarked, one of the reasons for the presence of different sociopolitical cultures in Italy probably lies in the different roles and outlooks associated with these family structures (Macry 1997). As someone who argued, not so long ago, that an important factor behind the industrialisation of much of northern Italy can be identified in the structure and behaviour of a specific family form – 'the pluriactive family form' – I am in total agreement with Macry (Bull and Corner 1993, see also Corner 1997). A similar interpretation has recently been put forward by Fukuyama, who has compared the Italian family structure prevalent in the 'Third Italy' with a Chinese family form (1995: 97–111). Others, such as Francks (1995), pointed out striking similarities between the 'pluriactive family form' of northern Italy and that prevalent in Japan. As is often the case with Italian society and culture, generalisations that are meant to apply to the whole of the country do not often work out, as they tend to obscure more than they can reveal.

Further studies at the micro/regional level are needed on this issue, in particular on the links between specific family forms and civic values and engagement, to move the debate forward.

A similar approach should apply to Catholicism and to its influence upon civic engagement. As Chapter 2 showed, contrary to Putnam's and Ginsborg's interpretations, Catholics in a traditionally 'white' area were found to be public-minded, active citizens who took a real interest in their local community. Catholic women, in particular, were found to possess solidarist, not familist, values. Once again, a generalisation meant to apply to the whole of Italy has led to distortions and misrepresentations. More importantly, though, socio-cultural differences between the 'red' and 'white' subcultural areas appear to persist in present-day 'post-ideological' Italy. Such differences were found to be qualitative rather than quantitative: they related primarily to the nature of social participation, of newspaper readership, and of political socialisation. As for different orientations regarding job satisfaction, worries about unemployment, and concern over the size and effects of extra-EU immigration, these can be accounted for by the socio-economic configuration of the two towns. I would therefore agree with Cartocci that traditional subcultural identities and solidarities are very resilient, although it was noticed that they may be weakening in Sesto, to be replaced not by individualist values, but by a revival of family and friendship ties and a loss of capacity for assimilating and integrating outsiders.

The persistence of territorial subcultures in Italy is reflected in the widespread presence of strong feelings of loyalty and belonging towards a sub-national entity, whether a town, a province or a region. It was found in Chapter 2 that civic engagement and associationism were high in both Sesto and Erba, yet in Erba public participation privileged the local dimension. According to Putnam, as we saw, social participation at local level is a positive sign of civic engagement, because it shows that the citizens take an active interest in their local community – this attitude, in turn, underpins democracy, by guaranteeing the correct functioning of democratic institutions. The underlying assumption is that support for democratic institutions at local level translates directly into support for national institutions. But what if civic engagement at local level is in direct opposition to national democratic institutions? As Cartocci wrote, 'The valorisation of local identities and communitarian values, *in opposition to a central state perceived as foreign and an enemy*, constitutes one of the original traits inscribed in the genetic code of our country' (Cartocci 1994: 117). (The emphasis is mine).

In both Sesto and Erba, as we saw in Chapter 3, national government and Parliament were judged negatively, in contrast to both local and regional governments. Thus in terms of 'evaluational orientation', that is, 'the judgements and opinions about political objects that typically involve the combination of value standards and criteria with information and feelings' (Almond and Verba 1963: 15), the local and regional levels of governance were not seen in harmony with the national level. There is, of course, nothing new regarding the low esteem in which national political institutions are held in Italy. As Sani (1980: 308) remarked, throughout the 1970s negative evaluations of their political system among Italians had actually increased since Almond and Verba's pioneering study. Sani explained this trend in terms of a growing dislocation between socio-economic change and political immobility, as well as the 'wide gap between popular expectations as to the role of government and perceived policy outcomes' (Ibid.: 309). In this context, it is quite remarkable that my own survey revealed persisting feelings of discontent with national political institutions at a time (1994) when political change had already begun and the national government was headed by a respected economist and ex-Governor of the Bank of Italy, Carlo Azeglio Ciampi. Admittedly, 'Parliament and the Ciampi government [...] were packed with representatives of the parties that had been so humiliatingly defeated [in the June 1993 mayoral elections]' (Gilbert 1995: 160). Nonetheless, the Ciampi government was 'technocratic' more than it was political, representing a far cry from previous DC-PSI-dominated administrations. As for local government institutions, previous surveys conducted in northern areas within both a 'white' and a 'red' subculture similarly established that they were held in high esteem, and were judged to function a great deal better than national government (Bagnasco and Trigilia 1984 and 1985, Barbagli and Maccelli 1985, Cartocci 1991).

In terms of 'affective evaluation' and feelings of belonging and common identity, the two towns differed. In Sesto the respondents' mistrust of central political institutions was mitigated by a strong sense of belonging to the national community. However, in Erba, the nation-state did not command the exclusive affection of respondents, who felt attached at least as equally to both subnational and supra-national entities. In both localities, as we saw in Chapter 3, there were no significant generational differences in the way people felt towards the various communities. Gender differences, however, were considerable. In particular, men of all ages in Sesto subscribed to the nation-state above their local community, whereas in Erba men put both collectivities on a par (and younger men put the local community first). Women's feelings of belonging were less clear-cut.

Thus localism and territorial subcultures were found to be stronger than religious and class affiliations or even generational change. In other words, respondents behaved and felt differently if based in Sesto or in Erba, even when they shared the same professional status (industrial workers) or religious beliefs (practising Catholics). The age of respondents did not seem to make much difference, either, in the sense that there was no clear cut generational divide. In many cases, as with participation in a trade union, readership of a local versus national newspaper and political socialisation, the dividing line between respondents could only be explained on the basis of the town they lived in and the specific local culture they partook of. Interestingly, it emerged that gender was more resistant to localism than either religion, class or age. Thus women, regardless of which locality they were from, participated mainly in apolitical associations, were largely indifferent to trade union activities and organisations and subscribed more often to solidarist values. However, in the case of newspaper readership and political socialisation, the 'pull' of the local subcultures proved stronger than gender, and women 'conformed' to the pattern prevalent in their locality. It seems clear, nevertheless, that women constitute weak links – 'weak ties', as Granovetter (1985) would say – within their respective territorial subcultures. On the one hand, Sesto women did not fully share the communist, politically-orientated, working-class values prevalent among male workers, while, on the other, Erba women did not entirely subscribe to localist and communitarian values branded in opposition to the nation-state. Men, by contrast, were fully embedded in their local subcultures, subscribing to a collective identity and presenting, in each locality, the characteristics of 'a strongly bounded group with a clear set of shared values' (Giddens, 1994). These findings go a long way towards explaining political attitudes and voting behaviour in both localities, as Part II will show.

Kinship and social networks also appear to transcend local subcultural identities. As argued in Chapter 1, family and social networks in Sesto have successfully outlived the period of large-scale industrialisation and appear to form an important source of 'social capital' which can, and indeed is, being used for the social and economic regeneration of the town. The concept of social capital, associated with the theoretical work of Bourdieu (1980) and Coleman (1988) and with the scholarly production of Putnam (1993, 1995a and 1995b), refers to the sum of resources or assets accrued through the possession of a network of relationships. There is compelling evidence that social capital can have positive effects on economic development, not least as provided by the case of the 'Third Italy'. A comparison with Vénissieux demonstrated that the persistence of strong kinship and social networks in Sesto may explain why the town, unlike other industrial conurbations around the world, can contemplate a remarkable switch from large-scale to small-scale industry. Despite comparable historical developments, Sesto and Vénissieux were found to be diverging. In terms of the continuing importance of primary associations, therefore, Sesto and Erba appear to have more in common than Sesto and Vénissieux. As discussed in Chapter 1, this indicates that traditional cultural and social identities and values are not necessarily displaced by economic modernisation. Indeed, the more people and communities can keep their cultural options open and conceptualise different – even contrasting – sets of values, the more they seem able to respond in a dynamic manner and adapt to socio-economic change. Conversely, those communities which have gone full steam down one specific socio-economic and cultural route are precisely those which find it more difficult to go in reverse gear and turn direction. It could be argued that they have lost some of their 'social capital' in the process.

Similar considerations can be put forward regarding the existence of multiple identities, or allegiances to different types and levels of community. As Diamanti and Segatti argued (1994: 18), the territorial identity expressed by a majority of Italians is both articulate and composite, a complex puzzle made up of a plurality of sub-national, national and supra-national referents. While the negative implications of this complex identity in terms of a weak sense of nationhood cannot be underestimated, the authors pointed out that it also amounted to a resource, in so far as 'it produces flexibility and adaptability in the face of changes and tensions which may involve different levels of the territorial system' (Ibid.: 21). As in the case of social identities, territorial ones in the Italian case appear to stand out above all for their complex interplay and their high degree of flexibility and multiplicity.

To conclude, my analysis of social identities at the micro level has confirmed that kinship and social networks continue to play a fundamental role in Italian society and to provide a most valuable source of social capital. The analysis has also established that the strength and intensity of these same networks do not correlate positively with familist and particularist values or 'uncivic' behaviour, at least in northern Italy. On the contrary, people who enjoyed strong kinship and friendship ties were also more likely to engage in horizontal associationism. The findings also showed that people can be civic-minded and public-spirited regardless of whether they hold secularist or religious beliefs. Indeed, Catholic values in traditionally 'white' regions of Italy were found to be conducive to horizontal associationism in the same way as 'secularist' values in traditionally 'red' areas. However, the research also showed that the nature of associationism in these two types of areas differed substantially and that this was to be attributed to the persistence of quite distinct subcultural identities. In the case of Erba, which was chosen as a 'model' for the 'white' subcultural regions, a strong subcultural identity was accompanied by deep feelings of attachment to a sub-national community. Furthermore, the trend appears to be in the direction of a strengthening of both sub-national (local, provincial and regional) and supra-national (European) allegiances. Multiple identities can have a positive role in a world increasingly shaped by the process of globalisation and the emergence of multi-level governance. This presupposes, however, that multiple identities are in a harmonious relationship with each other. Some of the Erba findings indicate that this was not the case and that sub-national and supra-national allegiances were being shaped in opposition to the central state, thus perpetuating what Cartocci considers, as we saw, an enduring trait in Italian social and political culture. Further analysis is needed to ascertain whether the more articulate or the more exclusionary version of territorial allegiances is on the ascendancy; or whether, to quote Diamanti and Segatti (1994: 21), 'territorial orientations have become an element of disruption in the complex mosaic that makes up Italian national identity'.

Part II will explore these issues in depth, when analysing political culture and electoral behaviour in the two localities. The decline of Christian Democracy and the success of the Northern League in areas like Erba will be assessed against the background of the prevailing pattern of social identities that has been identified and described in this part of the book. Similarly, the uncertain political and electoral fortunes of the parties of the left in Sesto will be related to the changing social values and sense of identity that the survey was able to detect in the town.

Part II: Political Cultures

Introduction

The end of the First Republic in Italy and the disappearance of many of the traditional parties have given rise to controversial interpretations concerning the political behaviour of the Italian electorate. At one level, it has been pointed out that the development of a new culture based on personal success and individual values in the 1980s and the demise of traditional political ideologies in the early 1990s should be interpreted as a sign of the emergence of a pluralist, fully modernised society, where voters express their preferences on the basis of party programmes and candidates, as well as their own personal interests, rather than ideological allegiances. In particular, voting behaviour linked to party identification, family loyalties and traditional political subcultures has been judged in serious decline (Mannheimer and Sani 1987 and 1994). Conversely, voters' mobility is considered on the increase, and the trend seems to point in the direction of voters exercising an individual rational choice without being influenced by the constraints of family, class, ideology or religion.

These recent trends can be interpreted as marking the completion of a process of social and economic homogenisation and cultural secularisation. Such an interpretation would appear to vindicate those sociologists who argued that economic development, with its interrelated processes of modernisation and urbanisation, would undermine ideologically-based conflicts and bring about more stable democracies along the Anglo-American model (Lipset 1960, Almond and Verba 1963).

It is easy to see how interpretations of this kind are in head-on collision with the opinions of scholars like Sapelli and Ginsborg who, as we saw in Part I, emphasised the continuing importance of family loyalties and values and the 'backward' modernisation

131

experienced by Italian society in the post-war period. One is left with the impression of a deep hiatus between academics from different disciplines, a hiatus which also appears to be predicated upon the political orientations and aspirations of the scholars themselves, following the turmoil of the early 1990s. The Italian 'revolution', which has seen the collapse of the political system characterised by a lack of alternation of parties or coalitions of parties in power, clientelism and corruption, was welcomed by many commentators as a liberating force, allowing, at long last, a modernised society to free itself from the constraints imposed by the exigencies of the Cold War and to set up new political institutions in its own image. Scholars like Sani (1992), Pasquino and McCarthy (1993), Diamanti and Mannheimer (1994), Pasquino (1995), and Vitali (1995) have all to an extent stressed the process of electoral change and the 'normalising' nature of the Italian political revolution, which was deemed to have brought about a much needed realignment of the political system to a society and an economy which are in no way different from those of other advanced countries. While one sympathises with their standpoint, one cannot help but feel that the pitting of a fully modernised Italian society against an archaic political system is somewhat wide of the mark. Italian society was by no means a passive victim of its political system, nor was it immune from clientelism and corruption. As della Porta (1996: 227, also 1992) observed, 'by running a generous and shrewd system of favours facilitated by the treatment of public office as a system of spoils, the corrupt politicians successfully obtained the complicity of civil society'.

As in the case of the German reunification process, Italian political events in the early 1990s fostered a strong sense of optimism and a conviction that there would be a speedy and decisive solution to long-standing problems. The initial period of euphoria, however, was followed by a bout of pessimism and a feeling that old weaknesses and failures were resurfacing. Gundle and Parker (1996: 15) summed up this feeling as follows: 'Whatever the solutions that are adopted, by the end of 1994 it was clear that the optimism that marked the early stages of the process of political reform had been excessive. The fall of an old political system that was bankrupt in every sense did not lead to a democratic rebirth, but rather to a protracted struggle for power in which most of the running was made by powerful vested interests that had much to lose from any redefinition of rules and procedures'. The new pessimism coincided with the rise of the Northern League, which brought territorial divisions to the fore, and the extraordinary success of Berlusconi's *Forza Italia*, which seemed to indicate a return to past practices and an attempt to put an end to any real modernisation of Italy's political institutions (Cartocci 1994, Farrell 1995). Conversely, the success of *Forza Italia* was also seen as pointing to a dealigned electorate, susceptible to be influenced by charismatic personalities and above all by the media (Mannheimer 1994, Bentivegna 1995). Thus, on the one hand, Italy was no longer being portrayed as an anomalous and exceptional case in Europe, but was directly being compared to other western democracies, including the U.S.A., France, and the U.K. On the other hand, scholars like Sapelli and Ginsborg put Italy squarely back in the Mediterranean basin and contrasted its immature and uncivic political culture to that of northern Europe and the Anglo-Saxon world.

As far as the former approach is concerned, Italy is seen as sharing the same research agenda as the rest of the western world. Indeed, the country's perceived process of socio-economic and cultural homogenisation was judged to provide a perfect case for vindicating the opinion of those who had argued that the West was witnessing the end of political ideology and a decline in the intensity of the political struggle (Bell 1988 [1st edition 1960]). One important aspect of this process is the decline of class voting as a European-wide phenomenon which, in the U.K. at least, has only partially been attributed to a decline in the size of the working class (Franklin 1985, Rose and McAllister 1986). It has also been attributed to what has been defined as 'partisan dealignment', i.e., a partial uncoupling between party preference and class (Crewe et al. 1977, Crewe 1984). The same argument was put forward for Italy (Barbagli et al. 1979; Corbetta et al. 1988). Various studies have also found that in modern western societies generational differences are now more important than socio-economic ones. Indeed for the U.K., Heath et al. (1991) no longer found a strong correlation between voting patterns and parents' party preferences. Some studies recorded a similar finding for Italy (Censis 1992). Parker (1996: 53) went as far as to argue that young people in Italy have generally lost interest in political activity, in sharp contrast to their parents, and that this 'chasm' is greater than in other European countries. Indeed, the process of socio-political change in western Europe, including Italy, has been judged so dramatic that some commentators have struck a warning note, seeing the demise of traditional ideologies and collective identities as a sign of social disintegration or `anomie'. This position was adopted by Todd (1991) for France, and was recently adopted for Italy by Revelli (1994: 668), who wrote that: `The sudden shift of large masses of voters [...] necessarily presupposes the breakdown of consolidated collective identities, the tearing of traditional communication networks, the "freeing" of social atoms deprived of stable referents and susceptible to powerful external signals'.

In contrast to the above, the more prudent and pessimistic approach to the events of the early 1990s focused on the persistence of older trends in Italian society and politics, and on the continuing anomalous nature of this country within the western world. In particular, the uneven support enjoyed by Italy's new parties within the national territory appeared to point to the persistence of locally- and regionally- based political subcultures, whose demise had been predicted by the proponents of developmental theories. This is not entirely surprising, given that both Catholicism and communism had for long represented political subcultures in some regions of Italy, notably the North East for Catholicism and the central regions for communism. Territorially-based subcultures have been found to be as strong today as in the past (Cartocci 1990 and 1994, Putnam 1993, Corbetta and Parisi 1994, Pisati 1997). Indeed the whole of Italy could be divided into four main regions in political terms: the South (and some other areas), where *Alleanza Nazionale* has revived the old populist tradition, the central regions still dominated by the solidarist culture of the PDS (the ex-Communist Party, now DS), and two Norths, one of which supports *Forza Italia* and the other the Northern League (Diamanti 1993 and 1994). In a major work on the Radical Right in western Europe, Kitschelt (1995: 183) distinguished between the southern-based, pro-nation-state MSI-*Alleanza Nazionale* and the northern-based, anti-nation-state Northern League and concluded that 'in a sense, both the neo-fascist MSI and the populist Northern League are *regionalist* parties with different constituencies'. [the emphasis is his]. The reappearance of territorial divisions led to a more prudent assessment of the likelihood and even the desirability of an end to consensual democracy in Italy (Calise 1993 and 1994).

It would be wrong to assume an over-simplistic view of developmental theories. Lipset (1960), for example, was well aware of the importance of political subcultures and fully recognised that allegiance to a political ideology could continue well beyond the break-up of the social structure which had allowed that same ideology to develop. Nonetheless, his underlying assumption was that such cultural and ideological continuities represented a 'political lag', so that adjustment to the new social reality at the political level would only be a matter of time. One outcome these theories do not contemplate, however, is the replacement of one subculture or political ideology by another in an advanced industrial society. Their approach remains rooted in the belief that the effects of modernisation are both universal and homogenising.

Whatever the findings of my survey in terms of political behaviour, Part I has already demonstrated that a new individualist and homogeneous society and culture have not so far supplanted in Italy more traditional family and friendship values and localist allegiances. Any hope of an Italian political regeneration cannot rest upon an alleged modernisation of this country's social identities along Anglo-Saxon lines, a prognosis which has consistently been proved false. As Diamanti and Segatti (1994: 34) concluded, after a survey of opinion conducted among a selected sample of Italian respondents in 1994, 'however deep political convulsions have been in the last few years, not only has the political culture of the Italian people not fundamentally changed compared to the past, it is also still deeply affected by the experiences of many decades. This confirms a truth that is well known to scholars but which is often forgotten [...]. The evolution of political culture and of its geo-political representations is not only slower than electoral processes, it is also partially autonomous vis-à-vis such processes. There is a structural gap between the former and the latter [...]'. This does not exclude the possibility that voting behaviour in Italy has come to resemble the attitude of informed consumers, as in other advanced countries. As McKie (1998: 19) put it for the U.K., 'where once people felt that to vote was a duty, just as they tended to vote out of rooted allegiances, we are now in the age of the shop-around vote, where a switch from Tory to Labour is more and more like switching from Sainsbury to Tesco'. Should Italian voters emerge in this part of the book as having entered this new age, we would have to conclude that there is no positive correlation between socio-political values and identities and electoral behaviour. Such a conclusion, in the light of the findings presented in Part I, seems rather dubious and far-fetched, although not impossible to contemplate. The opposite may be true, however, that is, that the extent of political and electoral change in Italy in the 1990s has been overestimated, and that continuity with past trends is just as much in evidence as change. This interpretation – neither optimistic nor unduly pessimistic – was recently put forward by various scholars, both within and outside Italy (Calvi and Vannucci 1995, Patrono 1995, Bull and Rhodes 1997, Maraffi 1997, Pisati 1997, Segatti 1997). Pisati, in particular, concluded his study of electoral behaviour in Italy in 1994 and 1996 by stating that 'in an age at times defined as "post-materialist", the main lines of segmentation of the Italian electorate follow the same dimensions of social differentiation which, according to Lipset and Rokkan's now classic study, emerged from the national revolutions and, later, from the industrial revolution. [...] both in 1994 and 1996 the main elements of differentiation among the electorate were the geo-political area of residence, religious practice, and occupational status' (Pisati 1997: 174). Other studies also reaffirmed the relevance of social class for voting, both in Italy and elsewhere (Bartolini and Mair 1990, Hout et al. 1995, Pisati and Barbagli 1996, Bellucci 1997). The definition of a social class, however, has been partially modified to take into account not only occupational status, but also sectional interests, distinguishing in particular between the private and the public sector (Kitschelt 1995, Bellucci 1997). The growing divergence of opinions regarding the extent of the process of electoral and political change in Italy has recently been mitigated by a general consensus that the country is still in a transitional phase of development and has not yet completed the passage from the 'First' to the 'Second' Republic (Pasquino 1994 and 1995, Bull and Rhodes 1996, Corbetta and Parisi 1997b).

Thus, there has been a tendency, which is now being partially rectified, to dichotomise arguments when analysing current political developments in Italy. These have been judged to have shown the emergence either of the pattern commonly known as 'rational choice voting', or a recreation of political subcultures under new guises – or even socio-political 'anomie'. The proponents of the concept of rational choice voting generally assume that voting behaviour is rational when it is the result of an individual's choice (Himmelweith et al. 1985, Hechter 1986, Fiorina 1990). This is not to say that voting takes place without reference to family, class, and/or values. It does mean, however, that associations such as the family are but one of the many factors which shape the formation of essentially individualised political values. These associations no longer function as communities. A political subculture, on the other hand, is predicated on the existence of group identity and a cohesive community. Rational choice theory emphasises the pursuit of rational interests at the individual level, while cultural approaches highlight collective behaviour and environmental constraints. Rational choice theory is not necessarily in conflict with cultural approaches, indeed the two can be viewed as complementary (Hechter 1986, Rex 1986, Eatwell 1997, Wildavski 1998). However, it is often the case that scholars privilege individual behaviour at the expense of group analysis or vice versa. In Part II I will put to the test and analyse the question of the persistence or demise of class-based and locally-based political allegiances, with a view to bringing to light both individual and group behaviour. For the electoral results of the 1990s to indicate a predominance of 'rational choice voting', my survey will need to show a high degree of voters' mobility, and a low degree of political and electoral loyalty to one's own class, family or religion. This is why my two case-studies are both highly relevant for such a study.

One of the reasons why Sesto was chosen as a case-study was precisely to gauge the impact of the phenomenon of 'partisan dealignment' upon a traditional working-class, left-wing stronghold (Cadioli 1964, Petrillo 1981 and 1992, Bell 1986). In Sesto at the 1994 political elections for the first time since 1946 the left parties did not obtain a majority of votes and the candidate of the right was elected. However, at the subsequent administrative elections the candidate of the left was elected Mayor. As we saw in Part I, the town has undergone substantial socio-economic changes in recent times, in particular the closure of some large industrial plants and the increasing attractiveness of its new housing estates to middle-class families, both for their affordable prices and for the town's proximity to Milan. These socio-economic changes, in particular the decline in the size of the Sesto working class, can to a certain extent explain the failure of the left at the 1994 general elections, indicating a pluralist, 'rational choice' approach on the part of an electorate which had no reason to feel loyal to a traditional subculture. Indeed, Berti and Donegà (1992) pointed out in 1992 that the communist subculture had been able to survive in the 1980s despite the disappearance of the socio-economic environment which had sustained it in the past. In this sense its persistence in the 1980s could be interpreted, in line with modernisation theories, in terms of a 'cultural and political lag', an expression which, as we saw, indicates the time needed for culture to adapt to societal changes.

Left-wing organisations in the town, however, have also started to change, after a period of predominantly defensive strategies in the 1970s and early 1980s (Regalia 1986). In particular, the

Democratic Party of the Left (PDS), which later became the Left Democrats (DS), the main heir to the Italian Communist Party, has begun to take on board the needs and demands of the middle-class electorate. It remains to be seen, however, whether the Sesto 'working class' itself changed allegiances and contributed to a large extent to the success of the right coalition, or whether it maintained its loyalty to the left. Another possible scenario is that Sesto workers have simply shown signs of disaffection for politics and a retreat to private concerns. To follow Hirschman's famous terminology (1970), I will try and establish whether industrial workers in Sesto have opted for exit, voice or loyalty, or indeed a combination of these. If they have changed allegiances, it is also necessary to establish whether there has been a process of 'partisan dealignment' or whether there is still strong identification with one political party, for example the Northern League.

Similarly, Erba was chosen as a good example for analysing the influence of religious beliefs upon political and voting behaviour. The town recently saw the rise of both the Northern League and *Forza Italia*, following the collapse of Christian Democracy. In 1994 the PPI (the main heir to the DC) polled 11 per cent, the League 26 per cent, and *Forza Italia* 26 per cent. In 1996 the Northern League obtained 32 per cent of votes, the *Polo* 36.9 per cent, the *Ulivo* 31.1 per cent. Is there a link between Catholic beliefs and the shift in votes to the Northern League and *Forza Italia*? If so, is the link provided by the fact that the town is representative of the northern Italian model of `diffused industrialisation', and that the Catholic subculture was closely correlated to the socio-economic configuration of this area (Trigilia 1986, Cento Bull 1989)? The questions to be addressed are, as in Sesto, whether the social groups who traditionally subscribed to the local Catholic subculture have become electorally mobile and now spread their votes more widely compared to the past, or whether they show a strong identification with a new political party.

In both localities attention has been paid to gender, in the context of the wider interpretative and theoretical issues outlined above. Traditionally, women have appeared to participate less in politics than men and, in Italy at least, as being more easily influenced by their families and by the Church when casting their votes (Dogan 1967, Weber 1977 and 1978). Indeed, in 1967 Dogan argued that in Italy there was a marked discrepancy between masculine and feminine voting behaviour, for religious reasons. The discrepancy was particularly noticeable, Dogan argued, in the case of peasant and working-class women, who voted in accordance with their Catholic beliefs rather than out of identification with a social class. However, in the large industrial cities the religious effect upon women voters was less noticeable. Since then, the process of secularisation of Italian society has weakened the influence of the Church upon voters. Already in the 1970s it was suggested that women's voting behaviour in Italy did not differ substantially from men's. In particular, it was argued, it was probably no longer the case that men voted more to the left and women more to the right (Parisi and Pasquino 1977).

As with increased voters' mobility and generational chasm, the gradual blurring of gender distinctions in voting behaviour is considered to be yet another sign of social and cultural modernisation. Thus for the U.K. it was recently maintained that gender differences do not affect the way people vote to any significant extent: 'gender has no influence upon voting in Britain today' (Rose and McAllister 1990: 51). The authors argued that 'the reason is straightforward. On matters that are salient to voting, men and women tend to share similar political values. On most major political issues men and women divide similarly – along lines of party or class, not gender' (Ibid.: 51). This is a relatively recent phenomenon, although the trend towards a homogenisation of gender voting patterns had been detected in the past (Sani 1977 and 1979, Barnes and Kaase 1979).

However, if we were also to take on board the opposite perspective on recent Italian political events, and accept that the emergence of new political parties with a populist and territorial appeal points to the persistence of locally-bound 'systems of solidarity', then the assumption that the dual process of modernisation and secularisation leads to social and cultural uniformity and political pluralism needs to be revised. Accordingly, it cannot be unquestionably assumed that gender voting patterns have become undifferentiated. Following the birth of new political parties in Italy, there have been signs that gender-based differences in voting behaviour may have re-emerged (Bellucci 1995 and 1997). Recent polls have suggested that the electoral success of Berlusconi's *Forza Italia* in the 1994 political elections was due partly to a preponderance of female voters, especially housewives (55 per cent women versus 45 per cent men supporters) (Diamanti 1994, Statham 1995). Conversely, the electorate of the Northern League was found to be predominantly male in the early days, although the party later attracted female voters in considerable numbers

(Mannheimer 1991). This is not a development unique to Italy. In the U.S.A, for example, a 'gender gap', in other words, considerable dissimilarities between the sexes in terms of political behaviour, was detected throughout the 1980s (Mueller 1988, Burrell 1993). Indeed, according to Mueller, 'a normative model of gender divergence now characterises much public discussion as well as some scholarly discussion' (p. 12). A gender gap has also been detected in Sweden, where women have voted increasingly for the left parties, and in Canada (Erickson 1993, Sainsbury 1993). As for France, it has been pointed out that in the 1981 presidential elections Mitterrand succeeded by appealing to the female electorate and attracting their votes in considerable numbers (Jenson and Sineau 1995). Even in the U.K., where its demise had been recorded, the gender gap was seen as re-emerging in the 1980s (Norris 1986), and finally reappeared at the 1992 general elections, with a considerably higher percentage of older women voting for the Conservative Party (Norris and Lovenduski 1993).

In contrast to the U.S.A, however, where the gender gap has taken the shape of a constantly higher level of support for the Democratic Party among women than men, so much so that some commentators have spoken of a 'voting bloc' (Mueller 1988: 25), in Italy women voters have been judged to form a 'mobile electorate', responsible to a large extent for the success of the centre-right alliance, the *Polo delle Libertà*, in 1994, and of the centre-left alliance, the *Ulivo*, in 1996 (*L'Unità*, 27 April 1996: 6, Segatti 1997, Zucchini 1997).

A question that needs addressing, therefore, is whether voting behaviour in Italy has become gender-neutral, as is generally maintained, although with increasing reservations, or whether specific gender differences are clearly visible. If a marked discrepancy exists, are women still attached to a traditional party and subculture, have they moved towards rational choice voting, or have they found a new collective political voice? Lastly, if voting behaviour differs substantially by gender, what are the nature of the differences and their consequences in terms of the political behaviour and influence of male and female voters?

The following sections will assess the extent of the process of partisan dealignment and individualism in voting behaviour or, conversely, the degree to which voters, both male and female, still subscribe to a territorial or class subculture and values. By establishing the political behaviour of Italian industrial workers in two traditional subcultural areas (one communist, the other Catholic) it should be possible to assess the significance of recent changes in voting patterns. Evidence of partisan dealignment would point to Italy's continuing process of secularisation and growing individualism. Evidence of the resilience – if not the revival – of political subcultures would need further explaining, particularly as far as their function in relation to specific social groups is concerned. The possible emergence of gender-based discrepancies in voting behaviour and values will also be explored, and their significance examined in terms of electoral outcomes and political influence.

4

Political Beliefs and Attitudes

Introduction

Part I analysed the social attitudes of respondents in Sesto and Erba; Part II focuses on political attitudes, as well as voting behaviour. Obviously, it is impossible to establish a clear-cut demarcation between the two, therefore in many respects this chapter picks up threads that have already emerged in the first half of the volume. However, the present chapter also aims to explore the more directly political implications of social beliefs and identities, looking specifically at respondents' opinions about policies and politics. The questionnaire that was distributed in the two localities privileged certain aspects of policy-making and politics. Prominent among these were the issues of taxation, privatisation, European integration, regional autonomy, federalism and immigration. Question 33 (a multiple question) dealt with most of these issues. It asked respondents whether they were prepared to pay higher taxes in exchange for better services or whether they would rather see taxes reduced, even at the expense of services. It also asked whether they thought that Italy needed a more decisive privatisation policy, or whether they considered such a policy a threat to the Italian economic situation. Respondents' opinion was sought on the merits of accelerating or slowing down the process of European integration, of giving Italian regions greater autonomy, and reorganising the Italian state along federalist lines. Question 38 (also a multiple question) asked respondents what policies they would adopt in relation to recent immigrants from outside the EU. Would they favour a policy of repatriation, social and cultural integration and 'assimilation', or the creation of a multi-cultural, multi-ethnic society? Finally, Question 39 probed the issue of citizenship rights, to whom and on what basis they should be granted.

There were two main reasons for limiting the number of questions on policy-making. The first was practical, the other was methodological. In practical terms, there was a clear need to keep the length of the questionnaire within reasonable limits. As it was, respondents were presented with a 12-page document to fill in, and I was both surprised and extremely grateful at the number of forms that were completed and returned in both localities. In terms of methodology (and of the research questions), there seemed to be no real need to probe every political issue one could think of: the main objective of the whole exercise was to obtain meaningful information on the extent of change or continuity in the attitudes of Italians towards politics and policy-making. Given the nature of the research which informs this book, particular attention was paid to topical issues which were being debated in Italy at the time of the survey. Taxation was an obvious choice, since the current level of fiscal pressure in Italy is high by European standards and is closely linked to the resilience of a 'social contract' which developed in the 1960s and 1970s. Privatisation was another straightforward choice. Italy has the largest public sector in western Europe, whose origins date back to the 1930s. For better or worse, this sector has played a major part in shaping the country's economic and political setting and the decision to dismantle it is proving a difficult one. One of the consequences of such a decision would undoubtedly be an increased rate of unemployment, although this would be offset by more efficient standards of services. European integration came next on the list. Italians have repeatedly expressed positive opinions regarding the EU and are among the strongest supporters of a single currency. It is not clear, however, whether this applies to all Italians in an undifferentiated way, or whether noticeable local and regional, as well as generational, patterns can be discerned. The survey aimed at ascertaining the existence of any such patterns. As for regional autonomy and federalism, these have become even more hotly debated in Italy since the time of the fieldwork underpinning this book. This situation is not unproblematic, since in 1994, at the time of the survey in Sesto and Erba, federalism was clearly considered 'League policy', whereas later the Northern League moved on to secessionism and the other political parties by and large embraced the concept of a federal state (although they disagree on what this means in practice). Nevertheless, the fact that federalism is no longer the prerogative of the Northern League indicates that it is seen as possessing certain intrinsic merits as a possible way forward for institutional change in Italy. It will thus be interesting to see whether respondents in Sesto and Erba looked favourably upon federalism irrespective of their party preferences, or whether there existed a close link between support for this idea and for the Northern League.

The questions referred to above can provide important indications as to the existence of a 'support for change' versus a 'resistance to change' mentality. In other words, a pattern may emerge where respondents can be grouped together on the basis of whether they seek to encourage and promote change, both in the economic and institutional spheres, or whether they try to resist and slow it down. Generally speaking, it is believed that certain social groups are more receptive to change than others, particularly the self-employed and those working in the service sector. By contrast, those on a fixed wage or salary, particularly traditional full-time manufacturing and public-sector employees, are thought to be reluctant to embrace new economic policies or to see an end to corporatist practices. In addition, generational differences are also felt to be significant, with older people less open to change than the young. Local and regional differences are also generally taken into account, but only to the extent that certain localities register a dominant presence of a specific social group, which may explain why they embrace a particular positioning vis-à-vis economic and political change. Thus a locality or region with a predominance of industrial workers employed in nationalised industries would show a higher than average resistance to change. However, as has been made clear in the course of this book, the Italian case has traditionally presented certain regional subcultural characteristics that are difficult to explain simply with reference to occupational status, and that may also prove relevant when accounting for people's opinions concerning the need for and the nature of political and economic reforms. This was another reason why respondents were chosen from the same socio-economic background, with the exception of a group of artisans and small entrepreneurs in Erba and a group of unemployed people in Sesto. The main objective was to explore whether the attitudes of these respondents to change were deeply influenced by the particular locality and subculture they lived in, irrespective of religious, gender and generational differences, or whether these latter factors, taken singly or indeed collectively, were more important in determining political attitudes and beliefs.

The importance of kinship and friendship networks in relation to political attitudes was also probed in the survey and the findings are presented here. In the questionnaire two questions dealt with this issue. Question 29 asked respondents how often they discussed politics with members of their families and friends, and whether they discussed it more or less often compared to five/ten years previously. Question 30 asked them the extent to which they shared their political ideas with family and friends. Responses to such questions indicate whether attitudes towards economic and political change are shaped primarily by individuals – albeit influenced to a certain extent by their social environment – or are actively promoted and sustained by primary social groups thanks to constant exchange of information and circulation of ideas. The findings therefore throw some light upon the alleged detachment of individuals from their primary groups in matters related to political attitudes and party preference, postulated primarily by rational choice theories, as discussed in the Introduction to Part II.

Family, friends, and political beliefs

As mentioned above, Question 29 asked respondents how often they discussed politics with family and friends. Opinion poll surveys tend to include questions which establish how interested people are in political issues. In this case, the question was more specific than in other surveys, since for the reasons outlined above it only referred to primary groups (Table 4.1).

In both localities, when asked if they discussed politics with family and friends, the majority of respondents stated that they did so 'quite frequently' or 'very frequently', as opposed to 'never' or 'a little' (Table 4.1). This was true of both men and women, and also applied across generations. However, when asked whether they discussed politics more or less often than they did five – ten years ago, more women than men indicated that they discussed it more often. This was mainly because many women had kept politics largely to themselves in the past. As Table 4.1 shows, the percentage of women discussing politics 'quite frequently' and 'very frequently' in 1994 was 59.4 percent, slightly more than that for men (58.5 percent), whereas in previous years many more men than women had discussed politics frequently. Furthermore, in 1994 many more women than men declared that they now discussed politics more

Table 4.1 Frequency of political discussions with family and friends (all respondents by sex)

			SEX		
			men	women	Total
frequency of	not at all	Count	62	37	99
political		% within SEX	12.0%	12.3%	12.1%
discussions with		% of Total	7.6%	4.5%	12.1%
family and	a little	Count	152	85	237
friends		% within SEX	29.5%	28.2%	29.0%
		% of Total	18.6%	10.4%	29.0%
	quite	Count	228	130	358
	frequently	% within SEX	44.2%	43.2%	43.8%
		% of Total	27.9%	15.9%	43.8%
	very	Count	74	49	123
	frequently	% within SEX	14.3%	16.3%	15.1%
		% of Total	9.1%	6.0%	15.1%
Total		Count	516	301	817
		% within SEX	100.0%	100.0%	100.0%
		% of Total	63.2%	36.8%	100.0%

often than in the past. In other words, women had 'caught up' with men in this respect.

When the findings were disaggregated by area (Table 4.2), the results were fairly similar: the majority of respondents in Sesto (58.3 percent) and in Erba (59.4 percent) stated that they discussed politics with friends and family 'quite frequently' or 'very frequently'.

However, a few significant variations were also noticeable, particularly the high percentage of young people aged between eighteen and thirty in Sesto who never discussed politics with family and friends (19.4 percent), compared to both young people in Erba (11.3 percent) and older people in Sesto. In previous years, young people in both localities had largely been uninterested in discussing politics with their primary groups. These figures indicate that we may be witnessing a process of increasing detachment of voters from the influence of their kinship and peer groups in Sesto, whereas in Erba this was not the case. Another difference turned out to be the higher percentage of women who discussed politics frequently in Erba (63.1 percent) in contrast with Sesto. Respondents' attitudes in both localities appeared to have changed quite considerably in comparison to previous years. In Sesto, it turned

Table 4.2 Frequency of political discussions with family and friends (by area and sex)

AREA					SEX		
					men	women	Total
Sesto	frequency of political discussions with family and friends	not at all		Count	29	20	49
				% within SEX	10.7%	16.4%	12.5%
				% of Total	7.4%	5.1%	12.5%
		a little		Count	79	36	115
				% within SEX	29.2%	29.5%	29.3%
				% of Total	20.1%	9.2%	29.3%
		quite frequently		Count	123	48	171
				% within SEX	45.4%	39.3%	43.5%
				% of Total	31.3%	12.2%	43.5%
		very frequently		Count	40	18	58
				% within SEX	14.8%	14.8%	14.8%
				% of Total	10.2%	4.6%	14.8%
	Total			Count	271	122	393
				% within SEX	100.0%	100.0%	100.0%
				% of Total	69.0%	31.0%	100.0%

Erba frequency of political discussions with family and friends					
not at all	Count		33	17	50
	% within SEX		13.5%	9.5%	11.8%
	% of Total		7.8%	4.0%	11.8%
a little	Count		73	49	122
	% within SEX		29.8%	27.4%	28.8%
	% of Total		17.2%	11.6%	28.8%
quite frequently	Count		105	82	187
	% within SEX		42.9%	45.8%	44.1%
	% of Total		24.8%	19.3%	44.1%
very frequently	Count		34	31	65
	% within SEX		13.9%	17.3%	15.3%
	% of Total		8.0%	7.3%	15.3%
Total	Count		245	179	424
	% within SEX		100.0%	100.0%	100.0%
	% of Total		57.8%	42.2%	100.0%

out that men had always discussed politics with family and friends to a great extent, whereas women had largely avoided to talk about such issues. Now, however, there was no longer much difference between them. In Erba, neither men nor women had discussed politics to any great extent in the past, but were now doing so.

Some preliminary conclusions can be drawn from these findings. The communist subculture in Sesto clearly relied not just on the workplace for political socialisation but also on the circulation of ideas within primary groups. This situation was almost exclusively male-orientated: we can infer from the data that it was primarily among male kin or male friends that political discussion took place. Nowadays both men and women exchanged political ideas in their primary groups, indicating an increased interest for politics among women after the demise of the traditional ideologies. The findings contrast sharply with those of a national survey carried out among Italian women in the 1970s (a decade of great political participation and turmoil), when 54 percent of respondents stated that they never discussed politics (Weber, 1981). The change suggests that gender differences have largely disappeared and that in this respect the electorate has become more homogeneous. However, kinship and social networks remain significant in terms of political socialisation – indeed, in some respects they have acquired a greater role, since they now influence women as well as men. From the point of view of modernisation theories, therefore, the findings are somewhat ambiguous, since the emergence of comparable patterns of behaviour among both men and women has been accompanied by a strengthening of the role and influence of primary groups in shaping political ideas and beliefs. Regrettably, the way the question was formulated does not give any indication as to whether nowadays political discussion takes place in gender-segregated or gender-mixed groups, which would have helped to establish the extent to which men and women influence each others' opinions.

Whether or not people in Sesto and Erba discussed politics with their primary groups, what is perhaps more relevant is how many of their relatives and friends actually shared the same political ideas (Tables 4.3 and 4.4).

As Table 4.3 shows, the larger group of respondents in both localities stated that a 'considerable number' of family members and friends shared their political beliefs (43.3 percent), followed by those who said that 'many' did so (18.4 percent). Only 11.2 percent declared that 'very few' did, while 10.8 percent said that the 'vast

Table 4.3 Percentage of family members and friends sharing the same political ideas (all respondents by sex)

			SEX		
			Men	Women	Total
Family and	just a few	Count	60	33	93
friends		% within SEX	11.5%	10.8%	11.2%
sharing same		% of Total	7.2%	4.0%	11.2%
political ideas	a considerable	Count	223	136	359
	number	% within SEX	42.6%	44.4%	43.3%
		% of Total	26.9%	16.4%	43.3%
	many	Count	104	49	153
		% within SEX	19.8%	16.0%	18.4%
		% of Total	12.5%	5.9%	18.4%
	the vast	Count	53	37	90
	majority	% within SEX	10.1%	12.1%	10.8%
		% of Total	6.4%	4.5%	10.8%
	don't know	Count	84	50	134
		% within SEX	16.0%	16.3%	16.1%
		% of Total	10.1%	6.0%	16.1%
Total		Count	524	306	830
		% within SEX	100.0%	100.0%	100.0%
		% of Total	63.1%	36.9%	100.0%

majority' shared their opinions. When the data was disaggregated by area, more people in Erba than in Sesto appeared to share their political ideas with friends and next of kin (Table 4.4). There were only minor differences in terms of age, but in terms of gender there was a noticeable difference. In fact in Sesto, more women than men (30.4 percent as opposed to 23.8 percent) appeared to share their political ideas with 'many' or the 'vast majority' of family members and friends, while in Erba the opposite was true. Indeed 37 percent of male respondents in Erba shared their political ideas to a large/preponderant extent, as opposed to 26.5 percent of women. The starkest difference, therefore, was between male respondents in Sesto and in Erba, a finding that once again evokes the differing role of primary groups in the two subcultures, the communist and the Catholic, in terms of political socialisation. As Chapter 2 showed, political ideas in Sesto had been shaped (for men) primarily at the workplace (and only secondarily in the

Table 4.4 Percentage of family members and friends sharing the same political ideas (by area and sex)

AREA				SEX		
				men	women	Total
Sesto	Family and friends sharing same political ideas	just a few	Count	37	18	55
			% within SEX	13.3%	14.4%	13.6%
			% of Total	9.2%	4.5%	13.6%
		a considerable number	Count	126	46	172
			% within SEX	45.3%	36.8%	42.7%
			% of Total	31.3%	11.4%	42.7%
		many	Count	43	20	63
			% within SEX	15.5%	16.0%	15.6%
			% of Total	10.7%	5.0%	15.6%
		the vast majority	Count	23	18	41
			% within SEX	8.3%	14.4%	10.2%
			% of Total	5.7%	4.5%	10.2%
		don't know	Count	49	23	72
			% within SEX	17.6%	18.4%	17.9%
			% of Total	12.2%	5.7%	17.9%
	Total		Count	278	125	403
			% within SEX	100.0%	100.0%	100.0%
			% of Total	69.0%	31.0%	100.0%

Erba	Family and friends sharing same political ideas				Total
just a few	Count	23	15	38	
	% within SEX	9.3%	8.3%	8.9%	
	% of Total	5.4%	3.5%	8.9%	
a considerable number	Count	97	90	187	
	% within SEX	39.4%	49.7%	43.8%	
	% of Total	22.7%	21.1%	43.8%	
many	Count	61	29	90	
	% within SEX	24.8%	16.0%	21.1%	
	% of Total	14.3%	6.8%	21.1%	
the vast majority	Count	30	19	49	
	% within SEX	12.2%	10.5%	11.5%	
	% of Total	7.0%	4.4%	11.5%	
don't know	Count	35	27	62	
	% within SEX	14.2%	14.9%	14.5%	
	% of Total	8.2%	6.3%	14.5%	
Total	Count	246	181	427	
	% within SEX	100.0%	100.0%	100.0%	
	% of Total	57.6%	42.4%	100.0%	

family), while in Erba the family had no rivals, for both men and women. Nonetheless, it is also clear that in Sesto there is no cleavage between primary groups and secondary associations and work environments, since even among Sesto men only a mere 13.3 percent declared that they shared their political ideas with 'just a few' family members and friends.

Positioning vis-à-vis economic change

Attitudes towards taxation were fairly clear-cut. It must be acknowledged at this point that surveys which probe taxation issues tend to attract unreliable answers, as people refrain from declaring their reluctance to pay taxes. Despite this caveat, respondents did not appear to shy away from these questions, and replies were consistent with the characteristics of the localities and the samples. When the two localities were considered together, a majority of respondents declared themselves in favour of paying higher taxes in exchange for better services, while only a small minority opted for favouring lower taxes even at the expense of public services.

However, whereas the majority opposed to tax cuts as a trade-off for services was overwhelming, the majority clearly in favour of higher taxes and better services was relatively low (only 50.6 percent). This figure suggested that the responses had to be disaggregated, since they probably concealed substantial differences related to gender, age or locality. When the data was broken down, people's beliefs did not appear to vary according to the locality (Table 4.5), but they did vary according to age.

There was no correlation between opposition to higher taxes and locality, but a significant positive correlation emerged between respondents' opposition to higher taxes and their age. Support for higher taxes was lowest among the youngest cohort (aged 18–30), increasing progressively to reach its highest level amongst the oldest group (aged 60 plus). In terms of gender, a majority of male respondents (52.9 percent) favoured higher taxes, as opposed to a minority of female ones (46.4 percent). This must be attributed primarily to the fact that there were more younger women than men in the samples, since there was no significant correlation between responses to the question related to tax and the sex of respondents. It thus appears that there is a generational divide among respondents, suggesting a mentality more receptive to change amongst the young. When the two areas were considered separately, a similar

Table 4.5 Respondents' views on higher taxes in exchange for better services (by area and sex)

AREA			men	women	Total
			SEX		
Sesto	agree strongly	Count	49	8	57
		% within SEX	20.9%	8.1%	17.1%
		% of Total	14.7%	2.4%	17.1%
	agree moderately	Count	80	40	120
		% within SEX	34.2%	40.4%	36.0%
		% of Total	24.0%	12.0%	36.0%
	agree a little	Count	43	24	67
		% within SEX	18.4%	24.2%	20.1%
		% of Total	12.9%	7.2%	20.1%
	disagree	Count	62	27	89
		% within SEX	26.5%	27.3%	26.7%
		% of Total	18.6%	8.1%	26.7%
	Total	Count	234	99	333
		% within SEX	100.0%	100.0%	100.0%
		% of Total	70.3%	29.7%	100.0%
Erba	agree strongly	Count	34	22	56
		% within SEX	15.6%	14.6%	15.2%
		% of Total	9.2%	6.0%	15.2%
	agree moderately	Count	76	46	122
		% within SEX	34.9%	30.5%	33.1%
		% of Total	20.6%	12.5%	33.1%
	agree a little	Count	39	34	73
		% within SEX	17.9%	22.5%	19.8%
		% of Total	10.6%	9.2%	19.8%
	disagree	Count	69	49	118
		% within SEX	31.7%	32.5%	32.0%
		% of Total	18.7%	13.3%	32.0%
	Total	Count	218	151	369
		% within SEX	100.0%	100.0%	100.0%
		% of Total	59.1%	40.9%	100.0%

picture emerged, with age divisions persisting in both Sesto and Erba (Pearson correlation between age and support for higher taxes: 0.269 in Sesto and 0.271 in Erba). Thus 55.4 percent of Sesto respondents aged 18–30 were opposed to higher taxes, as were 50 percent of those aged 31–40. All other age groups, by contrast, were predominantly in favour. In terms of gender, while 55.1 percent of male respondents were prepared to pay higher taxes, 51.7 percent of women were not. In Erba, as far as age was concerned, 59.8 percent of respondents aged 18–30 opposed higher taxes, as did 55.3 percent of those aged 31–40. The reverse was true for all the other age groups. As for gender, 50.5 percent of men favoured higher taxes, but 55 percent of women did not. In many ways this was quite an important finding, as taxation appears to be an area where localism does not play a part and where political opinions varied mainly on the basis of generational value-change, rather than the locality one happened to live in. Yet the findings are in some ways surprising, since a recent survey established that in Italy 'tax protest is very closely associated with self-employment, residence in the north-eastern regions, and support for the Lega Nord' (Ferrera 1997: 244). The most likely explanation is that the difference between the two surveys is due to the way the question related to taxation was formulated. In the survey cited by Ferrera, respondents had been asked whether or not they thought that taxes were too high with respect to the advantages they received. In my own survey, respondents were asked whether they were prepared to pay higher taxes in exchange for better services. It is therefore possible that people in the north-eastern regions feel primarily the need for better services, rather than simple tax cuts. This still leaves the question of whether it was Northern League voters who were predominantly opposed to tax increases, as indicated by Ferrera. The political beliefs and attitudes of Northern League voters will be examined in detail in Chapter 6, where it is demonstrated that there was no significant correlation between opposition to tax increases and Northern League voters in either Sesto or Erba.

Attitudes towards privatisation, on the other hand, re-established localism as an important factor in explaining political attitudes as well as attitudes towards economic change. Unlike attitudes towards taxation, opinions in favour of privatisation correlated positively with Erba (Pearson correlation: 0.200). Conversely, no significant correlation could be established between attitudes towards a policy of privatisation and age. Taking the two localities together, a majority of both men and women declared themselves in favour of giving greater impulse to a policy of privatisation (59.1 percent of men, 60.8 percent of women). As for age, clear support for such policy was in evidence only among young people aged 18–30. Once the data was disaggregated by area, however, a very different picture emerged (Table 4.6).

In Sesto, respondents were clearly split on this issue (49.7 percent in favour, 50.3 percent against), whereas in Erba they were clearly in favour (67.6 percent in favour). The split in Sesto was

Table 4.6 Respondents' views on the need to speed up the privatisation process (by area and sex)

AREA			men	women	Total
			SEX		
Sesto	agree strongly	Count	28	19	47
		% within SEX	14.0%	20.9%	16.2%
		% of Total	9.6%	6.5%	16.2%
	agree moderately	Count	71	26	97
		% within SEX	35.5%	28.6%	33.3%
		% of Total	24.4%	8.9%	33.3%
	agree a little	Count	62	16	78
		% within SEX	31.0%	17.6%	26.8%
		% of Total	21.3%	5.5%	26.8%
	disagree	Count	39	30	69
		% within SEX	19.5%	33.0%	23.7%
		% of Total	13.4%	10.3%	23.7%
	Total	Count	200	91	291
		% within SEX	100.0%	100.0%	100.0%
		% of Total	68.7%	31.3%	100.0%
Erba	agree strongly	Count	79	36	115
		% within SEX	36.9%	25.0%	32.1%
		% of Total	22.1%	10.1%	32.1%
	agree moderately	Count	67	62	129
		% within SEX	31.3%	43.1%	36.0%
		% of Total	18.7%	17.3%	36.0%
	agree a little	Count	34	28	62
		% within SEX	15.9%	19.4%	17.3%
		% of Total	9.5%	7.8%	17.3%
	disagree	Count	34	18	52
		% within SEX	15.9%	12.5%	14.5%
		% of Total	9.5%	5.0%	14.5%
	Total	Count	214	144	358
		% within SEX	100.0%	100.0%	100.0%
		% of Total	59.8%	40.2%	100.0%

reflected in the responses of both men and women, and a clear-cut position only emerged when age was taken into account. In Sesto both men and women opposed a policy of privatisation by a tiny margin. This margin became more substantial when different age cohorts were taken into account. Whereas 59.8 percent of young people aged 18-30 supported the idea of speeding up the privatisation process, a clear majority of all other age groups opposed it. In

Erba, by contrast, two-thirds of both male and female respondents supported such a policy, as well as two-thirds of all age groups, including people in their fifties and sixties. Furthermore, in Erba the policy found favour among all social groups surveyed, including industrial workers, as well as the sub-sample of artisans and small entrepreneurs.

The findings also differed sharply in the two localities when the issue of religion was taken into consideration. In Sesto, in fact, a majority of Catholic respondents declared themselves in favour of accelerating the privatisation process, however a majority of lay respondents did not. The fact that lay respondents in Sesto tended to hold left-wing beliefs clearly influenced their different positioning towards privatisation. In Erba, by contrast, both Catholic and lay respondents were supporters of this policy (Catholic respondents slightly more so). The findings are fairly unequivocal in pointing to the existence of patterns of values and attitudes which can only be explained with reference to the persistence of particular subcultures related to specific socio-economic and geographical areas. It may be argued that the findings can also be explained on the basis of 'market situations' (Kitschelt 1995: 5), that is, on the basis of the positioning of different industrial sectors vis-à-vis market pressure. Since small- and medium-sized firms in Erba tend to export much of their production, while large firms in Sesto produce mainly for the internal market, employees in the former locality may favour opening up to external competition to a much greater extent than employees in Sesto. This approach seems plausible, except that, according to Kitschelt, it represents a new theory of social preference formation which is applicable to post-industrial capitalist societies. Yet, ironically, a decisive positioning in favour of change in Erba masks a marked continuity with its traditional local culture, so much so that it finds support across different generations. As discussed in Chapter 3, the local culture in Erba has been predominantly private-sector orientated and 'entrepreneurial', revolving around the belief that people should count upon themselves and their primary groups rather than rely on the state for their living and/or welfare. This culture was shared by all social groups employed in the private sector, irrespective of their class status.

Once again, these findings are at best ambiguous and at worst fully contradictory in terms of theories of modernity and modernisation. On the one hand, we have a picture consistent with their main tenets in Sesto, where older working-class respondents continued to hang on to their traditional socialist beliefs and defend the nationalised industries, whereas the younger generation had moved on and no longer showed attachment to such ideals. On the other hand, we have a situation in Erba where older working-class people were just as eager as younger ones to promote economic change and to support economic policies generally associated with right-wing politics. Unbelievably, in both localities Catholics appear to be at the forefront of economic and capitalist modernisation! When we recall that Christian Democracy was the main beneficiary (and manipulator) of the Italian public sector and never ventured into free-market economic policies of the type advocated by neo-liberal thinkers, we have a clearer idea of the complexity of the Italian case and the inadequacy of linear interpretations based on simple opposite binaries. One of these binaries, which, as we saw, postulated that Catholic ideals clashed with modernisation while secularist values underpinned it, has thus been proved unfounded. This does not mean, of course, that such correlations may not be proved valid in other areas of Italy. My point is precisely that different combinations of 'pre-modern' and 'modern' values exist in different areas of Italy, and that religious beliefs are in this respect only a dependent variable subject to local and regional variations, in the same way as age and class (and to a much lesser extent even gender).

Positioning vis-à-vis institutional change

The survey confirmed that Italians of both sexes and all ages support the process of European integration, whatever their party or subcultural allegiances. Among all respondents, 80.9 percent declared that they were in favour of greater European integration, either strongly or moderately. Only 7.4 percent were strongly opposed. Men were slightly more European minded than women, and young people slightly more than the older generations. When the data was disaggregated by locality, there appeared to be more decisive support in Sesto than in Erba, but the differences were not marked.

The reverse was true in the case of support for granting the regions a greater degree of autonomy. There was general agreement that this was a desirable policy among all respondents of both sexes and all ages, but support was somewhat higher in Erba than in Sesto, and highest of all among Erba men. In Sesto, 78.9

percent of respondents agreed with this policy, of whom 42.2 percent 'strongly' and 36.7 percent 'moderately'. In Erba the figure for all respondents was 82.4 percent (49.1 percent and 33.3 percent respectively). A majority of male respondents in Erba (50.7 percent) agreed 'strongly' with this policy.

When asked whether they agreed with the idea of creating a 'Europe of the Regions', a majority of all respondents again replied favourably. In Erba, however, gender proved a divisive factor, since here a majority of men agreed with the idea but a majority of women disagreed. When it came to federalism (a contentious issue at the time as I explained above), gender persisted in proving the main divider, and really interesting findings began to emerge. Among all respondents, there was a split of opinions, even though a majority approved of this policy (52.2 percent), rather surprisingly perhaps given that federalism was clearly associated with the politics of the Northern League.

Nevertheless there was also substantial opposition to the idea of a federalist state, which turned out to be more marked among women: 55.8 percent of male respondents approved, while 52.9 percent of women disapproved. Gender divisions, however, only turned out to be really significant in Erba. In Sesto, in fact, the majority of both men and women rejected federalism (57.7 percent of men and 53.6 percent of women), whereas in Erba 66.8 percent of men were in agreement and 52.3 percent of women in disagreement (Table 4.7).

Thus only male respondents in Erba were fervent supporters of a federal state, in the same way as they had turned out to be fervent supporters of the local and regional dimension (see Chapter 3) and of greater regional autonomy. This indicates, once again, that gender is the only factor which is capable of consistently transcending subcultural allegiances, specifically because women did not conform to cultural and political localism to the same extent as men. No other factor had the same degree of influence. Generational differences, for instance, were negligible, so much so that all age groups in Sesto predominantly opposed federalism and all age groups in Erba predominantly supported it. Similarly, religion was not a factor of significance. A clear majority of both Catholic and lay respondents in Sesto opposed federalism, while a clear majority of both Catholic and lay respondents in Erba favoured it, with Catholics the more enthusiastic group (42.8 percent of Catholics strongly in favour and 18.5 percent moderately so, as opposed to 35.4 and 20.8 respectively among lay respondents).

Table 4.7 Respondents' views on the need to move towards a federal state (by area and sex)

AREA				SEX		
				men	women	Total
Sesto	agree strongly	Count		47	25	72
		% within SEX		22.6%	26.3%	23.8%
		% of Total		15.5%	8.3%	23.8%
	agree moderately	Count		41	19	60
		% within SEX		19.7%	20.0%	19.8%
		% of Total		13.5%	6.3%	19.8%
	agree a little	Count		32	14	46
		% within SEX		15.4%	14.7%	15.2%
		% of Total		10.6%	4.6%	15.2%
	disagree	Count		88	37	125
		% within SEX		42.3%	38.9%	41.3%
		% of Total		29.0%	12.2%	41.3%
	Total	Count		208	95	303
		% within SEX		100.0%	100.0%	100.0%
		% of Total		68.6%	31.4%	100.0%
Erba	agree strongly	Count		101	50	151
		% within SEX		46.3%	33.6%	41.1%
		% of Total		27.5%	13.6%	41.1%
	agree moderately	Count		49	21	70
		% within SEX		22.5%	14.1%	19.1%
		% of Total		13.4%	5.7%	19.1%
	agree a little	Count		21	23	44
		% within SEX		9.6%	15.4%	12.0%
		% of Total		5.7%	6.3%	12.0%
	disagree	Count		47	55	102
		% within SEX		21.6%	36.9%	27.8%
		% of Total		12.8%	15.0%	27.8%
	Total	Count		218	149	367
		% within SEX		100.0%	100.0%	100.0%
		% of Total		59.4%	40.6%	100.0%

The findings discussed above show that institutional change was less contentious than economic change, with the sole exception of federalism, and that there was support for it in both localities. In the same way as Part I has shown that most respondents possessed multiple identities and had, compared to the past, moved towards accepting both supra-national and sub-national dimensions, so now they did not object to either greater European integration or administrative decentralisation. The findings also give us an initial understanding of how respondents positioned themselves in relation to political parties, and to the Northern League in particular. In Sesto, respondents were clearly wary of the Northern League and rejected the one policy which at the time was closely associated with this political party, i.e., federalism. They were not, however, opposed to greater regional autonomy or even the idea of a 'Europe of the Regions' which in many ways could be interpreted as a prelude to a federal reorganisation of all European countries. In other words, they might even have accepted federalism were it not for the fact that at the time this policy represented the battle cry of an increasingly anti-national party. As we saw in Part I, respondents in Sesto were strongly attached to the idea of the nation, and this is consistent with their attitudes towards federalism as recorded in 1994, even though it is possible that such attitudes may be different today, as the idea of a federal state has now been taken on board by most parties. In Erba, by contrast, support for all three ideas was fairly strong, but an analysis of responses to questions of a 'Europe of the Regions' and federalism threw up a clear-cut gender divide, which was not matched by a generational or religious one. This indicates that support for the Northern League was also fairly strong in the locality, and that it was strongest among men of all age groups, including Catholics. As in the case of Sesto, such findings would be in line with respondents' attitudes towards the idea of the nation, as shown in Part I. While women harboured warm feelings for Italy as a nation, men were at best lukewarm, at worst hostile. The next chapter will fully substantiate these preliminary conclusions.

Attitudes towards immigration policies

Questions about attitudes towards immigrants are notoriously contentious and bring out the strongest defence barriers among survey participants. It is also the case that such questions may be flawed, indeed it is often argued that they can be biased and 'guide' respondents in a certain direction. Such concerns are legitimate, in my view, since surveys on this issue not uncommonly produce unsatisfactory or puzzling results. Furthermore, there are those who argue that a questionnaire is not the best tool for this kind of research, and that specific skills and a deep and proper understanding of the issues involved are required. The survey upon which this book is based did include a section on immigrants and immigration, however they were directed more at establishing people's perception of the extent of immigration in their locality and their attitudes towards specific policies than at probing the presence of racial tensions and racist feelings. This is not to say that responses should be treated as unproblematic, nevertheless they appeared to be largely consistent with the pattern of social identities and cultural values which had already emerged from an analysis of other parts of the survey.

Question 38 gave a list of possible policies for implementation in relation to extra-EU immigrants, simply asking people whether they agreed or disagreed with each. Policies listed included repatriation, helping immigrants to find housing and work in Italy, cultural assimilation, and the creation of a multi-ethnic, multi-racial society. Respondents clearly had difficulty with this section of the questionnaire, since a high percentage of respondents chose not to reply (ranging from 35 percent to 40 percent). Missing data was higher in Sesto than in Erba. Of those who replied, a large majority declared themselves against repatriation (63.5 percent), in favour of helping immigrants to find housing and work (74.1 percent), against cultural assimilation (56.3 percent), and in favour of a multi-ethnic society (69.8 percent). On the face of it, prevailing attitudes appeared to show an acceptance of immigration as well as rejection of the traditional approach directed at achieving cultural assimilation of the immigrants into their host society.

Were there substantial differences in attitudes between localities, or on the basis of other factors? Locality this time did not alter the findings, which were remarkably similar for every policy taken into consideration. Neither the communist tradition in Sesto nor the Catholic tradition in Erba made respondents adopt different solutions to the immigration phenomenon, a clear indication of the importance of the concept of solidarity in both traditions. Gender did not alter the findings, either, except that women in both Sesto and Erba were slightly more opposed to a policy of cultural assimilation and men slightly more opposed to the idea of creating a multi-ethnic society (particularly in Erba). Age proved a more discriminating factor, with young people in both localities, and especially in Erba, showing a lower propensity to accept that immigrants were in Italy to stay and that this situation required a different type of policy-making than simple repatriation (Table 4.8).

First, among young people a smaller percentage refrained from answering Question 38. Second, in Erba 45 percent of young

Table 4.8 Respondents views on a policy of repatriation of extra-EU immigrants (by area and age)

AREA			AGE				
			18–30	31–40	41–50	51–60	60+
Sesto	disagree	Count	43	31	69	12	1
		% within AGE	60.6%	66.0%	60.0%	63.2%	100.0%
		% of Total	17.0%	12.3%	27.3%	4.7%	.4%
	agree	Count	28	16	46	7	
		% within AGE	39.4%	34.0%	40.0%	36.8%	
		% of Total	11.1%	6.3%	18.2%	2.8%	
	Total	Count	71	47	115	19	1
		% within AGE	100%	100%	100%	100%	100%
		% of Total	28.1%	18.6%	45.5%	7.5%	.4%
Erba	disagree	Count	61	76	43	18	5
		% within AGE	55.0%	71.0%	71.7%	72.0%	62.5%
		% of Total	19.6%	24.4%	13.8%	5.8%	1.6%
	agree	Count	50	31	17	7	3
		% within AGE	45.0%	29.0%	28.3%	28.0%	37.5%
		% of Total	16.1%	10.0%	5.5%	2.3%	1.0%
	Total	Count	111	107	60	25	8
		% within AGE	100.0%	100.0%	100.0%	100.0%	100.0%
		% of Total	35.7%	34.4%	19.3%	8.0%	2.6%

people aged 18–30 actually agreed with a policy of repatriation, the highest percentage amongst all sub-groups; this figure contrasted with less than a third of most other age groups. In Sesto, the figure was slightly lower, nevertheless even here 39.4 percent of those aged 18–30 agreed with a policy of repatriation. Interestingly, in Sesto this figure represented less of a generational break than in Erba. As for helping immigrants find work and housing, 34.4 percent of young people in Sesto disagreed, compared to roughly 18–20 percent in the other age brackets, while in Erba 45 percent of young people disagreed, well above the figure registered among the other age groups (15–17 percent). Lastly, a multi-ethnic society commanded the support of a majority of young people in both Sesto and Erba, but in Erba only 60 percent of them actually approved.

There is little doubt, therefore, that in terms of attitudes towards immigration policies, there was much greater reluctance to accept change among young people, and that this was more in evidence in Erba than in Sesto. Such findings are not surprising in some respects, at least if one considers how people in Erba were attached to cultural and political localism, not to mention the racist undertones of the Northern League, a party, as we shall see in the next chapter, which found much support in Erba. The findings are, nevertheless, more important than they may appear at first sight, because they also clearly indicate a radicalisation of politics among the younger generation and a move away from the solidarity which characterised both subcultures. The findings are, in other words, the clearest sign yet that the traditional subcultures have been eroded and seriously dented in what constituted the 'core' of their value-systems. This was confirmed by the existence of a positive correlation between individualist values and support for a policy of repatriation, in contrast to both familist and solidarist values. In both Sesto and Erba, in fact, respondents who believed first and foremost in individual success predominantly agreed with a policy of repatriation, while people who put their faith in the family or in solidarity disagreed (Table 4.9).

The gap between the 'individualists' and the 'solidarists' was especially striking in Sesto, where 64.9 percent of the former agreed with a policy of repatriation, while 78.9 percent of the latter disagreed. In Erba, 50.8 percent of the 'individualists' agreed with a policy of repatriation, as opposed to 25.0 percent of the 'solidarists'. As discussed in Part I, the economic situation in the two localities was clearly perceived very differently by respondents and

Table 4.9 Respondents' views on a policy of repatriation of extra-EU immigrants (by area and life values)

AREA			Life values			
			individualist	familist	solidarist	Total
Sesto	disagree	Count	13	55	86	154
		% within				
		Life values	35.1%	55.0%	78.9%	62.6%
		% of Total	5.3%	22.4%	35.0%	62.6%
	agree	Count	24	45	23	92
		% within				
		Life values	64.9%	45.0%	21.1%	37.4%
		% of Total	9.8%	18.3%	9.3%	37.4%
	Total	Count	37	100	109	246
		% within				
		Life values	100.0%	100.0%	100.0%	100.0%
		% of Total	15.0%	40.7%	44.3%	100.0%
Erba	disagree	Count	32	80	87	199
		% within				
		Life values	49.2%	64.5%	75.0%	65.2%
		% of Total	10.5%	26.2%	28.5%	65.2%
	agree	Count	33	44	29	106
		% within				
		Life values	50.8%	35.5%	25.0%	34.8%
		% of Total	10.8%	14.4%	9.5%	34.8%
	Total	Count	65	124	116	305
		% within				
		Life values	100.0%	100.0%	100.0%	100.0%
		% of Total	21.3%	40.7%	38.0%	100.0%

this was linked to the way they viewed immigration. In Sesto, there was great anxiety among respondents concerning unemployment, which led them to state that immigration to their locality had been of large proportions and caused considerable social and integration problems. By contrast, respondents in Erba had appeared fairly relaxed about the economic situation and also about the impact of immigration, which they had considered 'negligible'. In one case, immigration had been constructed as a socio-economic threat, while in the other it was seen as largely irrelevant in terms of the economic and social well-being of the local residents. In my view, this helps explain why young people in Sesto were worried and the least prepared to accept that immigrants needed help with finding work and housing. It is more difficult to interpret the findings in relation to young people in Erba. In their case, unlike in Sesto, there does not seem to be a direct connection between support for a policy of repatriation and cultural assimilation of immigrants and fear of competition on the labour market or worries about the socio-economic situation. Fears that immigrants may represent a cultural threat were also less detectable among Erba respondents, including the younger generation. The only possible explanation is that anti-immigration attitudes in Erba correlate with support for the Northern League, which is to say, the reasons are political and not socio-economic. The issue of why people, particularly young people, voted for the Northern League in Erba will be explored in some detail in Chapter 6.

That attitudes towards immigration policies differed on the basis of perceptions of the economic situation was confirmed by Question 39 (a multiple question), as we saw in Chapter 3. Respondents were asked whether they agreed or disagreed that immigrants created competition on the job market and took away houses and services from Italian citizens. When responses were analysed together, respondents disagreed with all the above statements. However, when they were disaggregated by locality, respondents in Sesto were split on whether immigrants created competition in the job market, while two-thirds of respondents in Erba clearly disagreed. It was mainly Sesto men who were split on this statement, including young men aged 18–30.

Conclusion

This chapter has confirmed the relevance of kinship and friendship networks in the formation of political opinions in Italy. Such networks do not limit their influence to the personal and social sphere but play an important role in the circulation of information regarding politics and policy-making and the development of people's responses and reaction to them. The chapter has also highlighted the different positioning of respondents in relation to change. It has shown that the subcultural traditions associated with both Sesto and Erba account to a large extent for the apparent greater openness to change in the latter compared to the former. This was especially true as far as economic change was concerned. In terms of institutional change, respondents in both localities appeared well disposed both to the process of Europeanisation and to further decentralisation. They differed sharply, however, in terms of their views on the issue of federalism, with respondents in Sesto predominantly opposed to such a policy, and respondents in Erba predominantly in favour. I postulate that this was due to the close association this policy had with the Northern League party in 1994, and therefore with the political fortunes of this party in the two localities. This will be looked at in some depth in Chapters 5 and 6.

Finally, the chapter has considered respondents' opinions in relation to a variety of possible immigration policies. In this case the discriminant was no longer the locality or the particular subculture it was traditionally associated with, rather it was age (associated with different value-systems). As discussed in Part I, Catholicism and communism shared a belief in family values and in solidarity. Class solidarity allowed Sesto to open up to external influences and to respond positively to immigration from outside the locality. Universal, religion-based solidarity, on the other hand, was able to restrain Erba's strong sense of localism and high degree of demographic insularity. Nowadays, solidarity has been eroded in both localities. The younger generation has embraced individualist values to a large extent but it has simultaneously rejected tolerance for the 'other', which is often associated with greater cultural individualism. While in Sesto this rejection appears to be linked to perceptions of economic crisis and competition on the labour market, in Erba this is not the case. It remains to be seen, therefore, the extent to which such attitudes among the young in Erba are associated with the rise of the Northern League and/or with a politicisation and radicalisation of localism. If the latter proves to be the case, then we shall have to revise, in a different context than that examined in Part I, the 'virtuous' effects of cultural individualism. The persistence of localism seems to contradict all predictions of an end to Italy's exceptionalism and of the final completion of the country's modernisation process. The traditional subcultures may have been eroded, but it would be wrong to imply that they are being replaced by a homogeneous and 'modern' (i.e., open-minded and cosmopolitan) culture and society. This is not to say that other western European countries have reached a state of modernity that in some mysterious ways continues to elude Italy. On the contrary, the re-emergence of particularism and localism is a Europe-wide phenomenon, which it would be foolish to ignore or dismiss as pertaining only to the post-communist eastern countries.

5

Voting Behaviour

Introduction

The questionnaire distributed in both Sesto and Erba in 1994 dealt extensively with issues of electoral preference. Question 24 (a multiple question) asked respondents how they and their parents had voted at the 1987 and 1992 political elections. Respondents were asked to tick the party they had voted for, or they could opt for 'Abstained'. In the case of their father and mother, they were also able to give a 'Don't Know' answer. Responses to this question were surprisingly high, as mentioned in the Introduction, although they were considerably higher for the 1992 elections than for the 1987 ones. For 1987, 293 out of 443 respondents in Sesto (66.1 percent of the total number), and 301 out of 445 respondents in Erba (67.6 percent of the total) answered this question. For 1992, 365 out of 443 respondents (82.4 percent) in Sesto, and 385 out of 445 (86.5 percent) in Erba gave a clear indication of the way they had voted. Question 25 asked respondents for which party or coalition of parties they intended to vote at the March 1994 elections. The list of parties was much shorter than in Question 24, due to the fact that when the questionnaire was being devised it was not yet certain which parties would stand for election. Thus the smaller parties were all bundled together under the category 'Other'. Berlusconi's party, on the other hand, did figure in the list. Another category respondents could opt for was 'Undecided'. As it turned out, many more respondents chose this answer in Sesto than in Erba, due to the fact that the survey in Sesto was carried out in early February, whereas in Erba it took place in early March, thus nearer to the dates of the 1994 general elections. The rate of responses was once again remarkably high, with 382 people in

Sesto (86.3 percent of the total number of respondents), and 392 in Erba (88.1 percent) giving an indication of how they intended to vote or whether they were still undecided or wanted to abstain. Question 26 probed motivations for voting preference: respondents had to indicate to what extent, if any, various considerations had influenced their electoral choice. Question 27 asked respondents, who had opted for a different party in 1992 compared to the one they had voted for in 1987, to indicate the main reasons for their changed party preference, out of a list ranging from corruption to a desire for change. Question 34 dealt with the 1993 administrative elections, while Question 35 dealt with the reasons for respondents' electoral choice at these elections.

It is well known that there is a methodological problem with 'recall' questions, based on people's memory of how they voted in past elections (Van der Eijk and Niemöller 1979, Segatti 1997). First, respondents are reluctant to admit that they did not vote. Second, they tend to 'review' their past vote in the light of their voting behaviour in recent elections. Third, they may declare their preference for a party which happens to be popular at the time of the survey, projecting such preference onto the past. These are serious limitations which need to be taken into account. On the basis of the available data, there does seem to be an underestimation of the 'abstention' phenomenon. On the other hand, abstention rates were still rather limited in Italy in 1987 and 1992 and only became prominent at subsequent elections. High levels of uncertainty among respondents in the weeks preceding the 1994 elections (see below) are therefore in line with actual trends among the Italian electorate. It must also be said that respondents would have found it difficult to 'project' their current voting onto the past, at least in 1994, given that so many of the old parties had disappeared. The main distortion may therefore have revolved around an overestimation of the votes for the Northern League in 1987, given that many respondents may have projected backwards their preference for the Northern League in 1992. This is certainly a possibility, although the relatively low percentage of respondents who declared their voting behaviour at the 1987 elections suggests, rather, that many of them could not, or chose not to, remember how they had voted. Responses for 1987 should therefore be treated with care. Responses for 1992, 1993 and 1994 appear to be plausible. In addition, the time span between these elections is a relatively short one, thus minimising distortions.

Bearing in mind the above caveats, the high rate of responses to all the above questions made it possible to analyse in some depth voting trends over a crucial period of time (from the late 1980s to the middle 1990s), as well as the issues of voters' mobility, voters' reasons for party preference and voting patterns in relation to family strategies. The findings in relation to these specific issues will be presented in this chapter. Generational and gender differences will continue to be explored systematically alongside the question of the demise or resilience of the two political subcultures associated with the two localities. Results in terms of voting patterns will be presented separately for Sesto and Erba. This is partly, of course, due to the nature of the main research questions themselves in relation to subcultural voting, but it also received confirmation from the questionnaire data, since for 1992 there were significant positive correlations, as we shall see, between votes for the Partito Comunista Italiano (PCI), which later became the Partito Democratico della Sinistra (PDS), and Sesto as a locality. There was also a positive correlation between votes for both the Northern League and the Democrazia Cristiana (DC), which later became the Partito Popolare Italiano (PPI), and Erba as a locality.

Voting patterns in 1987, 1992 and 1994

Sesto San Giovanni

In Sesto the parties of the left experienced a dramatic decline between 1987 and 1994. The Communist Party had obtained 34.9 percent of the votes in 1987, but this went down to only 20.9 percent in 1992 and 21.9 percent in 1994, the latter figure rising to 29.7 percent if the votes for the Democratic Party of the Left (PDS) and those for *Rifondazione Comunista* are put together. Votes for the Socialist Party amounted to 18.6 percent in 1987, but a mere 1.3 percent in 1994. The full picture shows that, whereas in 1987 the parties of the left (including the Greens) obtained almost two-thirds of the votes, they managed only about a third in 1994.

Did the votes for these parties follow a similar trend among industrial workers? The answer, on the basis of the present survey, is no, although some interesting gender and generational patterns have emerged (Table 5.1).

As Table 5.1 shows, a majority of respondents voted for the left in the 1987 and 1992 elections and also declared that they intended to do so in 1994. The findings suggest the persistence of 'partisan alignment' among factory workers in Sesto, indicating that the decline of the communist subculture in the area ought to be attributed primarily to the decrease in size of the industrial working class (and to the parallel rise of the middle classes and/or of an

Table 5.1 Percentage of votes to the main parties in Sesto and among respondents

	1987	*1992*	*1994*
Official results			
PCI/PDS	34.9	20.9	21.9
Rifondazione	—	8.0	7.8
PSI	18.6	15.1	1.3
Verdi	4.2	4.4	2.9
DC/PPI	20.4	15.3	6.7
Lega	1.3	15.7	12.7
MSI/AN	4.6	3.7	5.9
Forza Italia	—	—	27.0
Others 16.0	16.9	13.8	
All respondents			
PCI/PDS	49.5	43.0	49.7
Rifondazione	—	6.0	2.4
PSI	12.6	7.9	—
Verdi	3.4	4.9	—
DC/PPI	9.6	7.7	5.0
Lega	4.1	12.6	7.3
MSI/AN	2.7	3.3	3.4
Forza Italia	—	—	9.7
Others	18.1	14.6	1.9
Don't Know	—	—	20.6
Total numbers	(293)	(365)	(382)
Male respondents			
PCI/PDS	57.4	50	54.5
Rifondazione	—	6.6	1.6
PSI	9.7	8.6	—
Verdi	2.6	3.7	—
DC/PPI	8.2	7.0	5.4
Lega	4.6	10.7	5.8
MSI/AN	3.1	3.7	5.5
Forza Italia	—	—	5.1
Others	13.4	9.7	0.3
Don't Know	—	—	21.8
Total numbers	(195)	(244)	(257)

Table 5.1—Cont.

	1987	1992	1994
Female respondents			
PCI/PDS	36.4	29.7	39.5
Rifondazione	—	5.4	4.4
PSI	17.0	5.4	—
Verdi	4.5	7.2	—
DC/PPI	12.5	9.0	3.5
Lega	2.5	17.1	10.5
MSI/AN	1.1	0.9	3.5
Forza Italia	—	—	21.1
Others	26.0	26.3	4.3
Don't Know	—	—	13.2
Total numbers	(88)	(111)	(114)

Sources: Comune di Sesto San Giovanni and 1994 survey. Please note that the number of all respondents is higher than the total number of male and female respondents, due to the fact that some respondents did not specify their sex.

underclass made up of precarious workers and the unemployed), rather than to a process of 'uncoupling' between party preference and class. There was a significant positive correlation (Pearson correlation: 0.315) between PDS voters (in 1992) and Sesto as a locality. The above data also shows the failure on the part of both the Northern League and *Forza Italia* to make any considerable inroads into this group.

There were, however, signs that the communist subculture was weakening even among factory workers, although this trend differed considerably in terms of gender and age. It was women whose voting behaviour showed greater discontinuity and who in 1992 had tended to 'betray' the ex-Communist and Socialist Parties, particularly the latter. Whereas in 1987 a majority of women had voted for the Communist and Socialist Parties (53.4 percent), in 1992 this percentage decreased to 40.5 percent (including *Rifondazione Comunista*). Women seemed to cast their votes in favour of new and/or smaller parties. In 1992 these types of parties (Northern League, Greens, Communist Refoundation and a variety of 'other' parties) attracted 56 percent of women's votes, as opposed to 30.7 percent of men's votes. As Figures 5.1, 5.2 and 5.3 show, the parties of the left (including PDS, Communist Refoundation and the Greens, but excluding the PSI), obtained more votes

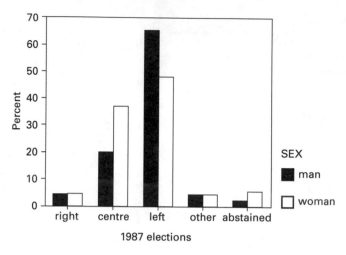

Figure 5.1 Voting behaviour at the 1987 elections (Sesto respondents by sex)

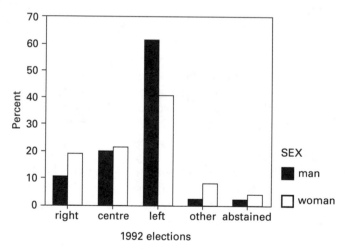

Figure 5.2 Voting behaviour at the 1992 elections (Sesto respondents by sex)

among male respondents than the other parties combined in both 1987 and 1992, and were on course to do the same in 1994.

By contrast, among women respondents votes for the parties of the right and the centre almost equalled those for the left in 1992, with the centre parties coming second and the right parties third

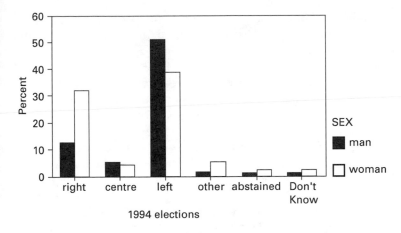

Figure 5.3 Intended voting behaviour at the 1994 elections (Sesto respondents by sex)

(Figure 5.2). In 1987, votes for the parties of the left among women had been above those for the centre and the right combined, with the centre parties a very close second and the right a long way behind (Figure 5.1). By 1994 (Figure 5.3), indications were that the parties of the right and centre combined were again on a par with those of the left, but this time the right came second, and the centre had moved to fourth place (after 'other parties').

The reasons why women and men voted for specific parties dif fered substantially, too. When presented with a list of motivations to account for their party preference in 1992, both men and women indicated 'ideals' and the 'party programme' as important factors influencing their choice. Men, on the other hand, also appeared to have been influenced to a large extent by considerations of loyalty. In fact, a third of all male respondents pointed to 'loyalty' as an important factor behind their vote. Considerations of loyalty also weighed heavily with men when voting at the 1993 administrative elections. By contrast, only a fourth of women mentioned 'loyalty' as a relevant factor for the 1992 political elections and even fewer referred to it for the 1993 administrative elections. Another major difference between male and female voters concerned the import-ance attributed to the level of competence of party candidates. Only 29 percent of men gave this factor any consideration, as opposed to 41 percent of women.

Voting behaviour also differed in terms of age. Young people generally did not vote for the parties of the left to the same extent as older people. The difference was particularly noticeable among male voters. While support for the PDS, PSI and *Rifondazione* in 1992 was well over 50 percent among the 31–40, 41–50 and 51–60 age groups, it stood at just over 30 percent among young men aged 18–30. Conversely, young male voters supported the Northern League and the ex-fascists (*Alleanza Nazionale*) to a much larger extent than older workers. In particular, 24 percent of men aged 18–30 voted for the League in 1992, as opposed to 5 percent in the 31–40 age group, 9 percent in the 41–50 cohort and 6 percent in the 51–60. The reasons for the younger voters' party preference differed from those of older voters. Considerations of loyalty played a lesser part, while the 'party programme' and 'ideals' were more frequently mentioned. Unlike women, therefore, who had tended to favour the smaller parties, young male voters had turned to the Northern League, a party whose territorial and communitarian appeal puts into question any interpretation of these data purely in terms of a more pluralist and individualist attitude on the part of young men.

Why women should have adopted a more pragmatic attitude than men and freed themselves from their class's and families' influence is an interesting question. One answer lies, in my view, in the fact that the communist working-class subculture was male-orientated, in the sense that it took for granted that politics was mainly reserved for men. Back in 1981, Weber (1981a: 204) suggested that the shift in women's party preferences from the DC to the PCI, which had been detected in the 1970s, should not necessarily be seen as 'an indicator of a secularisation process amongst Italian women. It could easily indicate a lack of information, emotional electoral behaviour and a preference for reassuring ideologies rather than cultural pragmatism'. In retrospect, it would seem that women were opening up to cultural pragmatism to a higher degree than was judged possible at the time.

It is interesting that further analysis of the questionnaires showed that a significant number of Sesto women respondents declared their intention of returning or starting to vote for the PDS in 1994, although on the basis of a pragmatic choice rather than on the basis of party loyalty or party identification. While men remained loyal to the party throughout the period, women's voting behaviour appears more varied and changeable. This is confirmed by a comparison between the 1987 and 1992 votes. Asked whether they had voted for a different party in 1992 compared to 1987, less than a fifth of male respondents said yes, as opposed to a third of women.

To sum up the findings in Sesto then, male workers over thirty showed loyalty to the Communist Party, while young men aged 18–30 were divided between the PDS, the Northern League and, to a lesser extent, *Alleanza Nazionale*. As for women, many continued to vote for the parties of the left, but had also adopted a more pragmatic and pluralist approach. They did not as yet subscribe to the phenomenon known as 'voters as consumers', since their motivations for changing allegiance in 1992 betrayed sentiments of impatience with the old parties rather than any degree of shopping around for the 'product' best suited to their needs. The phenomenon of partisan dealignment is also somewhat questionable, since many women changed party preference between 1987 and 1992 but remained within either the left or the right political spectrum. Interestingly, though, many more women than men were contemplating crossing the left-right boundary in 1994.

Erba

In Erba votes for the Christian Democratic Party (DC) – later *Partito Popolare Italiano*, or PPI – went down from 39.2 percent in 1987 to 27.3 percent in 1992 and 11.3 percent in 1994. The Northern League rose from 6.5 percent in 1987 to 27 percent in 1992 and decreased slightly to 26.2 percent in 1994 (Table 5.2).

The findings for Erba reveal a type of political behaviour which cannot be explained with reference to class voting but only with reference to the concept of a territorial political subculture. In Erba there was no relevant difference between the voting behaviour of manual workers, private-sector employees and the self-employed: among all three social groups in the sample the Northern League emerged as the largest single party. There was a significant positive correlation between Northern League voters and Erba as a locality, as well as a significant, though weaker, correlation between DC voters and Erba (Pearson correlation: 0.294 for League voters, 0.173 for DC voters). These findings confirm the persistence of a territorially-based political subculture in an area which until recently had been represented politically by a Catholic party. In other words, it appears that one party has been replaced with another among voters in the private sector but that there is also a substantial continuity with the past because the political consensus is still territorial and inter-classist rather than classist or representing individual choice. In Erba as a whole, however, the Northern League did not gain the same high percentage of votes as in the sample, due in my view to the following:

Table 5.2 Percentage of votes to the main parties in Erba and among respondents

	1987	*1992*	*1994*
Official results			
DC/PPI	39.2	27.3	11.3
League	6.5	27	26.2
PCI/PDS	15.1	7.4	7.7
PSI	16.2	11.8	1.1
Rifondazione	—	3.6	4.0
Verdi	2.5	2.6	2.5
MSI/AN	5.2	3.6	7.2
Forza Italia	—	—	25.5
Others	15.4	16.7	14.5
All respondents			
DC/PPI	29.2	20.3	13.3
League	19.9	40.5	34.2
PCI/PDS	13.3	10.6	15.6
PSI	9.6	3.9	—
Rifondazione	0.8	1.6	—
Verdi	3.7	2.6	—
MSI/AN	7.9	3.9	5.4
Forza Italia	—	—	14.5
Others	15.6	16.6	8.2
Don't Knows	—	—	8.8
Total numbers	(301)	(385)	(392)
Male respondents			
DC/PPI	26.0	18.8	13.3
League	23.7	46.0	40.0
PCI/PDS	12.7	10.3	14.2
PSI	8.7	3.1	—
Verdi	2.9	0.5	—
MSI/AN	7.5	6.3	8
Forza Italia	—	—	12.9
Others	18.5	15.0	5.9
Don't Knows	—	—	5.3
Total numbers	(173)	(224)	(225)

Table 5.2—Cont.

	1987	1992	1994
Female respondents			
DC/PPI	33.6	21.8	11.8
League	15.2	33.3	26.7
PCI/PDS	14.4	11.5	18.0
PSI	10.4	5.1	—
Verdi	4.8	5.8	—
MSI/AN	1.6	0.7	1.9
Forza Italia	-	-	17.4
Others	20.0	21.8	14.9
Don't Knows	-	-	9.3
Total numbers	(125)	(156)	(161)

Sources: Comune di Erba and 1994 survey. Please note that the number of 'Don't Knows' in Erba were considerably lower than in Sesto due almost certainly to the fact that the Erba survey took place at a later stage, nearer the time of the 1994 elections.

1. The Northern League's 'inter-classist', territorial appeal is strongest among that section of the population which identifies with the private 'productive' sector, regardless of people's status within it.
2. There are clearly also voters whose political opinion fluctuates and whose votes have been 'freed' by the collapse of the traditional Catholic subculture. Potentially these are 'rational choice' voters.

What is particularly interesting, though, is that among Erba's respondents, unlike in Sesto, a process of partisan dealignment seems to have been under way (1987 election results) but this process was reversed and replaced by new political alignments based, once again, on highly partisan criteria (territorial and racialised rather than Catholic and solidarist). If this were the case, we are faced with a situation where the process of partisan dealignment and individualist voting behaviour cannot be considered irreversible, as is often the assumption in industrial and post-industrial societies. New collective political identities can emerge and reverse that process. This finding seems consistent with the reverse post-materialist theory of populist and radical-right voting (Kitschelt 1995).

As in Sesto, women showed greater mobility in voting patterns, whereas men were more solidly behind one party, in this case the Northern League. In terms of left–right positioning, in 1987 male respondents opted for the parties of the centre, followed by the parties of the right, with the left trailing in third place (Figure 5.4).

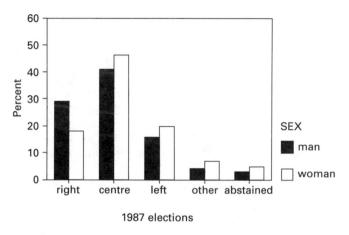

1987 elections

Figure 5.4 Voting behaviour at the 1987 elections (Erba respondents by sex)

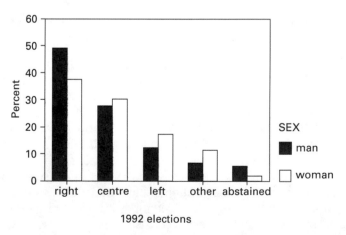

1992 elections

Figure 5.5 Voting behaviour at the 1992 elections (Erba respondents by sex)

Among women respondents the centre came first, followed by the left and then the right. In 1992, as Figure 5.5 shows, men opted for the right, followed by the centre, with the left still trailing behind. Among male respondents, votes for the parties of the right outnumbered those for the left and the centre combined. In the same year, women also voted predominantly for the right, but the centre came a close second. Also, among women votes for the right were heavily outnumbered by votes for the centre and the left combined. In 1994, both men and women opted for the parties of the right, with the left second and the centre third (Figure 5.6).

The main difference was that men were still voting predominantly for the Northern League, while women opted for *Forza Italia*. Unlike in Sesto, age did not represent a significant variable, since the Northern League attracted comparable percentages among all age cohorts, with the only exception of women aged 41–50, among whom Christian Democracy remained the largest party in 1992. In general women's reasons for voting for the League were more pragmatic than men's.

Given the territorial and localist appeal of the Northern League, and the fact that previous studies have shown that support for this party increases among Northerners, I decided to disaggregate the votes to the Northern League in 1992 on the basis of geographical

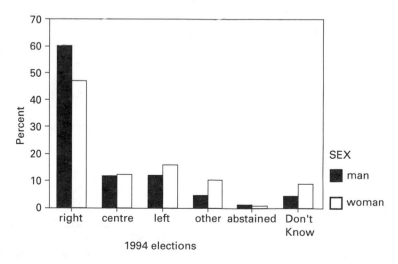

Figure 5.6 Intended voting behaviour at the 1994 elections (Erba respondents by sex)

origins. The results were quite striking, since I found that there was massive support for the Northern League in 1992 among respondents born in the North with northern parents, while there was a clear rejection of this party among people with southern origins (even if they themselves were born in the North). It was noticeable, though, that this distinction applied primarily to men, since women appeared to have voted for the Northern League irrespective of their regional origins. This suggests that the territorial, communitarian, quasi-ethnic appeal of the party was clearly perceived by and directly appealed to male voters, whereas it was not a principal factor among women.

A further difference emerged when the attitudes of Northern League voters were compared to those of voters of other parties. Whereas both male and female Northern League voters subscribed to the party's flagship ideas of a federal Italy and greater regional autonomy and supported its programme of privatisation, the orientations of non-Northern League voters differed considerably by gender (Table 5.3).

As Table 5.3 shows, men were generally much more receptive to the ideas and policies put forward by the Northern League, irrespective of their party preference. Indeed a majority of all men subscribed, either strongly or moderately, to the idea of a federal Italy (including a majority of supporters of the Socialist, Green and Radical Parties, as well as half of PDS and PPI voters) and of a Europe of the Regions (including a majority of PPI and PSI voters). By contrast, women were more clearly split, with only Northern League voters subscribing to the idea of a federal Italy or a Europe of the Regions. This finding suggests that the party may in future widen its appeal among male voters, whereas its female electorate is unlikely to increase. It also indicates that for men communitarian and localist allegiances as well as shared values continue to be very important and to cut across political party preferences.

Finally, in Erba, compared to Sesto, the influence of the Church upon voting behaviour was considerable, confirming the Catholic voters' switch from Christian Democracy to the Northern League. In Erba there were 194 respondents (44 percent of the total sample) who were practising Catholics and regular Church attendants. Of these, 166 indicated which party they voted for in the 1992 elections: 32 percent had voted for the Catholic Party, and 44 percent for the Northern League.

Table 5.3 Respondents' views on policy issues (Erba respondents by sex) (Percentages of respondents in favour)

	MEN				WOMEN			
	All	Strongly Northern League Voters	All	Moderately Northern League Voters	All	Strongly Northern League Voters	All	Moderately Northern League Voters
Wider Regional Autonomy	51	73	33	21	48	77	32	15
Federal Italy	46	73	22	19	34	74	14	13
Europe of Regions	29	36	37	43	18	38	27	33
Privatisations	35	45	30	31	25	38	43	43
Houses and work to residents	39	52	29	28	34	52	37	31

Voting behaviour at the 1993 administrative elections

Table 5.4 shows the way respondents in Sesto voted at the 1993 administrative elections compared to the 1992 general elections.

Respondents voted largely in the same way as they had done at the 1992 general elections. However, further analysis of voters' behaviour in 1992 and 1993 indicated that in some areas there were also signs of voters' mobility. The most loyal of all were PDS voters, since 91% of those who had voted PDS in 1992 continued to vote for this party in 1993. The PDS also made some considerable gains, mainly at the expense of Communist Refoundation and the Social Democratic Party. Also loyal were voters of the extreme right (MSI/*Alleanza Nazionale*): 83 percent of those who had voted for this party in 1992 reconfirmed their party preference in 1993. Next came Northern League voters (76 percent), PSI voters (76 percent) and Catholic party (PPI) voters (74 percent). The degree of loyalty to a specific party was therefore considerably high, although PSI, PPI and Northern League voters were considerably less loyal than PDS voters. While the PSI and the DC/PPI registered a net loss of votes, the League made a net gain. Voters of the Socialist Party and the DC had defected in various directions, with a few favouring the Northern League. The latter itself lost some voters but also made further gains at the expense of other

Table 5.4 Voting behaviour at the 1993 administrative elections (Sesto respondents)

		Frequency	Percent	Valid Percent	Cumulative Percent
Valid	DC	26	5.9	6.8	6.8
	PSI	29	6.5	7.6	14.4
	PDS	180	40.6	47.0	61.4
	Lega Nord	48	10.8	12.5	73.9
	MSI	15	3.4	3.9	77.8
	Other	67	15.1	17.5	95.3
	Abstained	18	4.1	4.7	100.0
Total		383	86.5	100.0	
Missing		60	13.5		
Total		443	100.0		

parties. Voters who defected both from and to the Northern League were scattered across the political spectrum.

In terms of gender, responses confirmed that men in Sesto were less likely than women to defect to other parties, although even among women voters the degree of loyalty to a specific party was high. Interestingly, the degree of loyalty among women PDS voters was the highest of all: 96 percent of female voters who had cast their vote for the PDS in 1992 reconfirmed their choice in 1993. It was mainly among women voters of other parties that the rate of mobility was higher than for men. Indeed, the gains registered by the PDS in 1993 compared to 1992 were almost entirely due to women voters switching their preference from a variety of parties to the PDS.

The main reasons for respondents voting as they did at the administrative elections can be seen in Table 5.5.

Nearly half of all respondents (44.9 percent) stated that they had voted on the basis of considerations of class interests. This figure was mainly due to PDS voters, 60 percent of whom pointed to this specific reason for their party preference. Next came the competence of the candidates (18 percent of all respondents), followed by considerations of local interests (17.7 percent) and loyalty (17.4 percent). PDS voters subscribed to loyalty as their main reason for voting PDS after class interests, followed by local interests. Conversely, Northern League voters indicated that the party's economic competence had been their primary motive for choosing it, followed by its commitment to local interests.

Respondents' votes at the 1993 administrative elections compared to the 1992 general elections in Erba show that the degree of

Table 5.5 Factors influencing voters in 1993 (Sesto respondents)

		Frequency	Percent	Valid Percent	Cumulative Percent
Valid	loyalty	61	13.8	17.4	17.4
	local interests	62	14.0	17.7	35.1
	economic competence	7	1.6	2.0	37.1
	class interests	157	35.4	44.9	82.0
	competence of candidates	63	14.2	18.0	100.0
	Total	350	79.0	100.0	
Missing		93	21.0		
Total	443	100.0			

loyalty to a specific party was high, just like it had been in Sesto (Table 5.6).

The main difference was that in Erba Northern League voters, as well as PDS voters, turned out to be the most loyal of all, since 95 percent of those who had voted PDS, and 88 percent of those who had voted Northern League in 1992, reconfirmed their party preference in 1993. The figures for the other main parties were also fairly high, with 74 percent of voters of the Catholic party and 79 percent of MSI/*Alleanza Nazionale* voters remaining loyal to their party. The only exception were PSI voters, of whom only 40 percent remained loyal in 1993. The rest defected to the PPI and the Northern League.

Voters who defected from the Northern League in 1993 gave their preference to the Catholic party, while voters who defected from Christian Democracy gave their preference to the Northern League (as well as to the smaller parties). This is another sign that both type of voters have a specific trait in common, which is their Catholic background. This aspect will be analysed in depth in the next section.

In terms of gains and losses, the Northern League was astoundingly stable. The Catholic party registered further losses, and the PDS gained, attracting new voters mainly from the left (Communist Refoundation and Green Party voters). As for gender, there was hardly any difference in behaviour among Northern League voters, while among voters of other parties women proved more mobile. In terms of their reasons for voting as they did, these can be seen in Table 5.7.

Table 5.6 Voting behaviour at the 1993 administrative elections (Erba respondents)

		Frequency	Percent	Valid Percent	Cumulative Percent
Valid	DC	69	15.5	17.8	17.8
	PSI	10	2.2	2.6	20.4
	PDS	52	11.7	13.4	33.9
	Lega Nord	151	33.9	39.0	72.9
	MSI	15	3.4	3.9	76.7
	Other	74	16.6	19.1	95.9
	Abstained	16	3.6	4.1	100.0
	Total	387	87.0	100.0	
Missing		58	13.0		
Total		445	100.0		

Table 5.7 Factors influencing voters in 1993 (Erba respondents)

		Frequency	Percent	Valid Percent	Cumulative Percent
Valid	loyalty	67	15.1	19.1	19.1
	local interests	110	24.7	31.3	50.4
	economic competence	11	2.5	3.1	53.6
	class interests	71	16.0	20.2	73.8
	competence of candidates	92	20.7	26.2	100.0
	Total	351	78.9	100.0	
Missing		94	21.1		
Total		445	100.0		

Most respondents (31.3 percent) indicated that the chosen party's commitment to local interests and issues had been their primary motivation. This was followed by the competence of candidates (26.2 percent), class interests (20.2 percent), and finally loyalty (19.1 percent). Northern League voters opted overwhelmingly (57 percent) for the party's commitment to local interests, followed by class interests. Voters for the Catholic party put considerations of loyalty first, on a par with the competence of candidates. PDS voters listed class interests as their main reason for voting for this party, followed by considerations of loyalty.

Voters' mobility

The issue of voters' mobility is crucial for an analysis of the behaviour of the Italian electorate in the aftermath of the collapse of the First Republic, as well as for an understanding of the likely fate of political subcultures in a decade of great political turmoil. Many commentators have focused on voters' mobility, as mentioned in the Introduction. While initially they tended to emphasise the extent of this phenomenon, thus heralding the emergence of a pluralist and individualist electorate, more recently there has been a cautious reappraisal of electoral trends. In important new work, D'Alimonte and Bartolini distinguished between intra-bloc and inter-bloc electoral volatility, and reached the conclusion that 'we should be careful in characterising the electorate as deprived of its historical identity and free to choose according to the rules of the market' (1997: 125). In particular, they argued that mobility had increased, however it was more pronounced in terms of parties' alliances than in terms of voters' shifts from one bloc to another: 'Parties have changed, but voters less so' (Ibid.: 132). Whatever mobility there had been, it had taken place at the expense of the centre parties, and it had favoured primarily the new centre-right groups, rather than the left parties (Ibid.: 124). This specific hypothesis will now be put to the test with reference to voters in subcultural areas. Questionnaire responses in both Sesto and Erba for the general elections of 1987, 1992 and 1994, as well as for the administrative elections of 1993, allowed a detailed analysis of both the extent and the specific nature of voters' mobility in each locality. What kind of picture emerges from the data?

Starting with the general elections of 1987 and 1992, the picture is one of high levels of mobility. In Sesto, the most stable voters were DC and PDS voters. 85.2 percent of respondents who voted DC in 1987 (twenty-three out of twenty-seven people) did so in 1992; two voters defected to the League. There were a few gains, but overall the DC lost one vote compared to 1987. Similarly, 86.7 percent of respondents who voted PCI in 1987 (124 out of 143) voted PDS in 1992; eight voted Communist Refoundation, and another seven defected to the Northern League. If we consider the votes for the PDS and Communist Refoundation together, there was hardly any change between 1987 and 1992. By contrast, only 51.4 percent of PSI voters remained loyal to their party (19 out of 37), whereas eleven defected to the Northern League and the rest to a variety of parties both on the right and on the left. As for the Northern League, 91.7 percent of respondents who had voted for this party in 1987 (eleven out of twelve) reconfirmed their preference in 1992; in addition, the party gained substantially from the PSI (eleven votes) and the PDS (seven votes), as well as from a variety of other parties both on the right and on the left, moving up to second place after the PDS.

In short, the data emerging from Sesto appears to confirm D'Alimonte and Bartolini's (1997) hypothesis. The voters lost by the centre parties (DC and PSI) favoured primarily the Northern League. The picture, however, is complicated by the fact that in Sesto the PSI was always in government with the Communist Party and tended to be seen primarily as a party of the left. If we consider that the Northern League gained votes from both the PSI and the PDS we can see that, rather than gaining from the centre, it succeeded in eroding the traditional left subculture of the town. The Northern League can nevertheless be considered an anomalous party of the right, since it is also a party with strong localist and regionalist connotations. It is helpful, therefore, to analyse how respondents intended to vote at the 1994 political elections, to see whether another party of the right, *Forza Italia*, was likely to gain from the centre and/or the left. Responses to Questions 24A and 25 were numerically high (357), which means that it was possible to draw a meaningful comparison from them. For reasons of clarity, it should be noted here that the total number of votes for each party will differ from that given above, which was based on a cross analysis of the 1987 and 1992 results. On the basis of a direct comparison between responses to Questions 24A and 25, the new Catholic Party, the PPI, was clearly going to lose votes, down from twenty-eight to nineteen, in favour of *Forza Italia* (four), the Northern League (two) and the PDS (two); it was also going to make a few gains from the PSI, while three people were undecided. The PDS was to gain substantially, up from 157 to 187, primarily at the expense of Communist Refoundation, followed by the Greens, PSI, the Social Democrats, the Radicals and even the Northern League. These figures confirm the party's newly found ability to shed its left-wing, subcultural image, and to attract votes from the centre, as well as from the left. Another eleven people who had voted PDS in 1992 were still undecided. The Northern League was going to lose quite heavily, down from forty-one votes to twenty-seven, in favour of both *Forza Italia* and the PDS. *Forza Italia* looked set to emerge as the second largest party, with thirty-six voters declaring their intention to choose it, gaining votes at the expense of the Northern League, the PSI, the DC and other smaller parties. On the basis of these figures, *Forza Italia* was gaining from the parties of the centre and of the right, but was not able to erode the predominance of the PDS, as the Northern League had started to do in 1992. The Northern League's force, however, appeared spent.

Who were the mobile voters in Sesto in terms of gender and age? They were mainly women and the young. Among men, mobility was predominantly intra-bloc. The only exception was a shift of votes in favour of the Northern League at the expense of both the DC and the PSI between 1987 and 1992. In 1994, compared to two years before, there was hardly any inter-bloc mobility: votes for *Forza Italia* came to a large extent from the Northern League and the DC, while the MSI/*Alleanza Nazionale* seemed destined to remain at a standstill. Among women, there was a shift of votes away from the PDS towards smaller parties of the left and the centre, as well as the Northern League, between 1987 and 1992. In

1994 many returned to vote for the PDS, but a large number also intended to shift to *Forza Italia* from a variety of parties from across the political spectrum (predominantly from parties of the centre and the right). It is thus extremely difficult to identify a clear pattern among women voters. The difference in voting behaviour between men and women was also noticeable among young voters. Young male voters, in fact, showed minimal inter-bloc mobility between 1992 and 1994, and looked set to favour the PDS. Those who had voted Northern League in 1992 were now split between this party and *Forza Italia*. Among young female voters, by contrast, *Forza Italia* was clearly going to emerge as the main party, gaining votes from left, right and centre.

To sum up, inter-bloc voters' mobility in Sesto was extremely limited among male voters, involving mainly a section of young male voters between 1987 and 1992. It was much higher among female voters, and highest of all among young female voters. Whereas among men mobility was largely restricted to the period 1987–1992, women voters continued to shift party preference between 1992 and 1994. As for the hypothesis put forward by D'Alimonte and Bartolini (1997), it is partly confirmed, in the sense that many DC and PSI voters moved to the right, and specifically to the Northern League in 1992 and to *Forza Italia* in 1994. Nevertheless, in Sesto PSI voters also moved to the PDS. More importantly, the Northern League appeared able to erode the left subculture among factory workers in 1992, whereas *Forza Italia* did not seem up to this task. Thus in 1994 the PDS was maintaining its core of supporters and attracting new support, a strategy which was to pay off at the 1994 local elections and the 1996 general elections.

In Erba, many voters also remained loyal to their party between 1987 and 1992, but PSI and DC voters by and large did not. The most loyal of all were Northern League voters, since fifty-five out of sixty people who had voted for this party in 1987 reconfirmed their vote in 1992. The Northern League overall gained very substantially, moving from sixty to one-hundred and sixteen votes, at the expense of the DC (eighteen votes), the PSI (thirteen votes) and the MSI (six votes), as well as the smaller centre parties. It also attracted the votes of previous non-voters (six). The second most loyal voters were PDS voters, with thirty-five out of forty voters reconfirming their preference to this party. The PDS overall was extremely stable, with forty votes in 1987 and thirty-nine in 1992. The PSI lost heavily, with only eleven voters out of twenty-nine recasting their vote for this party, while fifty-seven out of eighty-eight voters confirmed their preference for the DC. Overall the PSI fell to thirteen votes, and the DC fell to sixty-five votes. Thus the DC was the main party among Erba respondents in 1987, but fell to second place in 1992.

It is clear that the role of the Northern League in Erba mirrored that played by this party in Sesto, in the sense that in both cases the Northern League showed the ability to weaken the dominant subcultural parties. In Erba, however, it was not a question of an erosion of the dominant subculture, as of the completion of its break-up, which had already started in 1987. In Erba the Northern League triumphed at the expense of the DC and the PSI, that is, the two parties which had until then dominated local and national government. Indeed, whereas the DC was still, in 1987, the dominant party among Erba respondents, in 1992 its popularity had fallen so low that it had just above half the number of votes cast for the Northern League. Unlike in Sesto, there was no defection of voters from the left parties to the Northern League.

How were Erba respondents likely to cast their votes in 1994? To what extent was *Forza Italia* going to threaten the supremacy of the Northern League? A cross-comparison of responses to both Question 24A and Question 25 (376 respondents had replied to both questions) gives us a fairly clear indication of the way voters were going to behave. At that time, just before the 1994 general elections, 113 out of 152 voters declared their intention of recasting their vote for the League (74.3 percent). Loyalty to the Northern League was therefore still in evidence, but was not as high as between 1987 and 1992. A number of people (sixteen) were planning to switch to *Forza Italia*, whereas eight voters planned to defect to the Northern League from the PPI. Overall the Northern League seemed to be losing votes, down from 152 to 130, although eleven voters were still undecided. *Forza Italia* seemed set to gain fifty-six votes among Erba respondents, moving to third place after the Northern League and the PDS. It appeared on course to gain sixteen votes from the Northern League, nineteen votes from the PPI, seven votes from the PSI, and seven votes from a variety of smaller parties. The PPI appeared on the verge of falling into fourth place, losing votes to both *Forza Italia* and the Northern League. Finally, the PDS appeared set to move up into second place, gaining a substantial number of votes (up from thirty-nine to sixty-one) at the expense of a variety of parties from across the political spectrum, although predominantly from the left and the centre.

Thus among Erba respondents there was greater mobility than

had parents who also voted for this party. This was also true of young PDS voters (twelve out of fifteen). The ability of political parties to attract the votes of entire families, rather than individuals, emerges clearly from Table 5.8. This situation was even more in evidence in Erba, as will be shown below.

Women workers, however, did not vote like their parents to the same extent. Although this could be attributed at least in part to their husbands' influence, many women who did vote like their parents were married while a number of young unmarried women still living at home did not. As for the influence of the Church, neither men's nor women's voting behaviour appeared to be linked to their religious upbringing and beliefs, although this was more marked for women than men.

The more pluralist attitude on the part of women workers appears confirmed by other responses related to political socialisation and the role of the family and the Church. Despite the fact that many more women than men attended Church regularly and had formed their political ideas in the family, women were only slightly more likely than men to have voted for the Christian Democratic Party in 1992 and much less likely to have voted like their parents. Even young male voters voted largely in line with their parents in 1992, unlike young female ones. These findings appear to indicate a real cleavage between past and present women's political behaviour, since traditionally, as we saw, women were identified with political conservatism which in turn was attributed in great part to their degree of religiosity. The findings also indicate that for men, unlike women, political loyalty extended to their families as well as their class.

As for social networks, in Sesto the largest category of respondents stated that 'a number' of their friends shared their political opinions. This was true of all voters, although in the case of PDS voters an almost equal category said that 'many/the vast majority' of their friends shared their political ideas (Table 5.9).

Table 5.8 Respondents who voted in line with parents (Sesto) (1992 elections)

	All	Men	Women
Total number of respondents indicating parents' votes	(233)	(148)	(79)
of these, % voting like their parents	49	52	42
% voting PDS like their parents	69	73	47

Table 5.9 PDS voters sharing the same political ideas with family and friends (Sesto respondents)

			Voters		
			other voters	PDS voters	Total
family and friends sharing same political ideas	just a few	Count	41	15	56
		% within voters	15.8%	9.7%	13.5%
		% of Total	9.9%	3.6%	13.5%
	a considerable number	Count	117	62	179
		% within voters	45.0%	40.0%	43.1%
		% of Total	28.2%	14.9%	43.1%
	many	Count	30	34	64
		% within voters	11.5%	21.9%	15.4%
		% of Total	7.2%	8.2%	15.4%
	the vast majority	Count	17	25	42
		% within voters	6.5%	16.1%	10.1%
		% of Total	4.1%	6.0%	10.1%
	don't know	Count	55	19	74
		% within voters	21.2%	12.3%	17.8%
		% of Total	13.3%	4.6%	17.8%
Total		Count	260	155	415
		% within voters	100.0%	100.0%	100.0%
		% of Total	62.7%	37.3%	100.0%

Therefore it was among PDS voters that a sense of 'shared party preference' existed, which reflects the fact that it is the dominant local party. It also confirms that social, as well as kinship networks, reinforce class allegiances and have not been displaced by them.

As we saw in Part I, Erba respondents appeared to make much greater use of primary associations when it came to forming their political ideas and to exchange political opinions. Accordingly, there was greater evidence of families and even groups of friends voting en bloc in Erba than in Sesto, particularly when one takes into account the very considerable voting shifts registered among Erba respondents between 1987 and 1992. The Northern League, in particular, despite being a relative newcomer, had been able to attract the votes of entire families, rather than single individuals (Table 5.10).

A detailed analysis of the responses showed that in most of these cases family members switched simultaneously to the Northern League, and that in some cases it was young people who voted first for this party, *followed at a later election by their parents*. Thus, while in 1987 a majority of young Northern League voters had parents who had not voted for this party, in 1992 a process of political alignment within the family had taken place, with a majority of young Northern League voters having parents who did. Political socialisation thus seems to work in two directions, from parents to children but also vice versa, a possibility not contemplated by theories of rational choice voting. I will come back to this point in my conclusions.

In terms of friends, in Erba there were more respondents than in Sesto claiming that 'many/a majority' of their friends shared their political ideas. This was true of both DC and Northern League voters, but especially the latter. Indeed, a majority of all Northern League voters stated that most of their friends shared their political opinions (Table 5.11).

Table 5.10 Respondents who voted in line with parents (Erba) (1992 elections)

	All	*Men*	*Women*
Total number of respondents indicating parents' votes	(258)	(126)	(118)
of these, % voting like their parents	45	52	37
% voting DC/PPI like parents	74	85	61
% voting League like parents	51	47	56
% voting PCI/PDS like parents	6	74	29

Table 5.11 Northern League voters sharing the same political ideas with family and friends (Erba respondents)

			Voters	
		other voters	League voters	Total
family and friends sharing same political ideas	just a few			
	Count	32	6	38
	% within voters	11.5%	3.9%	8.8%
	% of Total	7.4%	1.4%	8.8%
	a considerable number			
	Count	139	52	191
	% within voters	50.0%	33.5%	44.1%
	% of Total	32.1%	12.0%	44.1%
	many			
	Count	36	55	91
	% within voters	12.9%	35.5%	21.0%
	% of Total	8.3%	12.7%	21.0%
	the vast majority			
	Count	25	24	49
	% within voters	9.0%	15.5%	11.3%
	% of Total	5.8%	5.5%	11.3%
	don't know			
	Count	46	18	64
	% within voters	16.6%	11.6%	14.7%
	% of Total	10.6%	4.2%	14.7%
Total	Count	278	155	433
	% within voters	100.0%	100.0%	100.0%
	% of Total	64.2%	35.8%	100.0%

There were significant gender differences, since women respondents did not share their political ideas with their friends to the same extent. The Northern League in Erba clearly mirrors the PDS in Sesto, in that its voters have a sense of 'shared party preference', indicating, once again, that this party has come to dominate local politics in a way that is cultural as much as electoral. Social networks thus appear to supersede class bonding in Erba, pointing to a form of political socialisation which cannot be explained with reference to either the 'class-based partisan alignment' or the 'rational choice' model.

A comparison between Erba and Annonay

In the same way as I introduced some of the findings on the French site of Vénissieux in Chapter 1, when discussing social identities, I will now present some of the findings on the other French locality which was matched with Erba, that is, Annonay. Even taking into account the less successful outcome of the questionnaire survey in France, in fact, there were macroscopic differences between Erba and Annonay in the voting behaviour of respondents which will contribute to a better understanding of Italian political subcultures.

Annonay is an industrial town characterised until the mid-1960s by an almost exclusive structure of family-owned firms in a variety of manufacturing sectors. Since then, there have been changes in the industrial structure of the town, including some take-over of local firms and the fragmentation of the textile sector. Annonay was and remains a working-class town, although many workers owned some agricultural land, and therefore enjoyed a semi-autonomous status, similar to Erba workers. In 1990, 60 percent of the active population were still classified as industrial workers. Sectoral divisions were more important than class divisions as the major determinants of local sub-systems, and there was a rigid vertical stratification around the town's two dominant sub-systems: leather versus paper (Ganne 1984). There was a strong corporatist culture, divided between the craft-based professionalism of the leather industry, and the Catholic paternalism of paper manufacturing. This set of sub-systems unravelled in the 1970s, provoking an identity crisis.

Despite its working-class base, Annonay was far from being a 'red' town. Politically, there was a 'tranquil dominance of the right' (Ganne 1984), and a gradual transition from a 'notable' system to one of 'local management' (Ganne 1987). There was also a strong streak of far-right anti-republican support in some areas (going back to the 1870s), reflecting Catholic ascendancy. The moderate right was mainly associated with the liberal professions and the presence of artisans and small entrepreneurs.

This brief description of the socio-economic and cultural charac- teristics of Annonay underlines both its similarities to Erba and dis- similarities compared to Vénissieux and Sesto. Yet in terms of voting behaviour Annonay differed sharply from Erba and pre- sented greater similarities to the other two localities. In Annonay there was a much greater percentage of votes for the parties of the left among respondents than was the case for the locality as a whole. This at one level was not surprising, since the largest group of respondents in the town were factory workers who appeared to subscribe to socialist and communist ideals in roughly the same way as, although to a lesser degree than, their fellow workers in Vénissieux and in Sesto. At another level, however, the results con- trasted neatly with the Erba ones. Despite the fact that the two towns shared a tradition of craft-based professionalism and Catholic paternalism, and although most respondents in Annonay were also employed in small- and medium-sized firms (with up to 500 employees), they did not seem to express the same political values as other social groups in the private sector. Indeed, when the Annonay sample was disaggregated according to occupational status (i.e., factory workers, self-employed, private-sector employ- ees), there was confirmation of this. In particular, a majority of respondents in the 'self-employed' category were found to cast their votes for the parties of the right, as opposed to factory workers who had voted predominantly for the parties of the left. Class voting therefore seems dominant in Annonay, where class is still defined in accordance with 'traditional' occupational status, rather than 'market situation', thus contradicting Kitschelt's approach (1995).

In Erba and Annonay there was no evidence of the existence of comparable political subcultures, despite comparable socio-econ- omic structures. Territorial subcultures based upon shared values and a sense of collective identity simply do not appear to have the same impact upon political behaviour in France as in Italy. Clearly in Annonay national, class-based cleavages prevail over any sense of local identity. This is not to say, however, that a sense of local iden- tity no longer exists, but rather that its effects upon political behav- iour differ fundamentally from those that have been detected in Italy.

Conclusions

To conclude, in Sesto men were still committed to the proletarian subculture, mainly out of loyalty, but they were also showing signs of contemplating 'exit' from public activity altogether, retreating to a private network of family and friends, driven by disappointment and disillusionment, according to the classic Hirschman's (1970) theory. There has been, however, no real political dealignment among them, so much so that one could envisage the situation changing if, for example, the unions were to adopt a higher profile or the latent fascist–antifascist tensions were to come to the fore. However, the decreasing size of the Sesto working class will alone ensure that the male workers' subculture will become increasingly entrenched.

As for women, they appear to have discarded any subcultural allegiances and, in so doing, to have 'emancipated' from Church influence and partially also from the influence of the family. Politically, this has led them to cast their votes more widely and to change party preferences more frequently. Loyalty to a group or a class is much less in evidence than among men. The Sesto findings seem to indicate that the recent collapse in Italy of the traditional ideologies may have had, as one of its major consequences, the effect of freeing women from the old constraints and making it easier for them to become detached from a subculture that has never really represented them directly. On the contrary, for male workers this collapse has marked the end of a dream and has resulted in great disappointment. The findings also confirm that women voters have become an increasingly mobile electorate, probably swaying the election results in the town in favour of the centre-right in 1994 and of the centre-left in 1996. A similar trend at national level is also plausible. Nevertheless, women voters seem to be lacking a collective identity and political 'clout', at least when compared to men's persisting 'bloc voting'.

Women's greater voting mobility does not mean that they will not vote for the PDS. On the contrary, they may be increasingly well disposed towards this party, now that it is striving to lose its subcultural connotations. When the PDS replaced the PCI, women delegates played a significant role in defining the new party, so much so that the new statute stated unequivocally that the PDS was a 'party for men and women' (Guadagnini 1993: 177). Since then, the PDS has shown itself open to women's membership and representation, following a trend already started by the old PCI. In

Sesto, too, the PDS impressed me with its will to attract new voters and members and to portray a new image, distancing itself from an all-too-close identification with a traditional working-class subculture. My interview with the PDS Mayor of Sesto, Sig. Pennati, (at the time he was only a candidate for the post) established quite clearly that he intended to steer his party away from the traditional proletarian subculture and any nostalgic vision of Sesto as the 'Stalingrad of Italy'. Although still considerably relying on the male workers' vote, and thus to their attachment to a subculture, the ex-Communist Party itself is now actively promoting partisan dealignment. The results of the 1994 administrative elections in Sesto went surprisingly well for the PDS after the negative results of the March 1994 general elections, a further sign that the increasingly middle-class local electorate is prepared to vote for it on the basis of its programme and past administrative record in the town. On this basis the Communist subculture is destined to die out slowly with the decrease in the size of the industrial working class, but the resilience of the PDS is assured. Unsurprisingly, at the 1996 political elections the Sesto constituency elected the candidate of the left, thus reversing the 1994 outcome.

In Erba, too, the recent demise of the traditional ideologies may be interpreted as having freed voters – both men and women – from the old constraints and made it easier for them to switch to a different party. There are, however, three important considerations to be made regarding this seemingly unproblematic interpretation of voters' behaviour in Erba. First, a substantial switch of votes from the PSI and the DC to the Northern League had already taken place in 1987, that is, *before* the Italian political system began to unravel and the old ideologies crumbled. Second, by 1992 voters' dealignment was replaced by realignment, around the Northern League party. Third, as in Sesto, men proved to be much less mobile voters than women. Once they shifted their votes to the Northern League, a process that was largely completed by 1992, they remained substantially loyal to this party. Among women voters, by contrast, mobility was as much in evidence between 1992 and 1994 as it had been in the period 1987–1992. The general impression is that in 1987 and 1992 men switched from one subcultural party to another, whereas women were more pluralist in their voting intentions. The fact that the Northern League was a new party probably explains why many women voted for it and even presented themselves as candidates, despite what has been defined as 'a party culture that favours traditional gender roles'

(Guadagnini 1993: 200). When *Forza Italia* appeared on the political scene, women voters, particularly the young, switched in large numbers to this party.

To sum up, the evidence appears to confirm that the Northern League is a new subcultural party (Cento Bull 1992 and 1993), but also indicates that this party enjoys a more limited though also much more clearly focused appeal compared to the old DC. Its appeal among industrial workers focuses sharply on northern males. As in Sesto, there was little evidence of partisan dealignment among male workers. The party they voted for may have changed, however political alignments continued to be based on highly partisan criteria (territorial and racialised rather than Catholic and solidarist).

In the next Chapter I will present an 'identikit' of PDS, DC, and Northern League voters in the two areas, with a view to establishing the cultural and political beliefs of these three categories of voters, and to identifying the main dividing lines, but also any commonality of ideas and aspirations, between them. Specifically, the aim will be to understand what attracted voters towards the Northern League from two subcultures at the opposite end of the political spectrum. In the case of Erba, it will also be important to examine whether the party represents a complete break from the Catholic subculture or whether there are shared values among both PPI and Northern League voters.

6

Political Ideologies and Localism

Introduction

In Chapter 4 it was found that the political attitudes and beliefs of respondents varied significantly on the basis of the locality they lived in, and to a lesser extent on the basis of generational and gender differences. The general hypothesis put forward was that this depended to a large extent on the specific subculture(s) people were embedded in. Both the socialist and communist subculture in Sesto and the Catholic subculture in Erba, with their emphasis on solidarity, largely appeared to account for attitudes of tolerance towards outsiders. In Sesto, class solidarity also appeared to account for the prevailing hostility towards neo-liberal economic policies, including privatisation and lower taxes, and aversion towards federalism, which at the time of the survey was closely associated with Northern League politics. Conversely, the market-orientated, small-business culture of Erba appeared to explain the greater favour neo-liberal policies encountered in this locality, among Catholic and lay respondents alike.

Chapter 4 concluded that solidarity had been eroded in both localities, with the younger generation embracing individualist values to a large extent but also demonstrating greater intolerance towards outsiders. It was postulated that attitudes of this type among the young were linked to the rise of the Northern League and the consequent politicisation of localism. The current chapter explores the extent to which different political and cultural values among respondents were associated with the political party they favoured at elections and the ideological view of the world it propagated. To this end the views and beliefs expressed by Democratic Party of the Left (PDS), Christian Democratic (DC), and Northern League voters are examined in depth and a profile of all three categories of electors is presented.

Class solidarity and localism: A profile of PDS voters in Sesto and Erba

PDS voters in Sesto (1992 elections) correlated positively with the male sex, whereas in Erba they did not correlate in any way with the sex of respondents. They also correlated positively with age, in other words, the older the respondents in Sesto, the more likely they were to vote for the PDS. No such correlation applied to Erba. This is another confirmation that the left subculture among the Sesto working class was predominantly male-orientated and that in 1992 it was showing signs of ageing, although, as we saw, this was partially being redressed at the 1994 elections. In terms of the geographical origins of respondents, PDS voters in both localities correlated positively with those who had non-northern birthplaces. Thus, people born in the Centre and, above all, the South, were more likely to vote for the PDS than people born in the North. Again, this confirms that the emphasis on class, characteristic of the socialist and communist culture, was welcoming to people who had migrated to another part of Italy and were in search of social and cultural integration.

In both localities PDS voters associated positively with considerations of loyalty and of the party programme. In Sesto there was also a positive correlation between PDS voters and considerations of interests, as well as PDS voters and their chosen party's perceived commitment to local issues. In Erba, neither of these aspects were associated with supporters of the PDS.

In terms of policy issues, PDS voters correlated negatively with a policy of privatisation, the idea of a Europe of the Regions, and federalism. In Sesto, but not in Erba, they were also fully supportive of the idea of paying higher taxes in exchange for better public services. As for immigration, in both localities PDS voters correlated negatively with perceptions of migrants as problematic and with the view that immigrants were creating competition on the labour and housing markets. They also overwhelmingly rejected a policy of repatriation, as well as any idea that their town had lost its identity due to immigration.

Not surprisingly, PDS voters in both localities subscribed in large numbers to solidarist values, although many more women than men opted for solidarity, while many more men than women put family values first. Indeed, PDS voters in Sesto subscribed to familist values ahead of solidarist ones, whereas in Erba the opposite was true. Furthermore, there was a significant positive correlation, which applied only to Sesto, between PDS voters and a perceived increasing importance of the family and of trade unions in recent years. These findings provide further confirmation that in Sesto the socialist and communist subculture represented values that were shared by factory workers both at the workplace and within their family. Indeed, PDS voters in Sesto (not in Erba) correlated positively with a high frequency of political discussions among family and friends. Thus family and work were not polarised environments, but reinforced each other, particularly since the communist subculture did not view the family as a centre of oppression, but rather as a centre of resistance against capitalist exploitation. Nevertheless, gender differences were also relevant, with female PDS voters declaring in larger numbers that trade unions had grown in importance in recent years, and male voters recording primarily a growing importance of the family. This is mainly due, in my view, to the fact that, as was pointed out in previous chapters, the collapse of the communist dream generated feelings of disappointment and disillusion vis-à-vis political action among male workers, while it simultaneously created sentiments of freedom and new hopes among women.

In terms of their judgement for political institutions, PDS voters in both Sesto and Erba associated with a positive view of the role of trade unions, and, in Sesto alone, also with a positive view of the role of political parties. In Sesto, unlike Erba, they also associated with a negative opinion of the role of employers' associations, banks, industry and the Catholic Church. Finally, in Sesto there was also a positive correlation between PDS voters and feelings of belonging to the nation-state, as well as between PDS voters and readership of the national press.

It could be concluded, on the basis of the evidence presented above, that PDS voters were not receptive to localism, as opposed to identification with a social class. Although this was generally the case, it was interesting that responses to issues related to immigration revealed the presence of a substantial minority of PDS voters, particularly in Sesto, who did not feel bound to extend their class-based solidarity to extra-EU immigrants. Thus 27.5 percent of all PDS voters in Sesto stated that immigration to their town had caused considerable social problems, a proportion only slightly smaller than among voters of all other parties (31.2 percent). By contrast, in Erba the corresponding figure for PDS voters was only 2.5 percent, as opposed to 13.9 percent of voters of all the other parties. Similarly, 40.4 percent of PDS voters in Sesto agreed, either strongly or moderately, that immigrants created competition on the labour market, while in Erba only 27.5 percent of PDS voters agreed. Among non-PDS voters, the corresponding figures were 46.9 percent in Sesto and 30 percent in Erba. Only when asked whether immigrants created competition on the housing market and for services, did PDS voters in both localities diverge markedly from voters of all other parties. The same divergence applied when a policy of repatriation was considered. Thus 74.5 percent of PDS voters in Sesto and 87.5 percent in Erba were opposed to such a policy, while only 54.1 percent of non-PDS voters in Sesto and 62.5 percent in Erba were opposed to it.

In conclusion, the socialist and communist subculture effectively encouraged the development of feelings of solidarity among factory workers which acted as a strong deterrent against any exclusion of people from different areas of Italy or even from different countries. Notwithstanding this noticeable achievement, sentiments of closure towards outsiders, particularly extra-EU immigrants, had surfaced even among respondents who identified more strongly with the left subculture. As Eatwell recently argued, in a paper on the extreme and radical right, 'some who vote for mainstream parties have views which are remarkably similar [to those of the insurgent right]' (1998: 30). In the same paper, Eatwell also pointed out that communist subcultures had proved fairly effective in stemming the rise of the extreme right: 'Anti-"fascism" has been a major factor preventing the FN [Front National] making greater inroads among communist working class voters in areas such as St. Denis: fascism was the historic "Other", and older voters especially can find it difficult to embrace the FN for this reason' (Ibid.: 26). The Sesto findings appear to confirm both interpretations. On the one hand, some exclusionary, even racist, views on immigration and identity clearly had managed to penetrate among supporters of the traditional left subculture. On the other hand, feelings of loyalty, class solidarity, and shared values at the workplace and in the family had acted as powerful constraints upon PDS supporters. The party itself, as well as the trade union movement, also played a major role in preventing people from switching political allegiance, at least judging from the positive view of these organisations which was prevalent among PDS supporters in Sesto. Thus unbroken trust between political institutions representative of the communist subculture and voters contributed to stem the rise of extreme or radical parties in the locality. From this point of view, the Sesto findings are emblematic of a wider pattern of political behaviour. As in Sesto, in the whole of northern and central Italy the left subculture was challenged by both the extreme right (MSI-*Alleanza nazionale*), and the radical right (Northern League) in 1992 and 1994, but neither was able to make considerable inroads into its strongholds (Melchionda 1995, Baccetti 1997).

Catholic solidarity and localism: A profile of DC/PPI voters

In contrast to PDS voters, DC/PPI voters correlated positively with Erba as a locality. They did not correlate in any way with the gender of voters, but they did associate positively with their age in Erba. Thus the older the respondents the more likely they were to vote for a Catholic party. Supporters of a Catholic party did not associate positively with place of birth or length of residence in either locality. As was to be expected, in both towns they associated positively with practising Catholicism.

In terms of their reasons for party preference, DC voters in both Sesto and Erba correlated positively with considerations of family and local traditions. In Erba alone, they also associated with considerations of morality. Conversely, considerations of interests seemingly played no part in determining the way they voted. In the 1993 administrative elections, DC voters in both localities voted primarily on the basis of considerations of loyalty. In Erba, local issues and the competence of candidates had also influenced their voting behaviour.

As far as opinions on policy matters were concerned, only in Sesto did DC voters correlate positively with a policy of higher taxes in return for better services. By contrast, only in Erba did they associate negatively with federalism. On any other policy issue, specifically with regards to privatisation, a Europe of the Regions, and further European integration, DC voters did not register either strong assent or dissent. Having said this, a majority of DC voters were in favour of a policy of privatisation and of further European integration, whereas there was a clear split concerning a

Europe of the Regions, and opposition to federalism, particularly in Erba. When it came to expressing judgement on the role of political institutions, DC voters in Erba (but not in Sesto) proved the most trustful and supportive of all. They were the only category of voters who associated with a positive judgement of both national Parliament and government, a judgement which had withstood the test of time, since, according to respondents, it had not substantially changed since five/ten years previously. Also in Erba alone, they associated with a positive view of local government and of political parties. Predictably, in both localities DC voters expressed a positive judgement of the role of the Church, and again this opinion matched what they thought of this institution in the past. As for immigration, DC voters in Erba (but not in Sesto) correlated negatively with a policy of repatriation and with the opinion that immigrants create competition on the housing and services markets. In Erba alone, they also associated positively with a policy of helping immigrants to find work and housing in Italy as well as with the idea of a multi-ethnic society.

Not surprisingly, DC voters in Erba put solidarist values ahead of familist ones, whereas in Sesto the reverse was the case. Also, more DC voters in Sesto than in Erba subscribed to individualist values, even though in each town it was a question of less than a fifth of voters. In both localities, DC voters correlated positively with a perceived increased importance of the family and decreased importance of the work environment. On the basis of these findings, DC voters in Erba ought to be considered as model citizens, supportive of both local and national political institutions, solidarist towards outsiders, expressing moderate, non-extremist views on both economic and political matters. Although they were politically conservative, they were not averse to change, being receptive to a policy of privatisation and further institutional decentralisation. While the family was clearly a very important institution for this category of voters, and it had grown in status in recent years, in no way did it detract from positive virtues of civicness and public-spiritedness.

Were DC voters in any way receptive to exclusionary, localist views and showing a weakening of their Catholic-based solidarity towards outsiders? In terms of feelings of belonging, they identified with both the local commune (in Erba alone) and the nation-state (in both towns). They read the local press as frequently as they read the national press. Thus in Erba their, undoubtedly strong, attachment to the locality was not to the detriment of feelings of allegiance to the nation-state. In terms of exclusion towards out-siders, very few DC voters in Erba subscribed to any such senti-ments, whereas in Sesto a substantial minority did so. In Erba, for example, 64.9 percent of DC voters stated that immigration to their locality had been minimal, while only 6.8 percent stated that it had been of considerable proportions, causing social problems. These figures were noticeably lower than comparative figures among vot-ers of all the other parties. In Sesto, too, DC voters were less anx-ious about the effects of immigration than voters of other parties, nevertheless here only 33.3 percent of them considered immi-gration to have been minimal. Similarly, in Erba 85.7 percent of DC voters opposed a policy of repatriation, compared to 60.5 percent of voters of the other parties. In Sesto, by contrast, only 53.3 per-cent of DC voters opposed such a policy, compared to 62.2 percent of voters of all the other parties. As for the idea of creating a multi-ethnic society, DC voters in Erba were massively in favour (80 per-cent, compared to 65.4 percent of voters of all the other parties), whereas DC voters in Sesto were split exactly 50:50 over this issue (compared to 73.6 percent of voters of all the other parties who were supportive of a multi-racial society).

Thus in Erba, unlike in Sesto, DC voters did not appear to have any views in common with the extreme or radical right. At first sight, this finding may appear very encouraging and be taken as a sign that the Catholic subculture had been even more effective than the communist one in promoting civicness and solidarity among its supporters and in creating moral barriers to the develop-ment of exclusionary feelings towards outsiders. In reality, though, DC/PPI voters in 1992 had become a minority among Erba respon-dents, with many who had voted for the DC in 1987 switching their allegiance to a different party (primarily the Northern League) in 1992. What had happened, therefore, was that the Catholic sub-culture had failed precisely where the communist subculture had succeeded, i.e., in stemming the transfer of supporters to a radical right, localist, party. We can infer from the findings – and this will become even more apparent when we consider Northern League voters – that many DC voters *had* come to harbour extreme views and that in their case the moral and institutional constraints imposed by the Catholic subculture had somehow proved ineffec-tive in retaining these people in the 'Catholic–solidarist' camp.

To conclude, DC/PPI voters in a 'white' subcultural area, who were predominantly regular Church attendants, stand out as stan-dard-bearers of civic virtues, in stark contrast to Putnam's and

Ginsborg's depiction of Catholicism as leading to particularism and having a stifling effect on public engagement, solidarity and trust. The Catholic subculture, based on universalist solidarity, had had a similar impact on people's values as the communist subculture, based on class solidarity. In either case, the development of feelings of solidarity among factory workers provided a powerful framework for the integration of outsiders, such as immigrants, mitigating the exclusive nature of the tightly cohesive networks produced by each subculture. The problem is that the Catholic subculture, which relied more heavily on the role of the Church, family and social networks than on political associations and institutions, appears to have been unable to mobilise effectively grassroots party-political organisations to stem the exit of voters and supporters.

Individualist values and localism: A profile of Northern League voters

Northern League voters associated positively with Erba as a locality. In Erba alone, they also correlated positively with male voters and negatively with age. In other words, the older the age of respondents, the less likely they were to cast their vote for this party. This was in stark contrast to both PDS voters in Sesto and DC voters in Erba. The propensity of young people to vote for the Northern League is well documented (Mannheimer 1991). Unlike PDS and DC voters, Northern League voters correlated positively with northern origins of themselves and their parents, as well as with long-term residency in the locality. Already we can see the signs of the emergence of a dual process of inclusion/exclusion, based on territory and geographical origins.

In terms of their reasons for party preference, Northern League voters associated positively with considerations of interest (in Erba alone), negatively with considerations of morality and of local political traditions (in both towns). Interestingly, Northern League voters in Sesto associated negatively with the view that their chosen party was well rooted in and committed to the locality, whereas in Erba they associated positively with such a view. As we saw earlier, the findings for PDS voters in the two localities were exactly the opposite, with PDS voters in Sesto, but not in Erba, judging their party's embeddedness in and commitment to local issues to have been an important factor behind their decision to vote for it. The different findings in the two localities can be seen as an implicit recognition that the Northern League in Erba had come to take on the role of a subcultural party.

In terms of policy issues, Northern League voters in both localities correlated strongly with a policy of privatisation and with federalism. In Erba alone, they also associated positively with the idea of a Europe of the Regions. Northern League voters in both towns associated positively with the view that extra-EU immigration had been of considerable proportions, creating social problems, as well as with the view that immigrants created competition on the job and housing markets. Northern League voters in both localities also associated with the view that extra-EU immigrants, as well as immigrants from the South of Italy, threatened the local culture. They also correlated strongly with a policy of repatriation of all immigrants. In addition, in Sesto (though not in Erba), Northern League voters opposed a policy of helping immigrants to find housing and work in Italy, while in Erba (though not in Sesto), they associated strongly with opposition to the idea of a multi-ethnic society. It is easy to see that these latter findings are in stark contrast to the values and attitudes expressed by both PDS and DC/PPI voters. Feelings of solidarity had been replaced by feelings of rejection and fear of 'outsiders', coupled with exclusive and 'racialised' sentiments of belonging to a community whose identity and culture were perceived as being under threat. The shift of votes to the Northern League from the PDS and the PSI in Sesto and from the DC and the PSI in Erba in 1992 and 1994 was thus accompanied by a change in values and a move away from an ideology of solidarity and universalism. This is confirmed by data referring to the reasons why respondents had shifted their vote in favour of the Northern League in 1992. In both localities, a majority of voters who had switched to this party indicated that 'their values had changed', while in Erba alone they also indicated that 'the new party takes a greater interest in local issues'. A perceived loss of identity on the part of their locality also appears to have played a role, with Northern League voters in both towns associating positively with the view that 'their commune had lost its identity due to extra-EU immigration', and the same voters in Erba (though not in Sesto) correlating with the view that their commune had already lost its identity prior to the period of migrations.

Was there a corresponding lack of faith in social and political institutions, both local and national, among Northern League voters? The answer is yes, particularly in Erba. Indeed, Northern

League voters correlated strongly in both localities with a negative judgement of the role of trade unions, and even more strongly with a negative judgement of the role of Parliament and national government. However, in Erba alone, they also associated with a negative judgement of local government, industry and the Church. It is interesting to see whether such negative perceptions of established institutions among Northern League voters were indicative of declining trust or simply a persistence of anti-system feelings. According to Eatwell, individuals are particularly receptive to the extreme or radical right when they experience 'a sense of declining trust in the socio-political system' (Eatwell 1998: 5). In other words, low trust is not a sufficient condition for explaining the sudden turning of substantial numbers of voters to the radical right, particularly in Italy where a low sense of trust in socio-political institutions had been a constant of the country's political culture in the post-war period. It is when people lose faith in the system that they become receptive to alternative proposals and 'solutions'. Once again, the findings confirmed this hypothesis. Northern League voters in Erba, in fact, correlated with a positive view of industry, local government and the Church in the past. In the case of Parliament and national government, these voters had held negative perceptions of the role of such bodies in the past, as well as at the time of the survey. However, their judgement of such bodies had worsened considerably over time, as indicated by the fact that the negative correlation between Northern League voters and perceptions of the role of Parliament and national government was much stronger in relation to their current than their past feelings. Furthermore, Northern League voters in Erba associated positively with the view that the importance of religion had decreased for them in recent times, whereas the importance of their work environment had become more prominent. If we consider that Northern League voters in Erba were predominantly practising Catholics and ex-DC voters, we can understand how their rejection of the Catholic subculture was linked both to a loss of faith in the Catholic Church and to declining trust in traditional Catholic sociopolitical institutions. By contrast, those voters who had remained loyal to the Catholic party had kept their faith in the Church and in local and national political institutions, as we saw earlier.

Loss of trust in the political system and a sense of loss of community identity can explain the rejection of sentiments of solidarity and the development of exclusionary feelings towards 'outsiders', which appear as the hallmark of Northern League voters, particularly in Erba. Declining trust, however, is only part of the explanation. A new faith, more precisely a new ideology, seems to have replaced the old value-system, based on a combination of individualism and localism. Indeed, Northern League voters in Erba, though not in Sesto, correlated negatively with solidarist values, positively with individualist ones. This finding seems to confirm a recent description of the electorate of the Northern League as being characterised by 'utilitarian individualism' and even 'hedonism' (Calvi and Vannucci 1995: 57–73). They were the only category of voters who read the local press in preference to the national one and who felt that they identified with the commune and with the region to a greater extent than with the nation-state. Readership of the local versus the national press thus appears to have emerged as a significant differential factor for Northern League voters. This finding points to the need for further research on the issue of the influence of the local media (not just the press) upon voters' political views and voting behaviour. This is not to say that the local press in Erba supported the Northern League, rather, that it may have helped this party by setting the agenda and framing the political debate and electoral campaign within territorial parameters. Calvi and Vannucci (1995: 34–38) established in their survey that Northern League voters were widely exposed to the media, particularly the radio and the press. Unfortunately, they did not differentiate between the national and local media, although their finding that Northern League voters listened in preference to private radio channels makes it plausible that they tuned into some of the many private local channels operating in Italy at the time.

Northern League voters in Erba were also well integrated socially, enjoying good family, neighbourly and working relations. In other words, these voters, at least in Erba, were not alienated, anomic individuals who had turned to the radical right in a desperate attempt to give a new meaning to their empty existence. Only in Sesto did Northern League voters report dissatisfaction with their current jobs and reply affirmatively to the question of whether they would prefer to change it – but then, this was true of a majority of all respondents in Sesto. By contrast, in Erba Northern League voters expressed satisfaction with their current jobs, and the vast majority stated that they did not want to change their work situation. More importantly perhaps, Northern League voters in Erba, unlike in Sesto, felt that they shared their political ideas with both family and friends. Indeed, they were the only category of voters where a clear majority indicated that their political ideas were shared by 'a large number' or 'the greatest number' of their relatives and friends. In Sesto, on the other hand, Northern League voters predominantly indicated that 'only a few' or at best 'a number' of their relatives and friends shared their political opinions. This is another sign that among factory workers and the self-employed in Erba, the Northern League had come to represent a diffused subculture, whereas in Sesto support for this party and its ideology was confined to a small group in defiance of the still dominant left subculture.

To conclude, Northern League voters originated politically and ideologically from the Catholic subculture, but they had moved radically away from its solidarist and universalist values. A loss of faith in the Catholic Church and in the socio-political system had precipitated a switch to a different ideology, whose principal traits were a belief in the work ethic and individual interests, coupled with an exclusionary commitment to the local and regional community. The findings presented thus far confirm what I wrote elsewhere concerning the Northern League (Cento Bull 1996: 178–183), that is, that the party had promoted a process of 'racialisation' of northern Italy's communities of small firms, becoming the political voice of the 'indigenous' population, to the exclusion of all 'outsiders'. Such communities, as we saw in Chapter 3, had produced high levels of trust and solidarity which were primarily born out of living in the same village, speaking the same dialect, sharing family as well as business ties, and having comparable social statuses. In other words, areas of diffused industrialisation tended to be characterised by a high degree of 'closeness' to the outside world, and even by a sharp division between one's own fellow-citizens and those perceived as 'strangers' (Becattini 1990: 39–40). This deep sense of localism had been, throughout the postwar period, tempered by the universalist nature of political Catholicism. The Catholic subculture, though locally- and regionally-based, was not localist or regionalist in content. With the rise and success of the Northern League, political localism has come to the forefront.

Conclusions

In his study of civic traditions and democracy in Italy, Putnam argued that social capital, which he equated with both norms of reciprocity and networks of civic engagement, is conducive to democracy. Part I raised the question 'Which type of democracy'? The tolerant and universalist version or the intolerant and parochial one? As Levi (1996: 51) remarked, 'Neighbourhoods (and certain other networks of civic engagement) are a source of trust and neighbourhoods are a source of distrust. They promote trust of those you know and distrust of those you do not, those not in the neighbourhood or outside the networks'. Similarly, the trust and social cohesion of northern Italy's communities of small firms, which have attracted the attention and even the admiration of so many economists and sociologists, presuppose distrust of outsiders. There is no denying that the social capital that these communities possess in abundance has been successfully converted into sustainable economic growth and development. What is much more questionable is whether it also systematically promotes and encourages the development of democratic institutions.

This chapter has clearly shown that social capital, taken by itself, is a weak predictor of the quality and strength of democratic institutions. In so far as it is linked to localism, social capital can produce exclusion as well as inclusion. Politically, this can lead to intolerant attitudes towards foreigners and immigrants and to a polarisation of 'Us' versus 'Them'. Both DC/PPI and Northern League voters in Erba possessed social capital. Both read the local press, participated in socio-political organisations, were extremely well integrated into their local community, were receptive towards economic and institutional change. Yet they were also poles apart in terms of their political values. DC/PPI voters were tolerant of and open to outsiders, identified with both their locality and the nation-state, had retained their faith in the socio-political system. By contrast, League voters were intolerant of both foreign and southern Italian immigrants, identified with their locality in preference to the nation-state, and had lost their faith in the socio-political system.

I would like to argue that social capital is a useful concept for analysing political developments, but it has to be decoupled from any uncontroversial association with 'democracy'. Social capital appears to be compatible both with participative democracy and with participative, potentially undemocratic, radicalism. The most fruitful association is that of social capital with localism. I do not mean this in a disparaging sense only. Localism in Italy has traditionally been linked to two political subcultures, socialism and communism and Catholicism, which successfully reconciled

embeddedness in a locality and a region with strong values of solidarity and cooperation which transcended the territory. What
needs to be examined is under which conditions 'community' and
'localism' become intolerant and exclusionary, at which point the
socio-economic advantages of social capital are offset by its threat
to political stability in that it provides ready-made channels of
information and communication which facilitate the rise of radical,
even extremist, political movements. As the present chapter and
the preceding one have shown, family and social networks contributed to the rapid radicalisation of politics, allowing for effective
circulation of information and build-up of intra- and inter-family
support for the League. Such an examination is outside the scope
of the present work, nevertheless the findings so far point towards
a crucial role played by a sudden loss of trust in political institutions and by ideology.

Conclusion to Part II

In Sesto I found evidence of the persistence of a class-based sub-culture among factory workers. However, the territorial and insti-tutional identity which had been built around working-class culture has been partially lost and there are also signs of a weaken-ing of the left culture among factory workers themselves, although with marked gender and generational differences. The PDS had reacted to this situation by moving towards the centre and increas-ingly appealing to middle-class voters, as well as de-emphasising the 'subcultural boundary'. As for Erba, a territorial subculture based upon shared values and a sense of collective identity and built around a specific socio-economic model ('diffused industrial-isation') continues to exercise its effects upon the local electorate.

My research findings raise some interesting questions related to the concept of 'rational choice voting' and the role of a political subculture. As we saw in the Introduction to Part II, rational choice voting considers voting behaviour as the outcome of individual choice and self-interest. The role of society and culture tends to be played down, while associations such as the family, a neighbour-hood, or even class are seen as no longer functioning as com-munities. 'Class once expressed itself precisely as community. Working-class groups often formed communities, whether in local villages or towns, or in clubs and educational associations. The remnants still exist, of course, but class division now much more often takes on individualised, or "biographical" forms. The "new poor", for example, such as single mothers or the chronically unemployed, don't form a community with one another' (Giddens 1994: 39, also Giddens 1990). Any voting behaviour which is embedded in social structures is, by implication, considered to be non-rational and not a free choice. Rational choice approaches to political and voting behaviour have recently been revised and viewed as complementary to, rather than in conflict with, cultural and ecological explanations. Wildavski (1998: 10), for example, argued that the concept of political culture can overcome the limits of a rational choice approach, by making 'why people want what they want into the central subject of inquiry'.

A specific assumption on the part of modernisation theorists is that a political subculture survives as a result of inertia, of the weight of tradition; in other words a voter in the context of a subculture tends to be a passive voter; conversely, a rational choice voter is an active voter, someone who exercises his/her will when voting. Once a subculture (and the 'community' to which it is linked, with its rules and constraints) disappear, political emancipation and individualised choice are seen as replacing passive obedience to the rules of the collectivity.

I have quite a few reservations regarding these assumptions. A subculture does not necessarily indicate irrational behaviour and/or the absence of choice. In a society where the family plays a crucial role and operates as a unit, it is perfectly rational that the vote is seen in the context of a family strategy and used accordingly and therefore collectively, rather than individually. This would explain why parents and children can influence each others' party preferences. There is nothing passive or traditional about this type of behaviour, even though it points to a persisting importance of the family. Similarly, a social group can make use of the vote collectively, because it perceives that it shares common needs and has greater chances of finding adequate political responses to its needs if it acts and votes as a group. This is just as much rational choice voting as is individualist behaviour. As for 'passive' voting, the survey findings relating to Erba indicate that the Northern League has 're-invented' a political subculture and a shared community, using as channels of political communication family and social networks, relying upon door-to-door canvassing, meetings in bars, village fairs, mass rallies, etc. Both voters and supporters have been 'activated'. This successful recreation of a subculture appears to indicate that individuals may *choose* to subscribe to a collective identity and to form a community – 'a strongly bounded group with a clear set of shared values' (Giddens 1994: 38) – with one another.

The connection between social identities, kinship and friendship networks, and electoral and political behaviour, established in the course of this volume, seems to point to a greater relevance of network theories over rational choice theories. Network theories set out to explain how individuals relate to one another and have drawn attention to the influence exercised upon electoral choices by groups of people who regularly exchange information and engage in symmetrical and equal or asymmetrical and unequal relations (Knoke and Kuklinski 1983, Huckfeldt 1984, Huckfeldt and Sprague 1987, Piselli 1997). Thus network theories encompass both 'horizontal' and 'vertical' associationism, spatial and non-spatial relations. Spatially-dense social relations tend to be milieux relations, which are largely confined to a locality or territory and can show a high degree of 'closure' to the external world (Bull et al. 1993). This degree of closure can be reflected in electoral behaviour and may help explain the continuing relevance of social and political subcultures.

What is interesting about my findings is that, whereas traditionally the Catholic and communist subcultures exercised a pervasive influence upon and successfully appeared to encompass the entire territorial community, nowadays a political subculture, given the increasing role choice has come to play, seems to represent the interests and needs of specific groups within a territory. The exclusionary aspect of a political subculture ('Us' versus the 'Others') has become more in evidence than its inclusionary one. It is mainly men who strive for partisan 'realignment' so as to perpetuate or recreate family and group ties. Women in Erba have given a more conditional support to the League than men. Women in Sesto have opted in greater numbers for a weakening of traditional subcultural values. In both localities there were distinct gendered voting behaviours. Male workers showed a high degree of continuity with the past and a determination, particularly in Erba, to preserve a familist and communitarian society represented politically by a subcultural party. Female workers continued to subscribe to family values and indeed to be influenced to some extent by the family in their voting allegiances (especially in Erba), but family and group ties as well as subcultural values had a much lesser impact upon them than upon men. Group ties, in particular, did not seem to exercise the same influence upon women as upon men.

This has two important implications, in my view. First, it indicates that women are increasingly withdrawing their support from political subcultures – whether Catholic or communist – which have traditionally placed them in a subordinate position vis-à-vis men. Second, it indicates that women have not found a political voice of their own, nor are they likely to find it in the foreseeable future, if by this we intend a collective representation at the political level. My findings show that, unlike men, women in areas previously dominated by subcultural parties are now likely to cast their votes widely across the political spectrum, distrusting collective representation. In this sense it is they, rather than male voters, who have become the new mobile electorate whose emergence at the 1992 and 1994 elections was heralded as proof of the social and political modernisation of the Italian people, as we saw in the Introduction. However, I would contend that in areas such as Sesto and Erba the discarding by women of a subcultural approach to voting does in itself amount to a collective aspiration and can be seen in direct opposition to men's collective political behaviour. In this context, it seems premature, at least for Italy, to speak of an individualist and gender-neutral voting behaviour. Unlike the U.S., however, the type of 'gender gap' that it has been possible to detect in the areas surveyed, cannot be easily translated into greater political influence. A similar conclusion was recently drawn from the outcome of the 1996 elections. Female voters may have contributed decisively to the electoral success of the centre-left in 1996, however, to quote an editorial in *La Repubblica* (19 April 1996: 10), 'women have come out of the electoral campaign defeated'. The editorial pointed out that women had failed to obtain greater political representation, arguing that this could only emerge as the result of women achieving 'female political subjectivity'. Interestingly, only the Housewives' Association, the *Federcasalinghe*, through their leader Federica Rossi Gasparrini, openly and skilfully publicised their conversion from the *Polo* to the *Ulivo before* the election. An electoral pact then followed, based on ten key demands put forward by the housewives' pressure group. After the elections, Ms Rossi Gasparrini boasted that the support of the association had been decisive for the success of the centre-left (*La Repubblica*, 23 April 1996: 6). At least one political party thus showed itself open to women's demands but only one women's group appears to have been able to use its members' votes as a political lever. If women's votes are 'unpredictable' and their political orientations vary considerably from one election to the next, men's persistent and reliable 'bloc voting' will continue to ensure that their own collective interests and aspirations are more effectively represented at the political level.

To sum up, it seems to me that the demise of collective identities and territorially-based subcultures in modern societies is not a foregone conclusion. Even if we agree that in some countries, such as Italy, they were historically determined and therefore able to rely to a large extent on the weight of tradition, the example of the Northern League shows that they have now become a political choice. Crucially, however, their role appears to have changed, precisely because of the new element of choice. Rather than encompassing the whole spatial community, the collective solidarity typical of a subculture is now increasingly functional to specific groups. It would therefore be more appropriate to suggest that in the struggle around competing material interests and values social actors (and voters) make use of different political instruments and that one of these instruments can take the shape of a political subculture built around a bounded group.

The above conclusions have wider implications regarding the resilience but also the changing nature of localism. The findings presented in the previous chapters have shown the existence of a direct link between the values and attitudes held by practising Catholics and localism. The survey has provided a sharp reminder of the importance of localist issues and values for Catholic people who reside in traditionally 'white' subcultural areas (Moia 1997, Rumiz 1997). In Erba there was clearly a vast reservoir of localist attitudes which the Northern League was then able to 'tap' and to utilise for a political project directly antagonistic to the one promoted by its rival subcultural party, the DC/PPI. It may be useful to list the main connecting elements between Catholicism and political localism in Erba:

- percentage of practising Catholics among League voters (77.8%), compared to non-League voters (72.1%). Practising Catholics among DC/PPI voters amounted to 91%.
- percentage of Catholics reading the local press on a regular basis and percentage of League voters doing the same, in comparison to non-Catholics and non-League voters. Among Catholics, 43.3% regularly read the local press, as opposed to 21.1% of lay respondents. Among Northern League voters, 43.3% read the local press on a regular basis, as opposed to 35.7% of non-League voters. The percentage of regular readers of a local newspaper among DC/PPI voters (43.8%), was almost identical to that of Northern League voters.
- percentage of practising Catholics with parents born in the northern province of Como, where Erba is located, and percentage of Northern League voters sharing these same geographical origins, in comparison to non-Catholics and non-League voters.

Among Erba respondents, 55.4% of practising Catholics had both parents born in the province of Como, as opposed to 45.8% of lay respondents. Among Northern League voters, 63% had parents born in this province, as opposed to 47.3% of non-League supporters. Among DC/PPI voters, 55.6% had both parents born in the province of Como.

- percentage of practising Catholics and of Northern League voters identifying with the local commune in terms of their affective orientation, again in comparison to non-Catholics and non-League voters. Among Erba respondents, 61.7% of Catholics identified strongly with the local commune, as opposed to just 38% of lay respondents. Among Northern League voters, 62.7% identified strongly with the local commune, as opposed to 52% of non-League voters. Among DC/PPI voters, 67.3% identified strongly with the local commune. The main difference between Catholic respondents, DC/PPI voters and Northern League voters consisted in their affective orientation towards the nation-state: while 60.1% of Catholics, 57.5% of non-Catholics, and 68.6% of DC/PPI voters identified strongly with the nation-state, the figure for Northern League voters was only 49%.

It is easy to see that for many Catholics switching from Christian Democracy to the Northern League was less of a jump in the dark and less of a momentary 'aberration' than it was thought possible in the early days. Whereas Christian Democracy subordinated localism to Catholicism, however, the Northern League has achieved the opposite, which is not surprising given the process of secularisation affecting Italian society since the 1970s. The Northern League is not just a neo-liberal, managerial type of party, it has also developed and popularised an 'ethnic', populist, even racist image of itself. These ideological and cultural components point to the existence of a shared system of values among party voters and supporters, which is one of the reasons why, in my view, it is substantially correct to identify the Northern League with a political subculture. The Northern League has taken on the political representation of the 'indigenous' productive community, with the effect of putting this same community into sharper contrast with both the outside world and the 'aliens within'.

In this context the anti-southernism of the Northern League – in many ways more marked than the xenophobia of many of this party's supporters and sympathisers – indicates both the persistence among southerners, at least in the eyes of the 'indigenous' population, of a system of values perceived as fundamentally different from the local one, and the non-integration of the southern immigrants into the entrepreneurial world which forms the basis of areas of small-scale industry. To this day the southern immigrants are present in large numbers in the public sector and almost totally absent from the group of artisans and small entrepreneurs. The social composition of Northern League voters and sympathisers confirms the predominance of people born and still living in the same village or town and the presence of a large proportion of the self-employed, as found in a 1989 survey of 234 Lombard residents (Cesareo et al. 1989). The survey showed that professionals, entrepreneurs and the self-employed amounted to 21.6 percent of the sample, whereas manual workers and teachers accounted for only 15.9 percent of the total sample. As for the remaining 52.5 percent, 23.3 were white-collar workers, 2.9 were managers and 36.3 did not work (pensioners, housewives, students, etc.). The socio-professional composition of the 1992 paid-up members of the Northern League in the province of Como (the only precise data of the kind I have been able to acquire for Lombardy) was even more striking: 38 percent were artisans, entrepreneurs or professionals, while 15 percent worked in commerce; only 4 percent were employed in the public sector. The remaining 43 percent were made up of wage earners (16 percent), white-collar workers (15 percent), pensioners (5 percent), and students (7 percent). More recent surveys have brought new evidence that the Northern League has been particularly successful among people employed in the private sector, be they entrepreneurs, artisans, or industrial workers (Calvi and Vannucci 1995, Bellucci 1997).

I therefore agree with Cartocci (1994) that the Northern League was a logical and in some ways predictable outcome of the weakening of Christian Democracy in its traditional strongholds. Localism is an integral component of the political culture of the Third Italy, and it cannot be discarded in any analysis or vision of political change in Italy. There are times when it is in the background, others when it is in the forefront. Its individual features may change, but it cannot be considered in decline, as various commentators have attempted to do ever since the unexpected success of the Northern League was judged to be on the wane (Diamanti and Segatti 1994, Brierley and Giacometti 1996, Diamanti 1996). While wishing away the League may well turn out to be a dream come true at some later stage, wishing away localism will prove much harder. As Bartolini and Mair (1990) recently reminded us, following Lipset and Rokkan's (1967) pioneering study of electoral stability in Europe, traditional socio-political divisions may persist even when the parties which had originally expressed them disappear.

In some respects, therefore, it can be said that, while localism can explain the Northern League, the party itself cannot explain localism. To put it differently, the Northern League has added a new dimension to localism, by turning it into an ideology (Diamanti, 1996) and developing the themes of ethnicity and self-determination, as well as emphasising exclusion at the expense of inclusion. The party, in short, has become one of the players (the PPI and the Catholic Church being two others) competing for political and cultural support within a boundary which is increasingly defined in territorial, sub-national, terms. In this context, localism has now acquired its own visibility, independently of the Northern League and of political Catholicism. This is now so blatantly true that the debate within Italy has recently turned to the existence of a 'north-eastern Question', to replace the old 'southern Question'. Whereas Padania (the northern nation invented by the Northern League) enjoys some publicity and recognition outside Italy, not least as a folklorist and entertaining phenomenon, it is in fact the North-East which has acquired a strong sub-national identity within the country, and which is being treated increasingly seriously. Comprising the regions of eastern Lombardy, Veneto, Friuli-Venezia Giulia and Trentino, the North-East has appeared to express, through its support for the League, a regional political class in pursuit of a regional political project. Indeed, a survey by Diakron (1996) found that, while only 8.6 percent of Italians were in favour of secessionism, the figure rose to 15.6 percent in the North and to 20.6 percent in the North-East. The focus of attention has therefore gradually shifted from the Northern League to political regionalism in the North-East. This was recently defined as 'fundamentalist' and 'integralist', with reference to its growing intransigence and radicalism. By contrast, others saw it as characterised by increasing pragmatism, in the sense that secessionism is being coolly taken into consideration, in these areas of Italy, as a possible viable alternative to the preservation of the nation-state.

After a period in which the 'selfish' interpretation of regional identity and the rise of the Northern League seemed to dominate the intellectual debate in Italy, leading to various attempts to demonise and stigmatise both phenomena, a growing body of scholars and politicians started to produce less emotional diagnoses and put forward more rational political solutions. Massimo Cacciari, the previous mayor of Venice and a leading exponent of the left, was one of the first to realise the significance of the emergence of a 'north-eastern question'. This led him to advocate openly the formation of a new regional party (*Il Partito del Nord-Est*), capable on the one hand of representing the needs of the local model of socio-economic development at the level of the central state, and on the other of stealing the thunder from the *Lega Nord* in the region. Cacciari has also become an ardent and vocal supporter of a Catalan-style solution for Italy's North-East, stressing the urgency of the creation of a federalist state. Thus Cacciari is trying to turn localism into a lever for the political renewal of Italy along federalist lines, where the multiple layers of identity consistently expressed by Italians can coexist harmoniously rather than battle with each other. He is also trying to channel the new synergies created by the new regionalist movement into a less radical and less exclusionary path than the one offered by Northern League politics, recuperating the more benign and acceptable face of localism. The crucial difference between Cacciari and other political actors and analysts is that he fully acknowledges the importance of localism in Italian political culture and strives to incorporate it into his quest for and vision of a new political system for Italy, as opposed to those who ignore it altogether, or who recurrently will it away. As Cartocci wrote (1990: 207), 'the subjective experience of modernity consists of an expansion of types of behaviour which are determined by individual choice rather than by destiny and/or tradition [...] Against this background forty years of elections in Italy lead to two possible conclusions: at the electoral level this modernisation has not taken place or it has taken place in the context of the particularism which characterises our culture, i.e., through the expansion of choices made on the basis of extra-political criteria'. At a time when Italy is faced with a choice of alternative institutional and political systems to replace the one rendered obsolete by the end of the Cold War and the collapse of the traditional parties, it is vital that the continuing influence of historical, sub-national, socio-cultural traditions is fully taken into account. Solutions which may appear ideally suited to the Italian case and yet are devised in the abstract or imported from abroad can easily backfire. In the next section I will discuss the implications of the major findings of this book for a realistic renewal of the Italian political system.

Conclusion

Reassessing modernity and modernisation

In the northern and central regions of Italy, until recently, Christian Democracy and the Communist Party successfully fulfilled a subcultural role. To their credit, they did not exploit their territorial embeddedness in order to deepen existing geo-political cleavages, which could have had the effect of adding to the very serious ideological cleavages that already endangered Italian democracy. As Corbetta and Parisi (1997b: 10) remarked, 'the solidity of the relationship between political parties and local socio-economic systems, far from showing the limitations of localism, had permitted these same parties to develop their national vocation'. Once the Catholic party's wider ideological appeal started to weaken, during the 1980s, the regional and subcultural nature of political allegiances in the DC strongholds was openly exposed and successfully exploited by the Northern League.

Seen against this background, the optimism, which, as we saw in Part II, dominated the intellectual debate in the early 1990s, was clearly misplaced, yet it was by no means entirely flawed. Ideology plays a much lesser role in Italian politics today, and there is a new commitment from various quarters to both economic and political liberalism. The problem lay elsewhere, namely, in the concomitant belief that subcultural and localist allegiances had evaporated together with the old ideologies, leaving behind a socially and culturally homogeneous electorate. Indeed the success of the Northern League in the 1992 general elections was seen primarily as born out of protest for the reluctance of the old parties to relinquish power, as well as a sign of an increasingly mobile electorate. When Berlusconi formed a new party, *Forza Italia*, in 1994, and went on to gain a substantial percentage of votes at the general elections held in the Spring of the same year, this was heralded as further proof that the Italian electorate had become uniform, even hopelessly standardised, thanks to the influence of television and the media. It was not until later that the political map of Italy was seen as having re-emerged with some of the old fault lines, with one party, the Northern League, dominating the North-East, another, the Democratic Party of the Left, dominating the Centre, and a third, *Alleanza Nazionale*, with its own territorial strongholds, particularly in the South. This raised the spectre of territorial cleavages replacing traditional ideological ones, and led to increasing doubts concerning the extent of social and political change in Italy. It also led to a reappraisal of the nature of the Northern League. When I put forward the hypothesis that this party was becoming the political voice of the Catholic-orientated areas of small-scale production (Cento Bull 1992), very few had looked at the connection. Since then various studies have confirmed this hypothesis, and a few have begun to address the issue of why these areas have raised their voice and even threatened to separate from the Italian nation-state. Before I discuss these new debates, I would like to come to some firm conclusions regarding the findings of this book in relation to the persistence of localism and political subcultures.

The first point that needs to be made is that, even though the old ideologies may have gone, small-scale industrialisation has clearly outlived them. So have particularism and localism, as witness the resilience of family values and social networks, as well as attachment to a local community. In some ways there is no contradiction between these findings and modernisation theories, provided the latter acknowledge the existence of different paths to 'modernity'. Once these are taken on board, the link between the socio-economic environment and cultural values could be simply extended to cover 'modern' societies characterised by small-scale, rather than large-scale, industrialisation. We would then correlate small-scale industry with particularist values and strong kinship and social networks, and large-scale industry with individualism and horizontal associationism. This would represent a relatively simple way to overcome the main weakness in the theory (i.e., the belief that modernisation has both a uniform and universal impact), and it is the one adopted by Sapelli with his distinction between a 'virtuous' and a 'bastard' modernisation, as we saw in Part I. Sapelli's terminology blatantly reveals where his sympathies lie, and in this he is by no means alone, nevertheless the type of modernisation associated with small-scale industry has also gained more than its fair share of admirers. Indeed it has been the tendency of all scholars interested in the Italian phenomenon of small-scale industrialisation to highlight, and to an extent romanticise, the social cohesion, cooperation and trust underpinning these communities of small firms. I will come back later to the question of the merits and demerits of both types of society. What I want to stress at this stage is that the findings presented in this book do not unequivocally support this relatively straightforward interpretation of socio-economic and cultural change. This I found somewhat surprising, since in my previous studies of areas of diffused industrialisation and the Northern League I had posited and largely demonstrated (or so I thought) a direct relationship between the socio-economic environment and political values and behaviour.

The second point, therefore, is that the type of industrialisation which characterises a given society is not necessarily a good indicator of its social and political culture. Chapter 1 showed very clearly that in terms of social identities and values Erba and Sesto were remarkably similar, while Vénissieux and Sesto differed quite sharply, whereas I would have expected the opposite, given the socio-economic configuration of the three sites. Nor can this 'anomaly' be explained away in terms of a 'cultural lag'. The socio-economic characteristics of Erba and Sesto date from the beginning of the century at least: how long can a 'cultural lag' reasonably be expected to last before we accept that the theory is flawed? The relationship between the two dimensions is more complex and less linear than modernisation theories allow for. In some instances it is not the socio-economic environment that determines cultural values and social identities, but rather it is the latter that are at the roots of the type of 'modernisation path' a given society will be able to follow. Thus in the Third Italy (as in Erba) localist and subcultural values, as well as strong kinship and friendship ties, pre-existed – and in turn influenced, even determined – small-scale industrialisation. In other instances it is the capacity of human beings to retain a multiplicity of cultural values which accounts for the complex coexistence of both particularist and universalist values, horizontal and vertical associationism, kinship and friendship ties and individualist behaviour (as in Sesto). In short, even though the socio-economic environment clearly shapes social identities and political culture, the reverse is also true, nor is the relationship between them immutable, inflexible or uni-dimensional. As Girvin

(1990: 32) wrote 'too much stress has been placed upon economic change [...] the roles of tradition, class, religion, and nationalism have also to be understood in the context of change and not as passive recipients of that change; the dialectic of change involves the interaction between both stable and unstable elements'.

The third point is that the demise of political subcultures in Italy and the erosion of traditional cleavages, as postulated with great confidence in the early 1990s, mainly on the basis of the emergence of an increasingly mobile electorate, appear to have rested largely on the assumption that there were no discernible gender differences in voting behaviour. Indeed, the disappearance of the traditional 'gender gap' in voting behaviour was part and parcel of the interpretation that saw the emergence of a fully 'modern' electorate in Italian politics. Yet, as Part II clearly showed, only the female electorate can be judged to have become relatively mobile. Male voters by and large continued to conform to a repeated pattern of voting behaviour. Subcultural allegiances have thus not weakened in terms of an increasing generational divide, but mainly in terms of an increasing gender divide. This finding has various important implications, but it is not in accordance with the hypothesis of the emergence of a uniform, modern, 'rational choice' electorate.

The fourth, and last, point, is that strong kinship and friendship ties and particularist and localist values are not an indication of a pre-modern society. The 'Italian' family may appear unchanged, but under the surface it has gone through considerable mutations and developed new forms and internal relations. Similarly, localism has also 'modernised'. As we saw in Chapter 4, people in Erba with strong localist values generally welcomed the European dimension, were in favour of a policy of privatisation and institutional decentralisation, participated in horizontal associations, and felt positive about various organisations generally associated with a modern liberal society, such as banks, industry and the media. By contrast, people in Sesto with weak localist values were in some respects more backward-looking, since they rejected privatisation, felt generally hostile towards banks and industry, and were more lukewarm regarding institutional change. It would be impossible to say which of the two localities is more 'modern'. As for the merits and demerits of each type of society, this is largely a misleading issue. Even if we agreed that Sesto, rather than Erba, represented a more desirable, open, tolerant, civic and individualist society, we could not model Erba (and innumerable other similar towns) along Sesto's values and culture, unless we believed that three into two will go. What we *can* do is bring out the more desirable traits in Erba's political culture and make sure that its less pleasant aspects are neutralised and played down, rather than pandered to. This means, to a large extent, neutralising the Northern League, which is not the same as demonising this party as an expression of selfishness, parochialism and cultural backwardness. It is precisely the modernity of the type of localism found in Erba which accounts in great part for the political success of the Northern League. What many often found puzzling and mystifying about this party, its being a mixture of the parochial and the neo-liberal, the folklorist and the managerial, is in fact a direct function of the modern relevance of localism, not just in Italy but in Europe. This brings me back to the more recent studies on the rise of the Northern League as the political voice of the north-eastern areas of small-scale industrialisation.

The modern face of political localism

Today we live in global times, which may be interpreted as the terminal death-knell for cultural and political localism. However, in reality, globalisation has given a new urgency to local economies and subcultures, and simultaneously reduced the space available to the nation-state. According to Cox (1994: 49), the state has been converted into 'a transmission belt from the global to the national economy, where heretofore it had acted as the bulwark defending domestic welfare from external disturbances'. Held (1995: 131) also stressed that 'it is much harder for individual governments to intervene and manage their economies faced with a global division of labour, the absence of capital controls and the operation of the world financial markets'.

One of the main political consequences related to the process of economic globalisation is the emergence of what is known as 'multi-level governance'. This term refers to the emergence of supra-national entities, or 'macro-regions', such as the European Community, which have acquired some of the powers previously reserved for nation-states because they are better placed to develop coordinated and collective policies to deal with the internationalisation of trade, production and finance. It also refers to the parallel emergence of sub-national constituencies, or 'micro-regions', partly as a result of increasing regional disparities due to the free movement of capital and labour and to the weakening of the national state's regulatory powers. As Held (1995: 133) remarked, strategies of regulation of economic activity will inevitably take place at local, as opposed to national, level. Multi-level governance has been accompanied by a reshaping of cultural and political identities, leading to 'the emergence, or re-emergence, of local movements seeking autonomy or even independence from present nation-states and a rush towards regionalism' (Sideri 1997: 43).

As I mentioned above, various studies have begun to address the issue of why Italy's Catholic-orientated areas of small-scale industry, located predominantly in the north-eastern regions, have raised their voice and even threatened exit from the Italian nation-state. Wild (1998) argued that the political programme of the Northern League and in particular its insistence on regional autonomy, must be considered a response to the constraints of scale faced by industrial districts, which need increasingly to develop new forms of regional cooperation, interaction and governance. Wild pointed out that the better performance of the communist-controlled local and regional political institutions in Emilia-Romagna and the central regions was an important factor in accounting for the continuing success of the heir to the old Communist Party in this part of Italy, in stark contrast to the collapse of Christian Democracy in the north-eastern regions. Anastasia and Corò (1996) also stressed the increasing importance of the regional milieux for the future development of Italy's North-East, and presented various possible future scenarios for the area, all of which contemplated the strengthening of the regional dimension in one form or another. They suggested that a regional strategy of development was the inevitable consequence of the process of economic globalisation. Various scholars have also shown how small- and medium-sized firms in the North-East have started to decentralise part of the production process to eastern European countries such as the Czech Republic, while also becoming sub-contractors to western European, predominantly German, firms. Some larger firms, such as Luxottica, have entered the capitals markets via the London and New York stock markets, in preference to the Milan bourse. According to Lago, the North-East has already started to think of itself in terms of a distinct macro-region, conscious of the fact that it is surrounded by strong and highly autonomous regions such as Bavaria: 'the institutional unification of the North-East is [...] an obligatory perspective along the road of achieving greater efficiency' (1996: 112).

The process of globalisation has accelerated regional disparities, creating both winners and losers. The process of European integration, on the other hand, has reduced the price regions have to pay if they want to acquire greater institutional and political autonomy, thanks to the abolition of internal customs barriers and the European single currency. In this context, the 'winning' regions welcome the possibility of loosening their bonds with the nation-state and are tempted to go it alone. The growth of the market has clearly contributed to the crisis of the nation-state, highlighting the growing dysfunction between the polycentrism of the former and the monocentrism of the latter. We now live in times when the primacy of economics over politics is being asserted increasingly forcefully. As Ohmae (1996) openly advocated, a new economic rationality is destined to prevail around the world, against which political and social interests and pressures will be of no avail. As for nation-states, 'the current paralysis of nation-states now shows them to have been a transitional mode of organisation for managing economic affairs [...] Given suitable autonomy, region states – by virtue of their unique ability to put global logic first – can provide precisely the kind of change agent the times require: effective engines of prosperity and improved quality of life for the people of the global economy' (Ohmae 1996: 149).

Ohmae's vision of the future, based on an analysis of the likely effects of the new globalising trends, puts the regionalism and localism of the Northern League squarely at the forefront of present-day economic and political thinking, while relegating modernisation theories, with their emphasis on homogeneous nation-states, among the category of the 'have-beens'. One could object that the political project of the Northern League, even though it makes sense in the context of economic globalisation and the advocacy of the supreme rationality of the new world order, relies heavily on emotional ties, a charismatic leader, and a populist style. However, many other 'modernising' parties have shared these same characteristics, including, to mention just one, the Conservative Party in Britain under Margaret Thatcher.

The secessionism of the Northern League, however, has been only one – albeit admittedly the most dramatic – of different ways in which the local dimension has reshaped its identity and found political expression in Italy. We should start from the premise that the process of globalisation has created anxiety in all regions, both winners and losers, as they are all having to adjust and respond to growing international competition. The findings presented in this book have shown that feelings of insecurity and defensiveness were present in both localities surveyed, leading to an erosion of their traditional solidarist cultures. While in Sesto such feelings went hand in hand with a 'resistance to change' mentality, in Erba the prevailing mood was in favour of neo-liberal policies and institutional change and, in the case of Northern League supporters, extreme individualism and localism as well as 'closure' to all outsiders. Yet this bold mood may have disguised a growing anxiety in a climate of increased competitiveness and volatile markets. In the North-East there are strong feelings that the regional model of development is at a cross-roads. After several years of economic growth, the region has been experiencing a slowdown in industrial production and a sustained exodus of its firms towards central and eastern Europe. Indeed the Northern League itself has in recent times shifted emphasis from an aggressively independentist and neo-liberal stance to a defensive and protectionist position, no longer arguing for 'Padania' to go it alone but to find its place within a wider Mitteleuropean entity.

As Kitschelt (1995: 267) wrote, 'ethno-cultural mobilisation is very much an interaction effect, a result of the conjuncture of primordial cultural collectivities, economic modernisation and communications, imbalances of resource control, and strategies of élite politics'. He added: 'Economic competition and élite strategies are complementary forces that account for the actual mobilisation where there was only a dormant sense of ethnicity before' (Ibid.: 267). The crucial importance attributed by Kitschelt to the role of élites suggests that competing and alternative élite strategies may yet make ethnicity (or, as in this case, ethno-regionalism), once again dormant. As Cacciari pointed out in an interview (*La Repubblica*, 13 July 1998: 9), a substantial part of the electorate of the North-East does not recognise itself in the Northern League, but is nevertheless putting forward a concrete and modern request for politics, a request which until recently clashed with the backward-looking attitudes of Italian political parties. This was confirmed by the findings of the Erba survey, which showed that there was considerable support for institutional and economic change, particularly for greater regional autonomy and a policy of privatisation, among voters of all parties. Even the concept of a federal Italy (at a time when it was clearly associated with Northern League politics) attracted some favour in Erba among all voters and both Catholic and lay respondents. In the Lombard provinces east of Erba and throughout the Veneto, support for federalism would have been even stronger. As Pansa (1997: 55) remarked some time ago, 'Rome does not understand that, in the Veneto, workers, entrepreneurs, trade-unionists, Cacciari, Carraro, the élites, those who are agnostic, those who feel nostalgic for the Venetian Republic, even rich and poor alike, have only one thing in common: they are radically federalist'. Thus a substantial constituency in the north-eastern regions, including areas of small-scale industry in Lombardy, is asking politics to perform a new role and to provide an innovative regulatory framework for dealing with and responding to economic globalisation. In this context, the ability of the Italian state to re-invent itself and set up a federalist structure may yet re-establish the primacy of politics over economics.

Modern politics for a 'modern' country

This is not a book on Italian politics, nevertheless the findings presented in the volume have some bearing upon current debates revolving around the merits and demerits of various political systems and institutions which Italy may introduce to replace those rendered obsolete by the end of the Cold War and the collapse of the traditional ideologies. The starting point is, once again, modernity. What do we mean by modernity and which political institutions fit a 'modern' country? I have argued throughout this book that modernity is not uni-dimensional or uni-linear. What is generally meant by modernity is the modern condition of Anglo-Saxon societies, which is taken as the paradigm of the modern condition the world over. In one of his latest books, Giddens (1990 and 1994), as we saw in Part I, made this position unequivocally clear, by listing kinship relations, social ties and the local community as contexts related to pre-modern societies and cultures. As a result, those countries which do not present similar traits to those offered by Anglo-Saxon societies are considered still on the way to 'modernisation proper', and countless explanations are put forward for their failures to exhibit the same characteristics as the truly 'modern' societies. Alternatively, every effort is made to interpret change in the non-Anglo-Saxon countries as denoting a decisive move in the direction of 'modernisation' proper. This has been precisely the fate reserved for Italy ever since the collapse of the old political system opened a debate as to the best way to modernise the country's institutions. As Eve (1996: 49) remarked, 'notions as widespread as "modernisation" and even many conceptualisations of "the state" or " the market" contain implicit comparisons with pre-modern situations where the state is not fully developed and the market not mature – comparisons which have their roots in comparisons between nations. It is better to make comparisons explicitly and methodically, using clear empirical examples, rather than risk using frameworks which contain elements of idealised contrasts or implicitly evolutionist binary distinctions'. What is in doubt is not the need to modernise Italy's institutions. The real issue is whether they need to modernise by importing a foreign model from one of the countries deemed to be already fully modern, or by setting up a political system which is both fit for the twenty-first century and able to build upon the social and cultural traits which are the unique and specific product of Italian history.

One of the worrying aspects of the desire to import a foreign model of political institutions in Italy is that it overlooks the extent to which other advanced countries are faced with the same dilemma of having to modernise their own political systems, following the end of the Cold War and of the world settlement associated with it. The U.K. is a fitting example. This country is still to a large extent relying on political institutions devised for the period when it was a world power and had a vast Empire. It has an old-fashioned and undemocratic House of Lords, an excessively centralised administration, a judicial system in disrepute, and an electoral system which, although it appears to work smoothly and continues to produce strong governments, is increasingly showing territorial fault-lines, remarkably similar to those which are generally considered an Italian peculiarity (Norris 1997). Indeed, it was to a large extent the complete irrelevance of the governing Conservative Party in Scotland for much of the 1980s and 1990s that made a Devolution Bill inevitable. The case for a radical transformation of British politics was made forcefully by Hutton (1996: 10): 'Britain in the 1990s has lost its sense of direction and its people are at odds with themselves. It needs to revitalise its economy, modernise its institutions, rewrite the contract between the members of its society and recover its self-esteem'. Ironically, the U.K. is moving gradually away from a political system which in the current political debate in Italy is still presented as a highly desirable model. There are similar lessons to be learnt from the fact that, as was mentioned in the Introduction to Part I, the U.K. had been looking eagerly at ways to import some of the traits exhibited by the 'Tiger economies', when it was caught off-balance by the sudden collapse of those same economies. Interestingly, the Italian model of small-scale industries had also been held for much of the 1980s as an example of a desirable and successful model that the U.K. should strive to import, somewhat regardless of its close links to social and cultural values and lifestyles which could not easily be replicated.

While other countries have been envying Italy its small-business economy, until recently Italian political experts and actors seemed eager to devise a political system which took little account of the needs and demands of this sector, preferring to demonise the way it had managed to raise its political voice in some areas of the country. In the vacuum created by this state of affairs, the Northern League opted for secessionism and discarded federalism as a solution to the problems created by globalisation and uneven regional development. In addition, the 'protectionist' stance adopted by the Northern League in the late 1990s, as well as the party's opposition to the war in Kosovo, had an adverse effect upon its electoral fortunes, judging by the poor results achieved by the party at the 1999 European and administrative elections and by the reactions of its supporters (*La Padania*, 1–2 July 1999). The results fuelled the hope – indeed, in some quarters, the certainty – that Berlusconi's *Forza Italia* would mark the end of the Northern League. Yet a careful analysis of the results of the 1999 administrative elections shows that the shift from the Northern League to *Forza Italia* was fairly minimal (Ministero dell'Interno. Direzione Generale per i Servizi Elettorali 1999). Many supporters of the Northern League chose to abstain, rather than switch to another party.

More importantly, secessionism provided a marked demarcation between the Northern League and the other parties, which managed to regain the initiative and moved to occupy the political space vacated by the Northern League. Nowadays federalism attracts the support of almost half of the Italian electorate (Mannheimer 2000: 9) and nearly all political parties. As Vassallo (1997: 694) wrote: 'At the time of the 1992 elections, only the representatives of the Northern League were "federalist" [...] By the 1996 elections all the main political groups had become convinced supporters of federalism, even though the term was generally linked to adjectives such as "solidarist" or "unitary"'. Federalism, however, means all things to all parties. For some it means further decentralisation not just to the regions, but also to the provinces and communes, so as to avoid the risk that the regions may start behaving like the central state vis-à-vis the lower tiers of government. For others, it simply means a new version of Italy's current administrative structure, with the important novelty of the granting of tax-raising powers to the regions. Still others reject the idea that the current regional structure can provide a sound basis for a federal state, and stress the need to create new macro- or meso-regions to replace the existing ones, which are considered too small to be viable.

It is clear that the relationship between the different tiers of government constitutes the main point of contention and the main obstacle towards a restructuring of the Italian state. This is not surprising, since in Italy strong municipal identities have long preceded the emergence of regional ones. Italy's large cities, in particular, have their own identities and do not generally form part of their own region's model of development or socio-cultural configuration. As Lago (1996) pointed out, Venice does not belong to the 'modello veneto', since it possesses a different socio-economic structure and cultural environment. Milan has very little in common with eastern and northern Lombardy, which, in turn, is undoubtedly part of the 'modello veneto'. Indeed Bagnasco (1996b: 1) pointed out, quite perceptively, that the regional capitals of northern Italy have not been capable of interpreting and representing the interests of their regions, precisely because they have little in common with the socio-economic systems which characterise the wider regional territory. My own survey demonstrated that in both Sesto and Erba the local commune commanded far greater allegiance than the region among respondents, including Northern League voters in Erba, even though the region had grown in stature and had gained more affection in recent years.

Another crucial obstacle to a decisive move towards political and administrative decentralisation is the perceived risk that it will exacerbate the gap between North and South. Some southern intellectuals have interpreted the disquiet felt by many in the region by calling for a renewed 'pact of solidarity' and putting forward a positive, albeit cautious, reappraisal of the policy of state intervention in the South carried out in the 1960s and 1970s, arguing (correctly) that it reduced income disparities between the two halves of the country (Bevilacqua 1993 and 1996, Compasso 1996). Other analysts, either from the South or sincerely concerned about the future prospects of economic and social regeneration in the region, have adopted a more innovative stance and argued that further decentralisation represents the best way forward for the South, too. Trigilia (1992: 189–90, also 1994) called for the introduction of greater regional autonomy coupled with greater financial responsibility at regional level. In this way, regional governments would become more directly responsible for allocating resources so that policy-making would be both visible and accountable to their electorates. Mutti (1992) also emphasised the need to promote collective action at local level. Leonardi (1995), following Putnam, analysed the prospects of the Italian South by adopting the concept of social capital, and concluded that, although this was largely absent in the region, it could not 'be established or accumulated if local communities are not empowered to determine their own outcomes' (1995: 178). Helliwell and Putnam (1995) further applied the concept of social capital to the Italian case and argued that regional governments in the 1980s had promoted greater wealth creation in the North but had also contributed to the economic slowdown registered by the South. As they put it succinctly, 'regions with better institutions grew faster' (Ibid.: 14). Contrary to what might be expected from their analysis, they concluded that the divergence between the two areas should be considered temporary, 'since the larger income gaps, and the associated differences in the effectiveness of government, will offer more good examples for the lagging regions to follow, and will probably increase the demands from their citizens that they should do so' (Ibid.: 14). In other words, they did not advocate a return to administrative and political centralisation but, rather, pointed to the virtuous effects that inter-regional competition and the diffusion of best practices might have on the weaker regions. Despite their divergences, most commentators agree, as we saw in Part I, that the South does not constitute an undifferentiated entity; on the contrary, it is made up of extremely diverse economies and socio-political cultures. It is also remarkable that, according to Mannheimer (2000: 9), there is now a growing demand for regional autonomy and even federalism in the South itself, even though it is less widespread than in the northern regions.

As was discussed in Part I, Italy's multiple identities can be seen as a resource, rather than a weakness or an obstacle. From this point of view Italy is better placed than other countries to devise an effective institutional response to the process of globalisation. What is required, however, is the ability to think innovatively and creatively on the part of the Italian state. One of the most ardent advocates of a 're-invention' of the state to make way for greater popular sovereignty is Piero Bassetti, President of the Milan Chamber of Commerce. In a recent book, he argued that the only possible response to the threat of the Northern League and, more importantly, to the challenges of globalisation, consisted in a new form of state, which he defined as a 'network' state without a centre, characterised by flexibility, pluralism and diversity (Bassetti 1996: 71–100, also Perulli 1995, Pichierri 1995).

It has been argued that, across the globe, 'the drastic transformations observed during the last two decades have created a double gap between the new economic requirements and the existing political order' (Boyer and Hollingsworth 1997: 466). Whilst governance structures ought to be able to facilitate transitions (Sabel 1997: 159), it is also the case that 'the incapacity of a society to alter its institutional configuration makes it vulnerable to absolute economic decline' (Boyer and Hollingsworth 1997: 455). This is precisely the kind of test the Italian state is currently facing. In this context, a half-baked and half-hearted commitment to a federal structure on the part of the government, may have the effect of hardening attitudes and increasing the attractiveness of the secessionist solution (Curi 1997: 52). Conversely, a decisive move towards political and fiscal federalism, accompanied by a solidarity pact to ensure that the less developed regions would not suffer if they fell behind in terms of economic growth, would defuse the threat posed by radical and ideological regionalism and re-establish the benign face of Italy's localist cultures.

Events in Italy are now unfolding rapidly. The Catholic Church has recently signalled its opening to a federal reform of the country's political institutions, partly under pressure from their grassroots clergy based in the north-eastern regions (Moia 1997). In February 1999 all weekly newspapers of the dioceses of Veneto, Friuli Venezia Giulia, and Trentino Alto Adige carried the same editorial, embracing federalism (Magister 1999: 75). The centre-left government has introduced substantial new measures of decentralisation and regional autonomy, including elements of fiscal federalism. In February 2000, Berlusconi's *Forza Italia* forged a new alliance with the Northern League, which hinges upon an agreement regarding a radical federalist restructuring of the Italian state and the abandonment of secessionism. Following this pact, the centre-right coalition went on to win the April 2000 regional elections, and now controls eight regions against the centre-left's seven. The elections also re-established territorial divisions, with the northern regions voting predominantly for the centre-right and the central regions voting predominantly for the centre-left. The

Presidents of the northern regions, all from the centre-right coalition, are already pressing hard for a rapid process of decentralisation, even raising concerns for the unity of the Italian state. Indeed, the President of the Italian Republic, Ciampi, repeatedly and publicly expressed his support for a federalist reform of the state without endangering its unitary framework. Conversely, within the Left Democrats (DS), a 'federalist war' is currently under way, following the poor showing of the centre-left at the regional elections, and the party leadership is accused by many northern members and officers of being excessively Rome-based and too fearful of causing divisions in the country (*La Repubblica*, 6 June 2000: 8). While it is impossible to predict the outcome of such heated debates, and it is understandable that the prospect of a federal Italy raises numerous fears and concerns, this book points to an uncontroversial conclusion. Unless the Italian political class chooses to adopt the solution of those scholars and political commentators who ignore the persistence of localism in Italian society and its growing credentials in these global times, it must engage in developing and promoting a new political system which builds upon the best traits of the country's political culture, including what its localism has to offer.

Appendix

Questionnaire

Q1) Sex   (a) Male [ ]   (b) Female [ ]

Q2) Age

          (a) 18–30   [ ]
          (b) 31–40   [ ]
          (c) 41–50   [ ]
          (d) 51–60   [ ]
          (e) More than 60   [ ]

Q3) Nationality

          (a) Italian   [ ]
          (b) European Union   [ ]
          (c) Other   [ ]

Q4) Status

          (a) Single   [ ]
          (b) Married/cohabiting   [ ]
          (c) Widowed   [ ]
          (d) Divorced/separated   [ ]

Q5) Education

          (a) Primary school   [ ]
          (b) Middle school   [ ]
          (c) Vocational qualifications [ ]
          (d) Secondary school   [ ]
          (e) University education   [ ]
          (f) University degree   [ ]
          (g) Self-taught   [ ]

Q15) Would you like to change job?   Yes [ ]   No [ ]

Q16) If yes, what kind of job would you like to do:

(a) Private sector employee   [ ]
(b) Public sector employee   [ ]
(c) Professional   [ ]
(d) Artisan, self-employed   [ ]
(e) Teacher   [ ]
(f) Other   [ ]

Q17) Which of the following statements best fits your beliefs?
(please choose only one)

(a) Personal realisation is most important in life   [ ]
(b) Family interests come before individual aspirations   [ ]
(c) The family is a handicap in terms of career success   [ ]
(d) Solidarity is the most important human value   [ ]

Q18) To what extent do you participate in the activities of one or more of
the following groups or associations?

	Regularly (A)	Sometimes (B)	Never (C)
(a) Sport/leisure groups	[ ]	[ ]	[ ]
(b) Religious associations	[ ]	[ ]	[ ]
(c) Voluntary associations	[ ]	[ ]	[ ]
(d) Artistic/cultural associations	[ ]	[ ]	[ ]
(e) Environmental groups	[ ]	[ ]	[ ]
(f) Charity associations	[ ]	[ ]	[ ]
(g) Professional associations	[ ]	[ ]	[ ]

Q19) In terms of religious practice, which of the following statements
best fits your and your parents' attitudes:

	Yourself (A)	Your father (B)	Your mother (C)
(a) Believer, regular Church attendant	[ ]	[ ]	[ ]
(b) Believer, irregular Church attendant	[ ]	[ ]	[ ]
(c) Believer, non-Church attendant	[ ]	[ ]	[ ]
(d) Non-believer, irregular Church Attendant	[ ]	[ ]	[ ]
(e) Non-believer, non-Church attendant	[ ]	[ ]	[ ]

Q20) How frequently do you read:

	Regularly (A)	Occasionally (B)	Never (C)
(a) A national daily newspaper	[ ]	[ ]	[ ]
(b) A local daily newspaper	[ ]	[ ]	[ ]
(c) A weekly magazine	[ ]	[ ]	[ ]
(d) A political party newspaper	[ ]	[ ]	[ ]

Q21) Are you and/or your parents members of:

	Yourself (A)	Your father (B)	Your mother (C)
(a) A political party	[ ]	[ ]	[ ]
(b) A trade union	[ ]	[ ]	[ ]
(c) An industrial/professional association	[ ]	[ ]	[ ]
(d) A co-operative	[ ]	[ ]	[ ]

Q22) To what extent do you participate in the activities of one or more of the following associations?

	Regularly (A)	Occasionally (B)	Never (C)
(a) A political party	[ ]	[ ]	[ ]
(b) A trade union	[ ]	[ ]	[ ]
(c) A cooperative	[ ]	[ ]	[ ]
(d) A local council	[ ]	[ ]	[ ]
(e) A neighbourhood council	[ ]	[ ]	[ ]

Q23) In the last ten years, how has the importance of the following environments changed?

	More important than before (A)	Same as before (B)	Less important than before (C)
(a) Family	[ ]	[ ]	[ ]
(b) Friends	[ ]	[ ]	[ ]
(c) Work	[ ]	[ ]	[ ]
(d) Religion	[ ]	[ ]	[ ]
(e) Trade Unions	[ ]	[ ]	[ ]
(f) Politics	[ ]	[ ]	[ ]
(g) Culture/sport/leisure	[ ]	[ ]	[ ]

Q24) For which political party did you and your parents vote in the last elections and in the previous ones?

		1 – 1992 Elections You Father Mother			2 – 1987 Elections You Father Mother		
		(A)	(B)	(C)	(A)	(B)	(C)
(a)	MSI	[ ]	[ ]	[ ]	[ ]	[ ]	[ ]
(b)	PLI	[ ]	[ ]	[ ]	[ ]	[ ]	[ ]
(c)	DC	[ ]	[ ]	[ ]	[ ]	[ ]	[ ]
(d)	PR1	[ ]	[ ]	[ ]	[ ]	[ ]	[ ]
(e)	PSDI	[ ]	[ ]	[ ]	[ ]	[ ]	[ ]
(f)	PSI	[ ]	[ ]	[ ]	[ ]	[ ]	[ ]
(g)	PR(radicals)	[ ]	[ ]	[ ]	[ ]	[ ]	[ ]
(h)	Greens	[ ]	[ ]	[ ]	[ ]	[ ]	[ ]
(i)	PCI/PDS	[ ]	[ ]	[ ]	[ ]	[ ]	[ ]
(j)	PCI/Refoundation	[ ]	[ ]	[ ]	[ ]	[ ]	[ ]
(k)	Northern League	[ ]	[ ]	[ ]	[ ]	[ ]	[ ]
(l)	Other	[ ]	[ ]	[ ]	[ ]	[ ]	[ ]
(m)	Abstained	[ ]	[ ]	[ ]	[ ]	[ ]	[ ]
(n)	Don't Know		[ ]	[ ]		[ ]	[ ]

Q25) For which party or coalition of parties do you intend to vote in the next elections?

(a) PPI on its own or as part of a coalition [ ]
(b) PDS on its own or as part of a coalition [ ]
(c) MSI on its own or as part of a coalition [ ]
(d) Northern League on its own or as part of a coalition [ ]
(e) Moderate coalition with Berlusconi [ ]
(f) Moderate coalition without Berlusconi [ ]
(g) Other [ ]
(h) I will not vote/spoilt ballot paper [ ]
(i) Undecided [ ]

Q26) To what extent did one or more of the following factors contribute to your party preference in the 1992 political elections?

	To a great extent (A)	To some extent (B)	Not at all (C)
(a) Loyalty to a party	[ ]	[ ]	[ ]
(b) Electoral programme	[ ]	[ ]	[ ]
(c) I share its ideals	[ ]	[ ]	[ ]
(d) Defends my interests	[ ]	[ ]	[ ]
(e) Family/local tradition	[ ]	[ ]	[ ]
(f) Morality	[ ]	[ ]	[ ]
(g) It has local roots	[ ]	[ ]	[ ]
(h) Competence of candidates	[ ]	[ ]	[ ]

Q27) If in 1992 you voted for a different party than in 1987, to what extent did one or more of the following factors influence your changed party preference?

	To a large extent (A)	To a certain extent (B)	Not at all (C)
(a) Corruption in the old party	[ ]	[ ]	[ ]
(b) Confused programme of old party	[ ]	[ ]	[ ]
(c) The new party looks after local interests	[ ]	[ ]	[ ]
(d) My ideals have changed	[ ]	[ ]	[ ]
(e) The new party defends my interests better	[ ]	[ ]	[ ]
(f) Desire for change	[ ]	[ ]	[ ]
(g) One party is like another	[ ]	[ ]	[ ]

Q28) Where did you form your political ideas? (you can give up to two indications)

(a) Family	[ ]
(b) Friends	[ ]
(c) Church and religious associations	[ ]
(d) School	[ ]
(e) Work	[ ]
(f) Trade Union	[ ]
(g) Political Party	[ ]

Q29) In your family and with your friends, nowadays do you discuss politics more or less frequently than in the past (5–10 years ago)?

	Today (A)	In the past (B)
(a) Not at all	[ ]	[ ]
(b) A little	[ ]	[ ]
(c) Quite frequently	[ ]	[ ]
(d) Very frequently	[ ]	[ ]

Q30) Among your relatives and friends, how many share your political opinions?

(a) Just a few	[ ]
(b) A considerable number	[ ]
(c) Many	[ ]
(d) The vast majority	[ ]
(e) Don't Know	[ ]

Q31) Please give your judgement of the following organisations and institutions, today and in the past (5–10 years ago):

	Today			In the past		
	Positive	Satisfactory	Negative	Positive	Satisfactory	Negative
	(A)	(B)	(C)	(D)	(E)	(F)
(a) Political parties	[ ]	[ ]	[ ]	[ ]	[ ]	[ ]
(b) Trade Unions	[ ]	[ ]	[ ]	[ ]	[ ]	[ ]
(c) Local Government	[ ]	[ ]	[ ]	[ ]	[ ]	[ ]
(d) Employers' Associations	[ ]	[ ]	[ ]	[ ]	[ ]	[ ]
(e) Banks	[ ]	[ ]	[ ]	[ ]	[ ]	[ ]
(f) Industry	[ ]	[ ]	[ ]	[ ]	[ ]	[ ]
(g) Catholic Church	[ ]	[ ]	[ ]	[ ]	[ ]	[ ]
(h) Local Media	[ ]	[ ]	[ ]	[ ]	[ ]	[ ]
(i) National Media	[ ]	[ ]	[ ]	[ ]	[ ]	[ ]
(j) Judiciary	[ ]	[ ]	[ ]	[ ]	[ ]	[ ]
(k) Regional government	[ ]	[ ]	[ ]	[ ]	[ ]	[ ]
(l) National Government	[ ]	[ ]	[ ]	[ ]	[ ]	[ ]
(m) Parliament	[ ]	[ ]	[ ]	[ ]	[ ]	[ ]

Q32) To which of the following collectivities do you feel you most belong today compared to the past (5–10 years ago)? (ranging from 0 = no feeling of belonging to 9 = maximum feeling of belonging)

	Today (A)	In the past (B)
	(out of 9)	
(a) The commune where you live	[ ]	[ ]
(b) The province where you live	[ ]	[ ]
(c) The region where you live	[ ]	[ ]
(d) Italy	[ ]	[ ]
(e) Europe	[ ]	[ ]
(f) The world	[ ]	[ ]

Q33) To what extent do you agree with the following statements?

	A lot (A)	A certain extent (B)	A little (C)	Not at all (D)
(a) I would pay higher taxes in exchange for better services	[ ]	[ ]	[ ]	[ ]
(b) I would pay fewer taxes at the expense of fewer services	[ ]	[ ]	[ ]	[ ]
(c) We need to speed up the privatisation process	[ ]	[ ]	[ ]	[ ]

(d) Privatisations aggravate the
   Italian economic situation [ ]   [ ]   [ ] [ ]
(e) We need a Europe of the
   Regions   [ ]   [ ]   [ ] [ ]
(f) European integration should
   proceed at greater speed   [ ]   [ ]   [ ] [ ]
(g) European integration has
   gone too far   [ ]   [ ]   [ ] [ ]
(h) The Regions should have
   wider autonomy   [ ]   [ ]   [ ] [ ]
(i) More autonomy to the
   Regions would aggravate
   territorial imbalances   [ ]   [ ]   [ ] [ ]
(j) The Italian State should
   become a federal State   [ ]   [ ]   [ ] [ ]

Q34) For which party did you vote at the 1993 administrative elections?

(a) DC   [ ]
(b) PSI   [ ]
(c) PDS   [ ]
(d) Northern League   [ ]
(e) MSI   [ ]
(f) Other   [ ]
(g) Abstained   [ ]

Q35) Which of the following factors influenced your choice of party?
(Choose one only)

(a) Loyalty to the party   [ ]
(b) It looks after local interests   [ ]
(c) Economic competence   [ ]
(d) Defends the interests of the social class to which I belong [ ]
(e) Competence of candidates   [ ]

Q36) In your view, which of the following constitute the main problems
affecting your commune today compared to the past (5–10 years ago)?
(Choose up to three answers in order of importance: 1 = most important
problem, 2 = second most important, 3 = third most important)

	Today (A)	In the past (B)
(a) Drugs	[ ]	[ ]
(b) Criminality	[ ]	[ ]
(c) Unemployment	[ ]	[ ]
(d) Environment: green space, pollution, traffic congestion	[ ]	[ ]

(e) Housing conditions	[ ]	[ ]
(f) Inadequate infrastructure	[ ]	[ ]
(g) Political corruption	[ ]	[ ]
(h) Immigration	[ ]	[ ]
(i) Deterioration of social relations	[ ]	[ ]
(j) Social and political conflicts	[ ]	[ ]

Q37) In your view, extra-EU immigration to your commune has been: (choose one only)

(a) Of minimal proportions	[ ]
(b) Considerable but without generating social problems or problems of integration	[ ]
(c) Considerable, generating social problems and/or problems of integration	[ ]

Q38) In your view, what kind of policy should be adopted towards extra-EU immigrants?

	Agree (A)	Disagree (B)
(a) Repatriation	[ ]	[ ]
(b) Help them find work and housing in Italy	[ ]	[ ]
(c) Respect their culture	[ ]	[ ]
(d) Cultural assimilation	[ ]	[ ]
(e) Create a multi-ethnic society	[ ]	[ ]

Q39) To what extent do you agree with the following statements?

	A lot (A)	To a certain extent (B)	A little (C)	Not at all (D)
(a) Extra-EU immigrants create competition on the labour market	[ ]	[ ]	[ ]	[ ]
(b) Extra-EU immigrants take away houses and services from Italian citizens	[ ]	[ ]	[ ]	[ ]
(c) Residents must have precedence for houses and jobs	[ ]	[ ]	[ ]	[ ]
(d) Citizenship must be granted on the basis of residence	[ ]	[ ]	[ ]	[ ]
(e) Citizenship must be granted on the basis of ethnicity	[ ]	[ ]	[ ]	[ ]
(f) An ethnic mix is not a good thing	[ ]	[ ]	[ ]	[ ]

(g) My commune has lost its
    identity due to extra-EU
    immigration   [ ]   [ ]   [ ]   [ ]
(h) My commune had already lost
    its identity prior to extra-EU
    immigration   [ ]   [ ]   [ ]   [ ]
(i) My commune has lost its
    identity due to economic
    recession   [ ]   [ ]   [ ]   [ ]
(j) Extra-EU immigrants threaten
    the local culture   [ ]   [ ]   [ ]   [ ]
(k) Southern Italians are well
    integrated in the town   [ ]   [ ]   [ ]   [ ]
(l) Southern Italians threaten the
    local culture   [ ]   [ ]   [ ]   [ ]

References

Alessandrini, S. and Dallago, B. (1987) *The Unofficial Economy. Consequences and Perspectives in Different Economic Systems*, Aldershot, MacMillan.

Almond, G.A. and Verba, S. (1963) *The Civic Culture: Political attitudes and democracy in five countries*, Princeton, Princeton University Press.

Almond G.A. and Verba, S. (1980) *The Civic Culture Revisited*, Boston and Toronto, Little, Brown and Company.

Ambrosini, M. (1992) 'Il lavoro degli immigrati. Analisi del caso lombardo', *Studi Emigrazione/Etudes Migrations*, 29, 105, pp. 2–20.

Amin, A., Johnson, S. and Storey, D. (1986) 'Small Firms and the Process of Economic Development', *Journal of Regional Policy*, October–December, pp. 493–517.

Anastasia, B. and Corò, G. (1996) *Evoluzione di un'economia regionale. Il Nord-Est dopo il successo*, Portogruaro, Ediciclo.

Baccetti, C. (1997) 'Pisa. Il "nuovo continuo"' in Corbetta and Parisi (eds) *Cavalieri e fanti.*

Bagnasco, A. (1977) *Tre Italie. La problematica territoriale dello sviluppo italiano*, Bologna, Il Mulino.

Bagnasco, A. (1988) *La costruzione sociale del mercato. Studi sullo sviluppo della piccola impresa in Italia*, Bologna, Il Mulino.

Bagnasco, A. (1994) 'Regioni, tradizione civica, modernizzazione italiana: un commento alla ricerca di Putnam', *Stato e Mercato*, 40, pp. 93–103.

Bagnasco, A. (1996a) *L'Italia in tempi di cambiamento politico*, Bologna, Il Mulino.

Bagnasco, A. (1996b) 'Bossi trenta in sociologia ma bocciato come leader', *La Repubblica Affari e Finanza*, 29 April.

Bagnasco, A. and Trigilia, C. (1984) *Società e politica nelle aree di piccola impresa: il caso di Bassano*, Venice, Arsenale.

Bagnasco, A. and Trigilia, C. (1985) *Società e politica nelle aree di piccola impresa: il caso della Valdelsa*, Milan, Angeli.

Banfield, E. (1958) *The Moral Basis of a Backward Society*, Glencoe, Free Press.

Barbagli, M. (1991a) 'Marriage and the family in Italy in the early nineteenth century' in J.A.Davis and P. Ginsborg (eds), *Society and Politics in the Age of the Risorgimento.*

Barbagli, M. (1991b) 'I genitori di lei e quelli di lui. Una ricerca sui rapporti di parentela in Emilia Romagna', *Polis*, 5, 1, pp. 71–83.

Barbagli, M., Corbetta, P., Parisi, A.M.L. and Schadee, H.M.A. (1979) *Fluidità elettorale e classi sociali in Italia: 1968–1976*, Bologna, Il Mulino.

Barbagli, M. and Maccelli, A. (1985) *La partecipazione politica a Bologna*, Bologna, Il Mulino.

Barnes, S. H. and Kaase, M. (1979) *Political Action*, Beverly Hills and London, Sage Publications.

Barraclough, R. (1996) 'The Northern League and the 1996 General Election: Protest vote or political entrepreneurship?', *The Italianist*, 16, pp. 326–50.

Bartolini, S. and Mair, P. (1990) *Identity, Competition and Electoral Availability. The Stabilisation of European Electorates 1885–1985*, Cambridge, Cambridge University Press.

Bassetti, P. (1996) *L'Italia si è rotta? Un federalismo per l'Europa*, Bari, Laterza.

Becattini G. (1987) (ed.) *Mercato e forze locali: il distretto industriale*, Bologna, Il Mulino.

Becattini, G. (1991) 'The Marshallian Industrial District as a socio-economic notion', in Pyke, Becattini and Sengerberger, *Industrial Districts and Inter-firm Co-operation in Italy.*

Bell, D. (1988, 1st edition 1960) *The end of Ideology*, Cambridge, Massachusetts and London, Harvard University Press.

Bell, D.H. (1986*) Sesto San Giovanni: workers, culture and politics in an Italian town, 1880–1922*, New Brunswick, Rutgers University Press.

Bellucci, P. (1995) 'All'origine delle identità politiche' in Parisi and Schadee (eds) *Sulla soglia del cambiamento.*

Bellucci, P. (1997) 'Classi, identità politiche e interessi' in Corbetta and Parisi (eds) *A domanda risponde.*

Belotti, V. (1990) (ed.) *Giovani a Vicenza*, Venice, Fondazione Corazzin.

Bentivegna, S. (1995) 'Attori e strategie comunicative della campagna elettorale' in Pasquino (ed.) *L'alternanza inattesa.*

Bergo, L. and Ferrazza, D. (1987) 'Inchiesta. Sesto: il futuro dopo l'età industriale', *Il moderno*, 1987, 14–23.

Berrington, H.B. (1984) *Change in British Politics*, London, Frank Cass.

Berti, L. and Donegà, C. (1992) *Sesto San Giovanni. Gli scenari del cambiamento*, Milan, Angeli.

Bevilacqua, P. (1993) *Breve storia dell'Italia meridionale dall'Ottocento ad oggi*, Rome, Donzelli.

Bevilacqua, P. (1996) 'New and Old in the Southern Question', *Modern Italy*, 1, 2, pp. 81–92.

Biorcio, R. (1991) 'La Lega come attore politico: dal federalismo al populismo regionalista' in R. Mannheimer (ed.) *La Lega Lombarda.*

Bourdieu, P. (1980) 'Le capital social', *Actes de la Recherche en Sciences Sociales*, 31, pp. 2–3.

Boyer, R. and Hollingsworth, J.R. (1997) 'From National Embeddedness to Spatial and Institutional Nestedness' in Hollingsworth and Boyer (eds) *Contemporary Capitalism.*

Brierley, W. and Giacometti, L. (1996) 'Italian National Identity and the Failure of Regionalism' in Jenkins and Sofos (eds), *Nation and Identity in Contemporary Europe.*

Bruckner, E. and Knaup, K. (1993) 'Women's and Men's Friendships in Comparative Perspective', *European Sociological Review*, 9, 3, pp. 249–265.

Brula, P. (1993) *Les résultats électoraux du PCF à Vénissieux de 1945 à nos jours* (unpublished PCF document).

Bull, A. and Corner, P. (1993) *From Peasant to Entrepreneur. The Survival of the Family Economy in Italy*, Oxford, Berg.

Bull, A. and Milner, S. (1997) 'Local identities and territorial politics in Italy and France', *European Urban and Regional Studies*, 4, 1, pp. 33–43.

Bull, A., Pitt, M. and Szarka, J. (1993) *Entrepreneurial Textile Communities. A Comparative Study of Small Textile and Clothing Firms*, London, Chapman and Hall.

Bull, M. and Rhodes, M. (1997) *Crisis and Transition in Italian Politics*, London and Portland, Frank Cass.

Burrell, B.C. (1993) 'Party Decline, Party Transformation and Gender Politics: the USA', in J. Lovenduski and P. Norris (eds) *Gender and Party Politics*.

Caciagli, M., Cazzola, F., Morlino, L. and Passigli, S. (1994) *L'Italia fra crisi e transizione*, Bari, Laterza.

Cadioli, P.L. (1964) *Sesto San Giovanni dalle origini ad oggi*, Sesto San Giovanni, Il Cavallino d'oro.

Calise, M. (1993) 'Remaking the Italian Party System: How Lijphart Got It Wrong by Saying it Right', *West European Politics*, 16, 4, pp. 545–560.

Calise, M. (1994) *Dopo la partitocrazia*, Turin, Einaudi.

Calvi, G. and Vannucci, A. (1995) *L'elettore sconosciuto. Analisi socio-culturale e segmentazione degli orientamenti politici nel 1994*, Bologna, Il Mulino.

Cartocci, R. (1990) *Elettori in Italia. Riflessioni sulle vicende elettorali degli anni ottanta*, Bologna, Il Mulino.

Cartocci, R. (1991) 'Localismo e protesta politica', *Rivista italiana di scienza politica*, XXI, 3, 551–581.

Cartocci, R. (1994) *Fra Lega e Chiesa*, Bologna, Il Mulino.

Cavalli, A. and de Lillo, A. (1993) *Giovani anni '90*, Bologna, Il Mulino.

Censis (1992) *La situazione sociale del Paese. Speciale 26 Rapporto*, Milan, Angeli.

Cento Bull, A. (1989) 'Proto-industrialisation, small-scale capital accumulation and diffused entrepreneurship: the case of Brianza in Lombardy', *Social History*, 14, 2, pp. 177–200.

Cento Bull, A. (1992) 'The Lega Lombarda. A New Political Subculture for Lombardy's Industrial Districts', *The Italianist*, 12, pp. 179–83.

Cento Bull, A. (1993) The Politics of Industrial Districts in Lombardy. Replacing Christian Democracy with the Northern League, *The Italianist*, 13, pp. 209–229.

Cento Bull, A. (1996) 'Ethnicity, Racism and the Northern League', in C. Levy (ed.) *Regionalism in Italy: History, Identity and Politics*.

Centre d'histoire et d'études, Municipalité de Venissieux (1992) Elections à Vénissieux (unpublished working document kindly supplied by its authors).

Cerase, F.P. (1992) *Dopo il familismo, cosa? Tesi a confronto sulla questione meridionale negli anni '90*, Milan, Angeli.

Cesareo, V., Rovati, G. and Lombardi, M. (1989) *Localismo politico: il caso Lega Lombarda*, Varese, La Tipografia Varesina.

CGIL Lombardia-AASTER (1991) *Le passioni e gli interessi dei localismi lombardi*. Milan.

Città di Sesto San Giovanni (1992) *Sesto San Giovanni e lo sport*, Sesto San Giovanni, Comune di Sesto.

Clark, D. (1989) *Urban Decline*, London and New York, Routledge.

Coleman, J.S. (1988) 'Social capital in the creation of human capital', *American Journal of Sociology*, 94, pp. 95–120.

Comune di Sesto San Giovanni (1993) *Piano regolatore generale*, November 1993 (Approved October 1994).

Compasso, F. (1996) *Scritti per il Sud. La solidarietà possibile*, Naples, Edizioni Scientifiche Italiane.

Corbel, M. (1983) *Vénissieux: du village à la cité industrielle*, Paris, Messidor.

Corbetta, P. (1993), 'La Lega e lo sfaldamento del sistema', *Polis*, VII, 2, pp. 229–52.

Corbetta, P. and Parisi, A.M.L. (1994) 'Ancora due Italie. Sulla natura della diversità meridionale nel referendum del 18 aprile 1996', *Polis*, 1, pp. 11–33.

Corbetta, P. and Parisi, A.M.L. (1997a) *Cavalieri e fanti. Proposte e proponenti nelle elezioni del 1994 e del 1996*, Bologna, Il Mulino.

Corbetta, P. and Parisi, A.M.L. (1997b) *A domanda risponde. Il cambiamento del voto degli italiani nelle elezioni del 1994 e del 1996*, Bologna, Il Mulino.

Corbetta, P., Parisi, A.M.L. and Schadee, H.M.A. (1988) *Elezioni in Italia. Struttura e tipologia delle consultazioni politiche*, Bologna, Il Mulino.

Corner, P. (1997) 'Thumbs down for the family? A comment on Paolo Macry' in *Journal of Modern Italian Studies*, 2, 2, pp. 218–200.

Corti, P. (1990) (ed) *Società rurale e ruoli femminili in Italia tra ottocento e novecento*, Annali, 12, Istituto Alcide Cervi, Bologna, Il Mulino.

Corti, P. (1991) (ed) *Le donne nelle campagne italiane del novecento*. Annali, 13, Istituto Alcide Cervi, Bologna, Il Mulino.

Cox, R.W. (1994) 'Global Restructuring: Making Sense of the Changing International Political Economy', in Stubbs and Underhill (eds) *Political Economy and the Changing Global Order*.

Crewe, I. M. (1984) 'The electorate: partisan dealignment ten years on', in Berrington, (ed.) *Change in British Politics*.

Crewe, I. M., Sarlvik, B. and Alt, J. (1977) 'Partisan dealignment in Britain', 1964–74, *British Journal of Political Science*, 7, pp. 129–90.

Curi, U. (1997) 'La Lega e l'eversione', *Micromega*, 4/97, pp. 41–53.

D'Alimonte R. and Bartolini, S. (1997) '"Electoral Transition" and Party System Change in Italy' in Bull and Rhodes (eds) *Crisis and Transition*.

Davis, J.A. and Ginsborg, P. (1991) *Society and Politics in the Age of the Risorgimento*, Cambridge, Cambridge University Press.

De Rose, A. (1992) 'Socio-Economic Factors and Family Size as Determinants of Marital Dissolution in Italy', *European Sociological Review*, 8, 1, pp. 71–91.

della Porta, D. (1992) *Lo scambio occulto. Casi di corruzione politica in Italia*, Bologna, Il Mulino.

della Porta, D. (1996) 'The system of corrupt exchange in local government' in S. Gundle and S. Parker (eds) *The New Italian Republic*.

Diakron (1996) *Italian People and Secession*. Milan, 6 September.

Diamanti, I. (1990), 'Partecipazione e orientamenti politici', in V. Belotti (ed.) *Giovani a Vicenza*.

Diamanti, I. (1993) *La Lega. Geografia, storia e sociologia di un nuovo soggetto politico*, Rome, Donzelli.

Diamanti, I. (1994) 'Lega Nord: un partito per le periferie', in P. Ginsborg (ed.) *Stato dell'Italia*.

Diamanti, I. (1996) *Il male del Nord. Lega, localismo, secessione*, Rome, Donzelli.

Diamanti, I. (1997) 'Identità cattolica e comportamento di voto. L'unità e la fedeltà non sono più virtù' in P. Corbetta and A. Parisi, eds., *A domanda risponde*.

Diamanti, I. and Mannheimer, R., (1994) *Milano a Roma. Guida all'Italia elettorale del 1994*, Rome, Donzelli.

Diamanti, I. and Segatti, P. (1994) 'Orgogliosi di essere italiani', *liMes*, 4, pp. 15–36.

Dickie, J. (1993) Representations of the Mezzogiorno in Post-Unification Italy (1860–1900). Unpublished doctoral thesis, University of Sussex.

Dickie, J. (1994) '*La macchina da scrivere*: The Victor Emmanuel Monument in Rome and Italian nationalism', *The Italianist*, 14, pp. 261–85.

Dogan, M. (1967) 'Political Cleavages and Social Stratification in France and Italy', in Lipset and Rokkan (eds) *Party Systems and Voter Alignment*.

Eatwell, R. (1997) *European Political Cultures. Conflict or Convergence?*, London and New York, Routledge.

Eatwell, R. (1998) 'The Dynamics of Right-wing Electoral Breakthrough', in *Patterns of Prejudice*, 32, 3, pp. 3–31.

Erickson, L. (1993) 'Making Her Way In: Women, Parties and Candidacies in Canada', in J. Lovenduski and P. Norris (eds) *Gender and Party Politics*.

Eve, M. (1996) 'Comparing Italy: The Case of Corruption' in D. Forgacs and R. Lumley (eds) *Italian Cultural Studies*.

Farrell, J. (1995) 'Berlusconi and Forza Italia: New Force for Old?', *Modern Italy*, 1, 1, pp. 40–52.

Ferejohn J.A. and Kuklinski, J.H. (1990) *Information and Democratic Processes*, Illinois, University of Illinois Press.

Ferrera, M. (1997) 'The Uncertain Future of the Italian Welfare State', in M. Bull and M. Rhodes (eds) *Crisis and Transition*.

Fiorina, M. (1990) 'Information and Rationality in Elections' in J.A. Ferejohn and J.H. Kuklinski (eds) *Information and Democratic Processes*.

Forgacs, D. and Lumley, R. (1996) *Italian Cultural Studies. An Introduction*, Oxford, Oxford University Press.

Frader, L.L. (1981) 'Grapes of Wrath: Vineyards Workers, Labour Unions and Strike Activity in the Aude, 1860–1913' in Tilly and Tilly (eds) *Class Conflict and Collective Action*.

Franchi, M. and Rieser, V. (1991) 'Le categorie sociologiche nell'analisi del distretto industriale: tra comunità e razionalizzazione', *Stato e Mercato*, 33, pp. 451–76.

Franklin, M. (1985) *The Decline of Class Voting in Britain*, Oxford, Clarendon Press.

Franks, P. (1995) 'From Peasant to Entrepreneur in Italy and Japan', *The Journal of Peasant Studies*, 22, 4, pp. 699–709.

Freedland, J. (1998) 'Britain's problem with corruption', *The Guardian*, 4 February, p. 17.

Fuà, G. and Zacchia, C. (1983) *Industrializzazione senza fratture*, Bologna, Il Mulino.

Fukuyama, F. (1992) *The End of History and the Last Man*, London, Penguin.

Fukuyama, F. (1995) *Trust: The Social Virtues and the Creation of Prosperity*, London, Hamilton.

Galli, G., Capecchi, V., Cioni Polacchini, V. and Sivini, G. (1968) *Il comportamento elettorale in Italia*, Bologna, Il Mulino.

Ganne, B. (1984) 'Gens du cuir, gens du paper', *Terrain*, March, pp. 4–17.

Ganne, B. (1987) Transformation des PME. Etude de cas d'Annonay. Unpublished paper, GLYSI, Lyon.

Ganne, B. (1991) 'Sistemi industriali locali: che cosa insegna una comparazione tra Francia e Italia', *Stato e mercato*, 31, pp. 47–76.

Garvía Soto, R. (1996) 'Asociationismo y catolicismo' (unpublished working paper, Universidad Carlos III de Madrid).

GEAS (1991) *GEAS. Passione sportiva e impegno sociale*, Sesto San Giovanni, Parma Editore.

Gentili Zappi, E. (1991) *If Eight Hours Seem Too Few. Mobilization of Women Workers in the Italian Rice Fields*, Albany, State University of New York Press.

Gérin, A. (1991) *Jeunes. Une chance pour une ville*, Paris, Messidor.

Gibbins, J.R. (1990) *Contemporary Political Culture. Politics in a Postmodern Age*, London, Newbury Park and New Delhi, Sage Publications.

Giddens, A. (1990) *Modernity and Self-Identity*, Cambridge, Polity Press.

Giddens, A. (1994) 'What's Left for Labour?', *New Statesman and Society*, 30 September, pp. 37–40.

Gilbert, M. (1995) *The Italian Revolution. The End of Politics, Italian Style?*. Boulder, San Francisco and Oxford, Westview Press.

Ginsborg, P. (1994) 'Familismo', in Ginsborg (ed.) *Stato dell'Italia*.

Ginsborg, P. (1994) *Stato dell'Italia*, Milan, Mondadori.

Ginsborg, P. (1995) 'Italian Political Culture in Historical Perspective', *Modern Italy*, 1, 1, pp. 3–17.

Ginsborg, P. (1996) 'Explaining Italy's crisis', in Gundle and Parker (eds) *The New Italian Republic*.

Ginsborg, P. (1998) *L'Italia del tempo presente. Famiglia, società civile, stato. 1980-1996*, Turin, Einaudi.

Girvin, B. (1990) 'Change and Continuity in Liberal Democratic Political Culture' in J.R. Gibbins (ed.) *Contemporary Political Culture*.

Golden M. (1988) *Labor divided. Austerity and Working-class Politics in Contemporary Italy*, Ithaca and London, Cornell University Press.

Gotman, A. (1989) 'Familles, générations, patrimoine. Une questione urbaine?', *Annales de la recherche urbaine*, Vol. 41, pp. 87–96.

Grancelli, B. (1987) 'Political trade-offs, collective bargaining, individual tradings: some remarks on industrial relations in Italy' in Alessandrini and Dallago (eds) *The Unofficial Economy*.

Granovetter, M. (1985) 'Economic Action and Social Structure: The Problem of Embeddedness' in *American Journal of Sociology*, 91, pp. 481–510.

Graziano, L. and Tarrow, S. (1979) *La crisi italiana*, 2 volls., Turin, Einaudi.

Gray, J. (1995) *Enlightenment's Wake: Politics and Culture at the Close of the Modern Age*, London, Routledge.

Gray, J. (1998) *False Dawn: The Delusions of Global Capitalism*, London, Granta.

Gribaudi, G. (1996) 'Images of the South' in Forgacs and Lumley (eds) *Italian Cultural Studies*.

Gribaudi, G. (1997) 'Images of the South: the Mezzogiorno as seen by Insiders and Outsiders' in R. Lumley and J. Morris (eds) *The New History of the Italian South*.

Gribaudi, M. (1987) *Mondo operaio e mito operaio: spazi e percorsi sociali a Torino nel primo novecento*, Turin, Einaudi.

Griffin, R. (1997) 'Italy' in R. Eatwell (ed.) *European Political Cultures*.

Griswold, W. (1994) *Cultures and Societies in a Changing World*, Thousand Oaks, London and New Delhi, Pine Forge Press.

Guadagnini, M. (1993) 'A "Partitocrazia" Without Women: The Case of the Italian Party System', in Lovenduski and Norris (eds) *Gender and Party Politics*.

Gundle, S. and Parker, S. (1996) 'Introduction: The New Italian Republic' in Gundle and Parker (eds) *The New Italian Republic*.

Gundle, S. and Parker, S. (1996) *The New Italian Republic. From the Fall of the Berlin Wall to Berlusconi*, London and New York, Routledge.

Heath, A., Jowell, R., Curtice, J., Evans, G., Field, J. and Witherspoon, S. (1991) *Understanding political change: the British voter, 1964–1987*. Oxford, Pergamon Press.

Heath, A., Jowell, R. and Curtice, J. (1985) *How Britain Votes*, Oxford, Pergamon Press.

Hechter, M. (1986) 'Rational choice theory' in Rex and Mason (eds) *Theories of Race and Ethnic Relations*.

Held, D. (1995) *Democracy and the Global Order: From the Modern State to Cosmopolitan Governance*, Oxford, Polity Press.

Hellman, J.A. (1997) 'Immigrant "Space" in Italy: When an Emigrant Sending Becomes an Immigrant Receiving Society', *Modern Italy*, 2, 1/2, pp. 34–51.

Hellman, S. and Pasquino, G. (1993) *Italian Politics: A Review*, London and New York, Pinter.

Helliwell, J.F. and Putnam, R.D. (1995) *Economic Growth and Social Capital in Italy*, Note di Lavoro 88/95, Fondazione ENI Enrico Mattei, pp. 1–16.

Himmelweith, H.T., Humphreys, P. and Jaeger, M. (1985) *How Voters Decide: A Longitudinal Study of Political Attitudes and Voting*, Milton Keynes, Open University Press.

Hirschman, A. (1970) *Exit, Voice and Loyalty*, Cambridge, Massachusetts and London, Harvard University Press.

Hollinger, F. and Haller, M. (1990) 'Kinship and social networks in modern societies: a cross-cultural comparison among seven nations', *European Sociological Review*, 6, 2, pp. 103–124.

Hollingsworth, J.R. and Boyer, R. (1997) *Contemporary Capitalism. The Embeddedness of Institutions*, Cambridge, Cambridge University Press.

Hout, M., Brooks, C. and Manza, J. (1995) 'The Democratic Class Struggle in the United States: 1948–1992', *American Sociological Review*, 60, pp. 805–828.

Huckfeldt, R.R. (1984) 'Political Loyalties and Social Class Ties: The Mechanisms of Contextual Influence', *American Journal of Political Science*, 28, pp. 399–417.

Huckfeldt, R.R. and Sprague, J. (1987) 'Networks in Social Contexts: The Social Flow of Political Information', *American Political Science Review*, 81, pp. 1197–216.

Hutton, W. (1996) *The State We're In*, London, Vintage.

Inglehart, R. (1990) *Culture Shift in Advanced Industrial Society*, Princeton, Princeton University Press.

Jenkins, B. and Copsey, N. (1996) 'Nation, Nationalism and National Identity in France', in Jenkins and Sofos (eds), *Nation and Identity in Contemporary Europe*.

Jenkins, B. and Sofos, S.A. (1996) *Nation and Identity in Contemporary Europe*, London and New York, Routledge.

Jenson, J. and Sineau, M. (1995) *Mitterrand et les Francaises. Un rendez-vous manqué*, Paris, Presse de Sciences Po.

Kay, C. (1997) *Globalisation, Competitiveness and Human Security*, London and Portland, Cass.

Keating, M. (1988) *State and Regional Nationalism. Territorial Politics and the European State*, New York, London, Toronto, Sidney and Tokyo, Harvester-Wheatsheaf.

Keating, M. (1998) *The New Regionalism in Western Europe. Territorial Restructuring and Political Change*. Cheltenham and Northampton, MA.

Kellner, P. (1997) 'Chase a tiger's tail and get bitten', *The Observer*, 21 December.

Kitschelt, H. (with A.J. McGann) (1995) *The Radical Right in Western Europe. A Comparative Analysis*, Ann Arbor, The University of Michigan Press.

Knoke, D. and Kuklinski, J.H. (1983) *Network Analysis*, Beverly Hills, Sage Publications.

L'Unita', 27 April 1996.

La Padania, 1 and 2 July 1999.

La Repubblica, 23 April 1996, 13 July 1998, 6 June 2000.

Lago, G. (1996) *Nordest chiama Italia: cosa vuole l'area del benessere e della protesta*. *Intervista di Gianni Montagni*, Vicenza, Neri Pozza.

Leonardi, R. (1995) 'Regional Development in Italy: Social Capital and the Mezzogiorno', *Oxford Review of Economic Policy*, 11, 2, pp.165–79.

Leonardi, R. and Kovacs, M. (1993) 'The Lega Nord: the rise of a new Italian catch-all party' in S. Hellman and G. Pasquino (eds) *Italian Politics: A Review*.

Lepre, A. (1994) *Italia addio? Unità e disunità dal 1860 a oggi*, Milan, Mondadori.

Levy, C. (1996) *Italian Regionalism. History, Identity and Politics*, Oxford and Washington, Berg.

Levi, M. (1996) 'Social and unsocial capital: a review essay of Robert Putnam's *Making Democracy Work*', *Politics and Society*, 24, 1, pp. 45–55.

Lijphart, A. (1977) *Democracy in Plural Society. A Comparative Exploration*, New Haven, Yale University Press.

Lijphart, A. (1984) *Democracies. Patterns of Majoritarian and Consensus Government in Twenty-One Countries*, New Haven, Yale University Press.

Lipset, S.M. (1960) [1976 re-edition] *Political Man*, London, Heinemann.

Lipset, S.M. and Rokkan, S. (1967) *Party Systems and Voter Alignment*, New York, Free Press.

Lovenduski, J. and Hills, J. (1981) *The Politics of the Second Electorate. Women and Public Participation*, London, Boston and Henley, Routledge.

Lovenduski, J. and Norris, P. (1993) *Gender and Party Politics*, London, Thousand Oaks and New Delhi, Sage Publications.

Lumley, R. and Morris, J. (1997) *The New History of the Italian South. The Mezzogiorno Revisited*, Exeter, University of Exeter Press.

Lyttelton, A. (1996) 'Shifting Identities: Nation, Region and City' in C. Levy (ed.) *Italian Regionalism*.

Macry, P. (1997) 'Rethinking a stereotype: territorial differences and family models in the modernization of Italy', *Journal of Modern Italian Studies*, 2, 2, pp. 188–214.

Magister, S. (1999) 'Dio, Papa e federalismo', *L'Espresso*, 11 February.

Mannheimer, R., (1991) *La Lega Lombarda*, Milan, Feltrinelli.

Mannheimer, R. (1994) 'Forza Italia' in Diamanti and Mannheimer (eds) *Milano a Roma*.

Mannheimer, R. (2000) 'La voglia di federalismo conquista anche il Sud', *Corriere della Sera*, 26 June.

Mannheimer, R. and Sani, G. (1987) *Il mercato elettorale*, Bologna, Il Mulino.

Mannheimer, R. and Sani, S. (1994) *La rivoluzione elettorale. L'Italia tra la prima e la seconda repubblica*, Milan, Anabasi.

Maraffi, M. (1997) 'Da un maggioritario all'altro: candidati e schieramenti nella transizione politica italiana' in Corbetta and Parisi (eds) *A domanda risponde*.

McKie, D. (1998), 'The secret party that nearly won the election', *The Guardian*, 22 January.

Melchionda, E. (1995) 'Il bipartitismo irrealizzato. Modelli di competizione nei collegi uninominali', in Pasquino (ed.) *L'alternanza inattesa*.

Membrino, Patrizia (1989) *Gli espulsi dal processo produttivo*, Comune di Sesto San Giovanni, Assessorato ai servizi sociali, assistenza e colonie.

Mingione, E. (1993) 'Italy: The Resurgence of Regionalism', *International Affairs*, 69, 2, pp. 305–18.

Ministero dell'Interno, Direzione Generale per i Servizi Elettorali. Servizio Elettorale. *Elezioni amministrative I Turno 13 giugno 1999 (Provinciali)*. http://195.120.182.34:8888/amm990613/PO89.htm.

Moia, L. (1997) *Federalisti di Dio? Incontri e scontri tra Chiesa e Lega*, Milan, Ancora Editrice.

Moioli, V. (1990) *I nuovi razzismi*, Rome, Editori Riuniti.

Moss, D. (1995) 'Patronage revisited: the dynamics of information and reputation', *Journal of Modern Italian Studies*, 1, 1, pp. 58–93.

Mueller, C.M. (1988) *The Politics of the Gender Gap. The Social Construction of Political Influence*, Beverly Hills and London, Sage Publications.

Mutti, A. (1992) 'La questione meridionale negli anni '90', in Cerase (ed.) *Dopo il familismo, cosa?*.

Norris, P. (1986), 'Conservative Attitudes in Recent British Elections: An Emerging Gender Gap', *Political Studies*, 34, pp. 120–28.

Norris, P. (1997) *Electoral Change since 1945*, Oxford and Cambridge, Massachusetts, Blackwell.

Norris, P. and Lovenduski, J. (1993) 'Gender and Party Politics in Britain', in Lovenduski and Norris (eds) *Gender and Party Politics*.

Ohmae, K. (1996) *The End of the Nation State: The Rise of Regional Economies*, London, Harper Collins.

Palazzi, M. (1990) 'Famiglia, lavoro e proprietà: le donne nella società contadina fra continuità e trasformazione' in Corti (ed.) *Società rurale e ruoli femminili in Italia*.

Pansa, G. (1997) 'Lega furbona, Roma tardona', *L'Espresso*, 2 October.

Parker, S. (1996) 'Electoral reform and political change in Italy' in Gundle and Parker (eds.) *The New Italian Republic*.

Parisi A.M.L. and Pasquino, G. (1977) *Continuità e mutamento elettorale in Italia*, Bologna, Il Mulino.

Parisi A.M.L. and Schadee, H.M.A. (1995) *Sulla soglia del cambiamento. Elettori e partiti alla fine della Prima Repubblica*, Bologna, Il Mulino.

Pasquino, G. (1994) 'Restaurazione nella transizione?', *Stato e Mercato*, 42, pp. 400–406.

Pasquino, G. (1995) *L'alternanza inattesa. Le elezioni del 27 marzo 1994 e le loro conseguenze*, Bologna, Il Mulino.

Pasquino, G. and McCarthy, P. (1993) *The End of Post-War Politics in Italy. The Landmark 1992 Elections*, Boulder, San Francisco and Oxford, Westview Press.

Patrono, M. (1995) *Maggioritario in erba. Legge elettorale e sistema politico nell'Italia che (non) cambia*, Padua, CEDAM.

Pavone, C. (1991) *Una guerra civile. Saggio storico sulla moralità nella Resistenza*, Turin, Bollati Boringhieri.

Penniman, H.E. (1977) *Italy at the Polls: The Parliamentary Elections of 1976*, Washington, American Enterprise Institute.

Perulli, P. (1995) 'Stato, regioni, economie di rete', *Stato e mercato*, 44, pp. 231–59.

Petrillo, G. (1981) *La città delle fabbriche, Sesto San Giovanni 1880-1945*, Cassago, CENB.

Petrillo, G. (1992) *La capitale del miracolo: sviluppo, lavoro e potere a Milano 1953–1962*, Milan, Angeli.

Pichierri, A. (1995) 'Stato e identità economiche regionali', *Stato e mercato*, 44, pp. 213–29.

Piore, M. and Sabel, C. (1984) *The Second Industrial Divide: Possibilities for Prosperity*, New York, Basic Books.

Pisati, M. (1997) 'Chi ha votato chi. Omogeneità e differenze fra gli elettorati dei diversi schieramenti politici' in Corbetta and Parisi (eds) *A domanda risponde*.

Pisati, M. and Barbagli, M. (1996) 'Classi sociali e comportamento elettorale a Bologna, 1984–1994', *Polis*, 1, pp. 39–59.

Piselli, F. (1997) 'Il network sociale nell'analisi del potere e dei processi politici', *Stato e Mercato*, 50, pp. 287–315.

Procacci, G. (1970) *La lotta di classe in Italia agli inizi del secolo XX*, Rome, Editori Riuniti.

Provincia di Milano (1988) *Il ruolo delle piccole imprese manifatturiere in un processo di riqualificazione del tessuto produttivo dell'area di Sesto San Giovanni*, Milan, Assessorato economia e lavoro.

Puccioni, M. (1998) 'Italians opt for equities over Armani as values change', *The European*, 1–7 January.

Putnam, R. (1993) *Making Democracy Work. Civic Traditions in Modern Italy*, Princeton, Princeton University Press.

Putnam, R. (1995a) 'Bowling alone, revisited', *The Responsive Community*, 5, 2, pp. 18–33.

Putnam, R. (1995b) 'Tuning in, tuning out: the strange disappearance of social capital in America', *PS: Political Science and Politics*, 28, 4, pp. 664–683.

Pyke, F., Becattini, G. and Sengerberger, W. (1991) *Industrial Districts and Inter-Firm Co-operation in Italy*, Geneva, International Institute for Labour Studies.

Quattrociocchi, L. (1996) 'Images de la famille italienne en mutation', *Population*, 51, 2, pp. 353–68.

Radio Times, 5 December 1984.

Ramella, F. (1975) 'Il problema della formazione della classe operaia in Italia', *Classe*, 10, pp. 107–25.

Rees, G. (1985) 'Class, Locality and Ideology' in Rees, Bujira, Littlewood, Newby and Tees (eds) *Political Action and Social identity*.

Rees, G., Bujira, J., Littlewood, P., Newby, H. and Tees, T.L. *Political Action and Social identity: Class, Locality, and Ideology*, London, MacMillan.

Regalia, I. (1986) 'L'area di Sesto San Giovanni', in Regini and Sabel (eds) *Strategie di riaggiustamento industriale*.

Regini, M. and Sabel, C. (1986) *Strategie di riaggiustamento industriale*, Bologna, Il Mulino.

Rengger, N. (1997) 'Beyond Liberal Politics? European Modernity and the Nation-State', in Rhodes, Heywood and Wright (eds) *Developments in West European Politics*.

Revelli, M. (1994) 'Forza Italia: l'anomalia italiana non è finita', in Ginsborg (ed.) *Stato dell'Italia*.

Rex, J. (1986) 'The role of class analysis in the study of race and ethnic relations' in Rex and Mason (eds) *Theories of Race and Ethnic Relations*.

Rex, J. and Mason, D. (1986) *Theories of Race and Ethnic Relations*, Cambridge, Cambridge University Press.

Rhodes, M., Heywood, P. and Wright, V. (1997) *Developments in West European Politics*, Basingstoke and London, MacMillan Press.

Richmond, A.H. (1988) *Immigration and Ethnic Conflict*, London, MacMillan.

Riffault, H. (1994) *Les valeurs des Francais*, Paris, PUF.

Rose, R. and McAllister, I. (1986) *Voters Begin to Choose*, London, Sage Publications.

Rose, R. and McAllister, I. (1990) *The Loyalties of Voters*, London, Sage.

Rumiz, P. (1997) *La secessione leggera. Dove nasce la rabbia del profondo Nord*, Rome, Editori Riuniti.

Rusconi, G.E. (1993) *Se cessiamo di essere una nazione. Tra etnodemocrazie regionali e cittadinanza europea*, Bologna, Il Mulino.

Sabel, C. (1997) 'Constitutional Orders: Trust Building and Response to Change' in Hollingsworth and Boyer (eds) *Contemporary Capitalism*.

Sabel, C.F. and Zeitlin, J. (1985) 'Historical Alternatives to Mass Production: Politics, Markets and Technology in Nineteenth-century Industrialization', *Past and Present*, 108, pp. 133–76.

Sainsbury, D. (1993) 'The Politics of Increased Representation: the Swedish Case', in J. Lovenduski and P. Norris (eds) *Gender and Party Politics*.

Sani, G. (1977) 'The Italian Electorate in the Mid-1970s: Beyond Tradition?' in Penniman (ed.) *Italy at the Polls*.

Sani, G. (1979) 'Ricambio elettorale, mutamenti sociali e preferenze politiche' in Graziano and Tarrow (eds) *La crisi italiana*.

Sani, G. (1980) 'Italy: Continuity and Change', in Almond and Verba (eds) *The Civic Culture Revisited*.

Sani, G. (1992) '1992: la destrutturazione del mercato elettorale', *Rivista italiana di Scienza Politica*, 22, pp. 539–65.

Sapelli, G. (1995a) *Southern Europe since 1945: Tradition and Modernity in Portugal, Spain, Italy, Greece and Turkey*. Translated by A. Fuller. London, Longman.

Sapelli, G. (1995b) 'The Italian Crisis and Capitalism', *Modern Italy*, 1, 1, pp. 82–96.

Sapelli, G. (1997) 'The transformation of the Italian party system', *Journal of Modern Italian Studies*, 2, 2, pp. 167–87.

Sartori, G. (1976) *Parties and Party Systems*, Cambridge, Cambridge University Press.

Seccombe, W. (1986) 'Patriarchy stabilized: the construction of a male breadwinner norm in nineteenth-century Britain', *Social History*, 2, 1, pp. 53–76.

Segatti, P. (1997) 'Un centro instabile eppure fermo. Mutamento e continuità nel movimento elettorale' in Corbetta and Parisi, *A domanda risponde*.

Shutt, J. and Whittington, R. (1987) 'Fragmentation Strategies and the Rise of Small Units, Cases from the North–West', *Regional Studies*, 21, pp. 13–23.

Sideri, S. (1997) 'Globalisation and Regional Integration' in Kay (ed.), *Globalisation, Competitiveness and Human Security*.

Snell, K.D.N. (1981) 'Agricultural Seasonal Unemployment, the Standard of Living, and Women's Work in the South and East, 1690–1860', *The Economic History Review*, 34, 3, pp. 407–37.

Statham, P. (1995) *The New Politics of Intolerance*, Leeds, Institute of Communications Studies.

Stubbs, R. and Underhill, G.R.D. (1994) *Political Economy and the Changing Global Order*, Basingstoke and London, Macmillan.

Tilly, L.A. and Tilly, C. (1981) *Class Conflict and Collective Action*, Beverly Hills and London, Sage Publications.

Todd, E. (1991) *The Making of Modern France. Politics, Ideology and Culture*, Oxford, Blackwell.

Tomassini, L. (1991) 'Mercato del lavoro e lotte sindacali nel biennio rosso' in Corti (ed.) *Le donne nelle campagne italiane del novecento*.

Topf, R. (1990) 'Political Change and Political Culture in Britain, 1959–87' in Gibbins (ed.) *Contemporary Political Culture*.

Trigilia, C. (1986) *Grandi partiti e piccole imprese. Comunisti e democristiani nelle regioni a economia diffusa*, Bologna, Il Mulino.

Trigilia, C. (1992) *Sviluppo senza autonomia. Effetti perversi delle politiche nel Mezzogiorno*, Bologna, Il Mulino.

Trigilia, C. (1994) 'Le basi sociali della crisi politica', *Stato e Mercato*, 42, pp. 406-12.

Van der Eijk, C. and Niemöller, B. (1979) 'Recall Accuracy and Its Determinants', *Acta Politica*, 3, pp. 289-342.

Vassallo, S. (1997) 'Il federalismo sedicente', *Il Mulino*, 46, 372, 4/97, pp. 694-707.

Vitali, O. (1995) *Il terremoto politico del 1994. Dal governo Berlusconi alla dissociazione di Bossi*, Rome, Viviani editore.

Weber M. (1977) *Il voto delle donne*, Turin, Biblioteca della Libertà.

Weber, M. (1978) 'Le casalinghe e la politica', *Argomenti radicali*, 2, pp. 45-56.

Weber, M. (1981a) 'Italy', in J. Lovenduski and J. Hills (eds) *The Politics of the Second Electorate*.

Weber, M. (1981b) 'La partecipazione politica femminile in Italia: evoluzione, determinanti, caratteristiche', *Rivista italiana di scienza politica*, 11, pp. 281-311.

Weiss, L. (1988) *Creating Capitalism. The State and Small Business since 1945*. Oxford and New York, Blackwell.

Welch, S. (1993), *The concept of political culture*, New York, St. Martin's Press.

Wild, S. (1998) The Italian Northern League: The Self Representation of Industrial Districts. Unpublished PhD Thesis, University of Bath.

Wildavski, A. (edited by S-K Chai and B. Swedlow) (1998) *Culture and Social Theory*, New Brunswick and London, Transaction Publishers.

Willson, P. (1993) *The Clockwork Orange. Women and Work in Fascist Italy*, Oxford, Clarendon Press.

Zincone, G. (1985) *Gruppi sociali e sistemi politici: il caso donne*, Milan, Angeli.

Zucchini, F. (1997) 'La decisione di voto: i tempi, l'oggetto, i modi' in Corbetta and Parisi, *A domanda risponde*.

Index